Information Technology
as Business History

Information Technology as Business History

Issues in the History and Management of Computers

James W. Cortada

Contributions in Economics
and Economic History, Number 177

GREENWOOD PRESS
Westport, Connecticut • London

Library of Congress Cataloging-in-Publication Data

Cortada, James W.
　　Information technology as business history : issues in the history
and management of computers / James W. Cortada.
　　　　p.　cm.—(Contributions in economics and economic history,
　　ISSN 0084–9235 ; no. 177)
　　Includes bibliographical references and index.
　　ISBN 0–313–29950–1 (alk. paper)
　　1. Business—Data processing—History.　2. Information technology—
Management—History.　3. Electronic data processing—History.
I. Title.　II. Series.
HF5548.2.C675　1996
658'.05—dc20　　　96–3644

British Library Cataloguing in Publication Data is available.

Library of Congress Catalog Card Number: 96–3644
ISBN: 0–313–29950–1
ISSN: 0084–9235

First published in 1996

Greenwood Press, 88 Post Road West, Westport, CT 06881
An imprint of Greenwood Publishing Group, Inc.

Printed in the United States of America

The paper used in this book complies with the
Permanent Paper Standard issued by the National
Information Standards Organization (Z39.48–1984).

10 9 8 7 6 5 4 3 2

Contents

Preface

In 1976, Peter Drucker commented on computers in a disturbing way: ''The main impact of the computer has been the provision of unlimited jobs for clerks''—discomforting words, because we tend to think of computers as tools to aid productivity. Barely a decade later (1984), Lewis H. Lapham declared that ''no businessman these days dares to embark upon the journey of incorporation without first acquiring a computer so huge and so omniscient as to strike terror into the software of its enemies.'' In 1995, *USA Today* led off a cover story with the headline ''PCs Power '90s Renaissance.'' Nothing boring about computers around this American society! But how much do we really know about computers or, more importantly, about information processing? What these quotes do suggest is that we know very little about what computers really have or have not done. What should we know? How do we approach the topic? Why do we care?

It turns out we should care. You get paid by a computer; the nation spends up to 10 percent of all its money on the care and feeding of these ''engines of the mind.'' Our children love them, teachers are ignorant of them, but the future of both is linked to a technology-based pedagogy. We fight wars effectively with computers dropping ''smart bombs'' on supposedly ''dumb'' enemies. Word processing on a computer is about the only way you can write a letter, an article, or a book today. And now the telephone company, in partnership with our cable or utility company, wants to make our television sets programmable. We are moving from a society that keeps its information on paper to one that hides it in computers, from the days when going to the library meant driving to a building filled with books, to logging onto the ''information highway.'' In short, computers are about as important an influence on our lives as taxes, health, and the economy.

This book is intended for those who have to make sense of this new technology. Largely, I think this is a small community of historians, economists, journalists, and those interested in the history of computers. But I keep bumping into information processing managers who display an historical perspective in making decisions about this technology. As senior executives increasingly come to power with experience in using computers, I find yet another community with "war stories" and an historical perspective—some accurate, much of it in need of a good dose of realistic analysis. This is not a history of computers, but it is a book about the computer's history. It is a guided tour of the critical issues in the history of computers. Along the way, we will see castles of technology, get a sense of the historical figures and the issues they faced, and hear sermons about lessons learned and opportunities gained and lost. Lots of data are thrown at you and many questions raised but not answered. It is also a charge to future historians about what they must study, and yet a caution that glib answers do not serve us well. Information processing is serious business—over a trillion dollars a year now—but also a pervasive influence on our lives.

For those quick to condemn computing's lack of productivity, watch out—your analysis may be wrong. For those who buy and use computers, this may be a welcome change from the normal fare from computer experts, many of whom do not even realize that there were computers before the Personal Computer (PC)! Some people quickly run to such phrases as "this is the 'Age of the Computer.' " But when we study the history of computers, we examine one of the most important infrastructures of the second half of the twentieth century, and yet we have not figured out completely how to go about the task of studying the history of computing, or what questions to answer. We have barely begun to even acknowledge that computers have a history, let alone see what it teaches us.

This book, therefore, is a taste of computer history. We will sample issues, demonstrate approaches, and call out issues. Chapter 1 is a general introduction to the study of the subject, from the caveman to the present. Caveman to the present? "Cavemen didn't have computers, did they?" Of course not, but from the beginning humans have tried to manage and preserve data. So that chapter is broad in scope, the "big picture." Chapter 2 is an introduction to what the contemporary information processing history looked like, from the 1950s to the present. This chapter is very economic, with lots of data on who sold what to whom, how many, and why. This chapter attempts to demonstrate major trends in the business of computers. But why do we care about this kind of discussion? Simply put, it is an industry that delivers a technology to a society in a form that is useful and becomes important. Inventors invent, companies manufacture and sell machines, and you and I buy and use them. So we need to understand how computers came to market. This chapter is a taste of the topic, presenting some broad comments about the industry we came to call such things as data processing, management information systems, the computer industry, and the PC business.

Since computers were extensions of earlier office machines used to add, calculate, and tabulate, we need to understand computing within a broader context. Chapter 3 serves that purpose by placing computers within the over 100-year history of mechanical devices used in modern times to do data processing. Why do we care? Many of the ways you and I receive computers, buy them, and use this technology were worked out in companies that existed ten, thirty, even fifty years before the first commercial computer was available. Did you know that National Cash Register (NCR) and Burroughs—in time both peddlers of computers—had been selling information-handing machines over 100 years ago— or, that International Business Machines Corporation (IBM) has been around since before World War I? Historical context is so important; computers have a lot of it, and its patterns of behavior are described in this chapter.

Given an introduction to the history of computing, its industry, and its office appliance heritage, we should be ready for the first direct sales pitch of this book, the case for studying the history of how computers were used. That is the purpose of Chapter 4. Short on length, my intent is to begin the process of suggesting not only that it be studied (we suggested that idea in earlier chapters), but that we follow the Biblical stricture to teach someone to fish, not simply feed them fish. This chapter describes a strategy for the study of the topic. Chapter 4 will then appear as a demonstration of the process and serve as a one-stop supply of basic information on the modern industry.

In Chapter 5 I illustrate the strategy in a brief form by addressing what I consider to be the biggest hole in our understanding of information processing's history: what people used computers for. Can you imagine it? Computers in themselves are meaningless, other than as a demonstration of humankind's ability to invent things. But put it to a use that changes the way humans work and play, and then you have a real story! The chapter introduces my suggestion that use of computers be studied initially by looking at how they were used by industry, not simply by function. In other words, for example, go find out how and why bankers use computers before you write histories of automatic teller machines. I have tried to be as broad as possible without writing a book on the theme. I demonstrate the research process and the issues involved by looking at some one dozen industries.

Chapter 6 is a very short, to the point, discussion of the issues that need to be studied in the broad area of the management of information processing. It catalogs key strategic issues in the historiography of the general theme of managing computing. Subsequent chapters then demonstrate the themes in action.

In Chapter 7 I take my historian's hat off (well at least tip it) as I move back into my role as a member of the information processing community. In business, from the very earliest days of the computer, executives began developing the idea that information, like money, inventory, and employees, was a corporate asset and in time developed various practices for treating it as such. It is a concept alien in the histories of computing. Yet even more basic than applications or their management is information and how we use it. Information is what gives meaning to the existance of computers, so this chapter describes management's view of information as a corporate asset, with trends. I want those who study the industry to have a solid grounding in this concept of information as a corporate asset. They can then apply it as they hunt through the relics of the past, where the notion will be found in different forms but always for the same reasons.

Chapter 8 is intended to address another area almost totally ignored so far by historians: how companies managed the acquisition and use of computers. We know virtually nothing about the history of data processing managers, the rise of programmers or systems analysts, or the evolution of the computer center operator. Yet millions of people had these jobs. The good news is that over the decades many "how to" books on these functions—what I will call "business anthropology"—were published that can serve as ammunition for the historian. So, much like Chapter 5 is intended to demonstrate how a topic can be approached, Chapter 8 is used to illustrate the issues involved and a strategy for addressing them. After writing it, I had the same reaction as after Chapter 5: Slap my forehead with the palm of my hand and say, "Ah, I could've written this a decade ago!" Some historian is going to figure out that a career can be built writing history books on this theme.

So there you have it. The front end of the book is an introduction, Part I exposes you to a variety of industry-related issues, Part II to an applications perspective, Part III to the management of this technology. Most of the chapters are heavily laden with notes that direct you to the critical bibliography and are intended to serve as an additional research tool.

This book, like its topic, also has a history. Most of these chapters appeared in some earlier version as articles, prefaces to books, introductions, and so on, but have all been totally rewritten and brought up to date. I corrected errors of fact and judgment, and took advantage of the fact that I have learned additional things along the way. Some of the chapters are completely new creations (e.g., Chapters 6, 8), while the others barely look like the original versions. All, as you can see, are very much related to each other. The one thing you will not accuse me of is being fixated on the history of machines, but I am willing to be charged with worrying about the management and use of technology—my central concern in my research on computers and office equipment.

You are also entitled to know something about me. I live in two worlds: that of the historian and that of a user of technology within the information processing industry. I was formally trained as an historian but have spent nearly a quarter century working for IBM in sales, marketing, and consulting. I would sell computers by day, write history books by night. In the late 1970s I began to write books on how to manage information processing, an effort I have continued down to the present with the result that I have had to look at the practical day-to-day issues of using computers across multiple decades. By the early 1990s I also became very enamored with quality management practices, the area I thought was generating the most useful and productive new management tools and techniques at the time. As with everything else that catches my eye, I also began commenting in print on that topic. It ties back to everything else because central to many of such practices is the effective use of information technology (I/T). The effective use of computers, in turn, is tied to certain best practices of the past. The history of computing, in turn, is also a function of what occurs in science, technology, business management, and contemporary economics. So while some readers (usually professors, not executives) will think I dabble in several fields, I don't. To me it is all one big pot of stew because each affects the other. That perspective has formed my views as expressed in each chapter.

Let me bring you back to where I began: This is an eclectic tour through a garden filled with the flowers of computing's history. It is not comprehensive, but I am confident you know why. This tour would not have been possible without the continued support of my colleagues at Greenwood Press. Over the past two decades we have worked on many projects together, some of which have involved works of reference on the history of computing (encyclopedias, bibliographies, etc.), others more monographic in nature. Special thanks goes to the Institute of Electrical and Electronics Engineers (IEEE) for granting me copyright permission for using an article published in the April 1996 issue of the *Annals of the History of Computing*, the basis of Chapter 5. I also want to take this opportunity to thank John Donohue and his team at Rainsford Type for efficiently guiding this book through the production process.

In the final analysis, errors of judgment and fact are my fault. This book is an extended essay, a cathedral under construction. I challenge you to say you can do better—then go out and do the work that lies ahead of us. If you are not an historian, treat this as your short lesson about computing's importance and exploit its messages to better use this technology.

Information Technology
as Business History

1 _____

A General Introduction to the Study
of Computing History

Computers have now been with us for over half century. They have gone from being highly experimental, one-of-a-kind devices found in university laboratories at such locations as The Massachusetts Institute of Technology (MIT) and the University of Pennsylvania to being ubiquitous, even the icon of the late twentieth century. So it is no wonder that historians and economists have barely had a chance to turn their attention to a technology that snuck up on them so quickly. Early historical studies on computing were written by the engineers who built the machines themselves and later by journalists. As recently as 1983, when the first version of this chapter was written, we were hard put to find many professional historians at work on the topic.[1] That has all changed, as computers joined the mainstream of the history of computing. The history of technology has also come into its own, emerging from under the umbrella of the history of science and amateur of devices, to join in the mainstream of historical analysis. Today it is common for historians of computing to be asking questions that reflect the significance of computers.

In a way, the popularity of the history of computing has complicated the topic. There was a time—which has yet to completely pass by—when the thing to do was to write histories of machines. In fact, that class of historical research will probably never go away. The history of clocks and other machines has demonstrated that point. What is changing are the issues being addressed. These range from institutional histories of vendors to studies of how computers have been used, finally to the effects of such technologies on society at large and over longer periods of time. We have also come to recognize that computers were simply one of many technologies that became available for the manipulation of data.[2]

For many historians perhaps one of the most promising starting points is the nineteenth century because of its many similarities to our own era. One of its most obvious characteristics was the explosive growth in the use of technology and the consequent rapidity of change in society that grew out of new inventions both in Europe and in North America. When compared to earlier centuries, the nineteenth and twentieth saw more changes and experienced less stability. Looking back at the 1800s thus has helped many historians to define the impact of changes and technology of our century on society, even at the risk of practicing Whiggish history. People of letters during the last century were at least as cognizant of historical forces at work around them as individuals are today. The effects of the Industrial Revolution and the impact of technology were not lost to them. Herbert Spencer noted that "progress was not an accident" but simply a "necessity." Worrying about the consequences of change on historical research and the attitude that change and progress were causing each other, Lord Acton reminded historians that "truth is the only merit that gives dignity and worth to history." Yet, in our changing world of computers, space, medicine, and science his precept seems always difficult to live by. For historians and commentators of science and technology the subject to be studied keeps changing along with their concerns and perceptions and thus the meaning of truth. The problem facing historians today nowhere seem so evident as in the study of information processing history. It seems as if everything has yet to be done!

A NEW FIELD OF STUDY

Complicating matters is the fact that the history of information processing has become a viable field of research only within the past twenty years. Prior to that the only information processing literature available was contemporary; that is to say, materials on activities then taking place. Computers and information processing in themselves have only been perceived as existing within the past few years. And since historical investigation of events is always after the fact, we are waiting for the past to become. Newness is a real problem for historians, although as proof that they are finally recognizing computing as having a past I submit the fact that in the decade between 1985 and 1996, well over a thousand publications (articles, books, and videos) appeared on the history of computing.[3] But it is this newness of the subject on the one hand and the traditional historical concerns for scholarship, truth, and perspectives of time on the other that give meaning to any discussion of information processing history and set the challenges for future research.

Even what to call the topic has been a continuous problem, no thanks to the industry that spawned the technology because it, too, could not settle on a label. In the 1930s and 1940s, the word computer was hardly used, other than to describe mathematicians who computed. Usually we think of Vassar College mathematics graduates in army uniforms calculating firing tables during World War II. In business organizations, the department responsible for using information processing equipment might be called the "tabulating department" or the "IBM department." Adding machines and desktop calculators were not dignified by having a name for themselves; the closest was the "Accounting Department." In the 1950s and 1960s, "electronic data processing" or, more simply, EDP, became the phrase to use, reflecting by the second half of the decade the growing migration of information processing to electronic digital computers. By the mid-1970s, the more popular term was "Management Information Systems," or MIS, reflecting the changing mission of EDP from simply crunching numbers and data to offering analysis and help in decision making. In the 1980s we saw the slow migration away from EDP and MIS to "information technology" or I/T by the start of the 1990s. We are currently stuck on I/T.

We also are dealing with the name of the devices we are talking about! In the 1930s and 1940s the term used was calculator. Purists will want to debate the difference between a calculator and a computer; and users see computers as simply large calculators. By the end of the 1950s we see the acceptance of the term computers as evidenced by titles of books and articles of the period and the language in them. Then we specialized. By the mid-1970s these devices were "mainframes" and "minis." In the 1980s we got "micros," "microcomputers," and "personal computers," not to mention derivative phrases like "Macs" and "PCs." If you are a futurist, you would have to conclude that we are not finished coming up with new names for the industry and its technology!

Despite the confusion and evolution of names, it may seem odd to pause and justify the historical significance of information processing history as a field of research, although suggesting where we are and what lines of investigation might prove profitable to explore does make sense. After all, Americans alone have spent over $4 trillion on computers and sink about 10 percent of their gross national product (GNP) into this technology.[4] But it is a necessary exercise to conduct from time to time if historians are to define the history of information processing in terms relevant to their generation and to the society of which they are a part. Truth, change, technology, and research are all variables in a complex formula which changes with this topic. If we accept the notion that information processing is having a profound impact on the nature of society in the last quarter of the twentieth century, then we have no choice but to define carefully what needs to be studied and how. No study of this century can seriously avoid the issue of information processing history. Careful questioning of this industry's technology and history makes it possible for archivists and librarians to start collecting the kinds of materials future scholars will need, while offering researchers today an opportunity to define events while they are still fresh in our minds.

Although I still refer to information processing as a relatively new field for historical research, that is not to say that historians have remained strangers to computers. Quite the contrary, like other members of society historians have been "users" of computers for nearly three decades. In fact, the emergence of quantitative history as a giant sub-field of historical inquiry was made largely possible by access to computers, beginning in the late 1960s and getting up a full head of steam by the mid-1970s. PCs in the 1980s just fed the fires more, particularly in the 1990s when large numbers of statistical processing tools became convenient and inexpensive to use. In fact, dependence on computers to perform historical research has gone so far that one of the first leading spokesmen of quantitative historians, Robert W. Fogel, admonished his colleagues in 1975 not to overuse it.[5] Yet despite his plea that other research techniques be used with computers, hardly any significant socio-historical study today is conducted without the use of computers.[6]

When we flip the issue of information processing and history over on its other side—the historical study of information processing—we find that little substantive historical scholarship has been published. There are signs of newness around us. The Charles Babbage Institute, the key archival center for the study of computing's history, is a product of the 1970s, while the *Annals of the History of Computing* only began publication in 1979. The important historical works on information processing have all been published within the past several years.[7] A quick survey of the historical literature on computing reveals that fewer than 500 articles and four dozen books have been published by historians. An additional 3,000 plus titles examined by this author are critical to the study of information processing (seminal pieces, memoirs, for example). Oral interviews with key people represent fewer than 400 titles.[8] This observation should not be confused, however, with the massive literature on information processing which historians could employ in their research. The Charles Babbage Institute, at the University of Minnesota, is currently acquiring vast quantities of materials (published and unpublished) useful to historians. Yet the harsh fact remains, almost everything in the way of historical research has yet to be done, a conclusion I first reached in 1983 and which remains true as of this writing (1996). The good news is that we no longer are prisoners of information processing history being contemporary; we now have over a half century of history behind us just for computers, and for related equipment and applications more than a century. It is time to get on with the work of the historian.

Even historians have a difficult time, however, accepting the notion that this industry has been around for a long time. While I hope I put that issue to bed with publication of *Before the Computer*, the fact represents a new paradigm that will take time to sink in. The data processing industry, or that of information processing, has, after all, been around since the late nineteenth century. While historians will refer to abacusses, looms, other automata, and the explosive growth in mathematics since World War I, the mass use of information processing only began at a significant level with card input/output devices of the Hollerith type. That technology dates from the 1880s. The use of such devices remained essentially unchanged and limited until after World War II. Although scientific literature is salted and peppered with several hundred articles about research on devices (written during the 1920s and 1930s) that eventually evolved into computers, this knowledge was hardly applied before World War II to any

significant degree. Much more massive was the use of adding machines, calculators, cash registers, and hundreds of specialized billing and accounting machines that dwarfed the use of punch card technology right up through World
War II.[9]

Considerable attention has been paid to developments in electronic computing
during World War II, much of it sensational and highly eclectic. Yet other than
for some highly specialized devices made during the war for cryptography and
weapons controls in Great Britain, Germany, and the United States, many gaps
remain in our understanding of the early development of information processing.[10] What we think of as a data processing industry (the name it had in the
1960s–early 1980s) with large numbers of users, a wide variety of products and
applications, and a rapid stream of technological innovations came only after
World War II and not really until the mid-1950s and running unrelentlessly to
the present. Today, for example, over a third of U.S. homes have personal
computers, and over two-thirds of all American business enterprises. Therefore,
while data processing has a pedigree dating back thousands of years, its significance to the study of history is hardly two generations old. Newness again
explains why all the work for historians lies ahead of them.

In many ways the evolution of information processing and the historical literature which is beginning to follow behind it parallels earlier historical situations. Three very common examples (for comparative purposes) involve the
wool trade of the Middle Ages, the Industrial Revolution of the eighteenth and
nineteenth centuries, and the automobile industry after World War I. In all three
cases, these highly defined industries, along with their communications links,
economic bases, and historical importance, emerged almost overnight. Within
two generations each grew out of virtual insignificance to become major economic factors in society, influencing standards of living and the political and
military powers of states, and affecting the attitudes of leaders and thinkers. In
all three, participants recognized the importance of their work and kept records
for future use while others wrote memoir literature. And in each case, historians
were at work from the earliest days reacting to the phenomenon in question,
raising the same concerns anyone would expect for any period of history.

While executives, for example, in major automobile companies wrote their
memoirs in the 1950s and 1960s, and thousands of articles appeared in the
contemporary press, historians simultaneously defined the historical issues requiring further study.[11] A similar litany could be sung about either the Industrial
Revolution or the wool trade. To cite a quick example from information processing, think of Herman Goldstine's *The Computer from Pascal to von Neumann*, which combines memoirs and historical investigation, or the more recent
case of Emerson W. Pugh and his colleagues with *IBM's 360 and Early 370
Systems*.[12] In short, the way historians react to vast new changes in a society
beset with different and important economic ventures is a familiar situation—
information processing is no exception. It would be interesting, maybe important, to understand to what extent the first historians of a new technology in the

nineteenth or twentieth centuries were both an historian and a member of the industry, before all the research was done by historians who were not participants in the subjects they wrote about.[13]

One IBM pamphlet on the history of the company's technology tumbled across one of the great surprises about the historical significance of information processing. Hitting the proverbial historical nail on the head, its title *It Was to Have Been the Nuclear Age. It Became the Computer Age*, told the story.[14] The explosion of the atomic bomb a half century ago drew to a close the age of free security and focused attention on a new technology. The literature on atomic energy and its applications today number in the hundreds of thousands of titles. It was only in the 1970s, however, that writers, scientists, politicians, and historians recognized that the real story lay with computers, not with atomic energy—not to be confused with the topic of the Cold War. In the two previous decades scientists kept introducing new technologies and products. Companies like IBM, The Radio Corporation of America (RCA), and others made products while governments, universities, and all major corporations installed and used large numbers of computers. By the early 1970s, most companies in the industrialized world were spending about 2 percent of their budgets on computers and related software and people, closer to 5 percent by 1995. The figure for communications and information handling in general approached 30 percent by the early 1980s.[15]

Looking at the significance of the issue from the point of users defines the case even more dramatically. In the United States alone, the U.S. Department of Labor predicted in 1975 that by 1985 over 70 percent of the workforce in the industrialized sector would be dependent on computers to perform their work. A negligible number were so dependent in 1960. The forecast was made and surpassed. Historians, caught up in the use of computers like everyone else, were surprised at how quickly information processing became a fundamental force in our society. The scientific and futuristic characteristics of Alvin Toffler's books, which seemed so fictional just two decades ago, are commonplace today.[16]

The speed and scope with which information processing became such a profound part of our lives therefore provides the first and most important reason for historians to study the subject. It simply affects so many people today. Therein lie questions of historical significance that have yet to be answered, despite the fact that we have known what mountain was to be climbed for over a decade. How did information processing become so important in such a short period of time? Why? Although these questions have not been answered definitively, pieces of the punchline are coming together. I made that observation in 1983 and it still holds today. Clearly the development of reliable, cost-effective technology is a major contributor to the answer. Many of the articles that have appeared in the *Annals of the History of Computing* have discussed this very point: the development of one kind of computer or another and the evolution of various types of software (languages, operating systems, and, more recently, applications). Other authors have pursued the software issue thoroughly insofar as operating systems and programming languages are concerned, to the point that much of what happened during the 1940s and 1950s is reasonably well understood today.[17] Although much of this literature is memoir in nature and sometimes mimics chronicles of the Middle Ages, the quality is such that we have a good picture of the early years. Much more needs to be done, but some of the key issues and questions have been identified, at least the issues relevant to historians of the 1990s.

Another line of questioning that has been pursued, although less satisfactorily, is institutional histories. The most obvious example is IBM, the subject of a growing body of literature.[18] Yet good histories of other vendors (for example, Sperry, Honeywell, Data General of the mainframe and minicomputer era) are still needed. However, histories of PC companies written by journalists were appearing at the rate of about one every three or four months during the 1990s.[19] We need to understand how so many companies were formed and run, how products were developed and sold, who used them and why, and what the effects on society in general were. What we have learned since the 1970s has been the importance of studying technological developments within the context of engineering, business, and institutional history, and of the role of customers and government officials, rather than in the isolation of engineering developments.[20]

The broader issue of society raises a more fundamental point. In the October 1982 issue of the Charles Babbage Institute's *Newsletter*, its director, Arthur L. Norberg, clearly raised an important point: "There has been some concern recently for too much attention to hardware development, with a small amount of simultaneous analysis of software, and too little attention to industrial activity."[21] In the mid-1990s we can say some progress has been made in addressing his concern, although doctoral dissertations continue to be written that focus on hard technical "box" histories. Those historians who have been working with the subject of computer history, however, have moved on to broader issues, even when they write about machines.

But it seems as if the historians have gently tiptoed around the obvious problem: the impact of computers on society. It is a challenging issue given the newness of the subject which does not lend itself to the benefits of perspective that the distance of time offers. Norberg recognized part of the problem by acknowledging that much work had to be done in writing biographies of key people and in preparing institutional histories and other monographs on various devices and software (especially application programs), so that historians could then move on to the difficult issues involving the general role of information processing in society and in the world economy. Indeed the narrower, more parochial monographs and articles will be required as building blocks before any broad study of any significance can be attempted. In this requirement the history of computing is no different from any other field of historical research. Basic work on narrow subjects is the early and necessary step that must be taken. What helps is the fact that there is a growing body of sociological and economic studies on the use and effects of computers that historians will eventually exploit; they have not done so yet.

The temptation to look at global issues (as I am guilty of in this chapter!) is difficult to resist and indeed is an important step, but a dangerous one because of the lack of data upon which to base judgments. For example, the Industrial Revolution of the eighteenth and nineteenth centuries could not be appreciated in its global and broadest social context until after World War II—a century and a half after the process began![22] With respect to information processing, a history was written of the computer industry which, while interesting and informative, illustrated how risky it is to write on a broad theme when basic material is not available for research.[23] Various industry surveys illustrate how desperately we need basic information about the subject of computers, effects on society, and consequences on economies of the world.[24] The need to analyze what is already a large mountain of information is perhaps still the biggest challenge of all. It is that requirement that makes existing surveys weak, not the efforts of the scholars in question.

In 1983 I generated a list of fundamental issues requiring the attention of historians and the list could have gone on for many pages. In looking at it in 1996, I found it still held true and therefore I present it as food for thought. It is not definitive, but the topics are crucial to the field of information processing history. Simply put it includes:

- biographies of key inventors, businessmen, and users
- institutional histories of vendors of hardware, software, and services
- institutional histories of companies, universities, and government agencies describing their use of data processing
- analysis of technical issues concerning the development of hardware, software, and management techniques
- applications and their evolution in various economic or industry sectors (office, factory, defense, public utility, insurance, banking, accounting, etc.)
- impact of information processing on society (covering many of the issues suggested by Toffler but also its effect on education, defense, and business practices)
- use of computing in war and peace (diplomatic, World War II, Korea, and Vietnam)
- role of communications (why stop with the telegraph and the telephone, or even railroads and automobiles?)
- effect of rapid communications and information processing on social values and attitudes
- nature of change and the "technological imperative"
- comparative analyses of the evolution of information processing and other historical phenomenon.

The good news is that since the early 1980s we have seen important articles and books appear on each topic and many are being written. The greatest progress has been made in technical histories, biographical encyclopedias, company histories, and, most recently, histories of applications. In short, the debate is becoming broader in scope and long on research, just what is needed at the moment!

One of the most important questions may involve change itself. We know that information processing is a major contributor to change coming at a time when the world economy is going through a two-phase shift—Third World economies from agricultural to industrial, and industrial to service based— driven at a heated pace within the context of global competition. All of that, of course, has been largely facilitated by technical advances in computing and telecommunications.[25] Why is change faster today than it was 100 years ago? How has information technology contributed to this situation? What are the effects of change? What is change? These kinds of fundamental historiographical questions can be partially answered through the careful study of information processing itself. One good first attempt that can serve as a jumping off point for scholars is James R. Beniger's *The Control Revolution*, in which he demonstrates how society's need for control over information with which to run businesses and other organizations made the need for computational devices necessary.[26] If your taste runs more toward business history rather than biosocial perspectives, an excellent model is JoAnne Yates' *Control through Communication*, which looks at specific companies and how they managed information and, like Beniger, covers both nineteenth- and twentieth-century trends, rather than just those of a short period (e.g., the age of the computer).[27]

We can quickly review the progress made in addressing many of the issues listed above and identify some opportunities if we accept an artificial and arbitrary set of periods with which to work. For the sake of argument, I have selected the following historical periods as a framework for reviewing some developments and opportunities for continued research:

- Information processing from ancient times to the Age of Napoleon (to about 1800)
- Nineteenth and early twentieth centuries (to 1939)
- Birth of the modern computer (1939–1955)
- Era of information systems (1955 to the present)

These breakdowns are convenient in that they reflect obvious clusters of existing literature and areas requiring further research. The period to around 1800 takes into account the development of calculating devices and fundamental work in mathematics. It also encompasses the initial reactions of the scientific community to the Industrial Revolution (with looms and counters, for example). Nineteenth-century developments, when carried on to the start of World War II, although not exactly a clean and neat set of chronological boundaries, do at least take into account the development of various engines, calculators, additional work in mathematics, and, of course, the introduction and wide use of punch card technology, particularly in scientific research and in industrial and office applications. In this period the two giant developments that have already been studied now to a great extent are the work of Charles Babbage and Herman Hollerith.

The years from 1939 to 1955 were seminal in the development of the electronic digital computer along with the creation of operating systems, programming languages, and applications. The period following represents the explosive use of information processing in all sectors of industrialized society, no longer limited to the laboratory or to a few government and industrial users. We may also be seeing the emergence of yet another historical watershed, beginning in the early 1980s with the massive adoption of personal computers—a class of computers that is rapidly overtaking the more traditional mainframe approach to the processing of information.

INFORMATION PROCESSING FROM ANCIENT TIMES TO THE AGE OF NAPOLEON

I am narrowing the focus of this section to counting devices, although information processing (tablets, books, etc.) will eventually have to be put into a broader context of information handling and its impact on society. The more we learn about the functioning of the brain and the evolution of the human species, the more obvious it becomes that humankind was as much information-handling creatures as it was tool users. The importance of data manipulation with tools outside the brain is a story that has yet to be pulled together properly. That effort will give old counting methods and devices new meaning set solidly into the framework of what we know of human thinking today. The Age of Napoleon is a convenient cutoff because with the wars of the late 1700s and early 1800s, work on relevant information management, counting, and mathematical issues, and by important groups of people, slowed down. There is a marked pause in developments caused by these wars, in sharp contrast to the spurt triggered by World War II, the Korean conflict, and the Vietnam war. The Industrial Revolution, from the point of view of technological innovations, was a fruitful period. One of the by-products of this era was what we might today call programmable looms or process control, developed before 1740 with significant advances achieved by the end of the 1760s. Work on mathematical calculators peaked in the 1770s, not to be advanced significantly until after the Napoleonic Wars. Mathematics as a field of study benefited richly from the Enlightenment of the 1700s; its development would be further renewed by the second decade of the 1800s, leading to new forms of mathematics critical to the future of computers (e.g., Boolean logic, statistics).

If you were to take a bird's-eye view of the literature dealing with automata primarily, the field below would show pockets of rich material and also much barren countryside. Large mountains of documents and publications would appear concerning tablets, illuminated manuscripts from the Middle Ages, and finally the history of the technology of printing. Even the history of writing and languages has been well studied, and frequently. These topics need not concern us because what is of greater interest is the evolution of counting (computing) technology, the ancestor of the computer. Through that narrow lens we can see where opportunities for additional research and analysis exist.

Briefly put, there is a growing body of literature covering the inventions of Baron Gottfried Wilhelm von Leibniz (1646–1716), John Napier (1550–1617), Blaise Pascal (1623–1666), Wilhelm Schickard (1592–1635), and Gaspard Schott (1608–1666), not to mention the work of a variety of people on looms in the 1700s. This documentation includes good biographies, technical descriptions of various devices, and works about the evolution of mathematical principles.[28] As individual historical outcroppings on the landscape, these materials are good and cover important issues—intellectual background of the people involved and technical explanations of their devices—and are based on solid archival and other primary materials. Equally important, this work has been placed into context with other scientific and technological developments of the age.

Yet in spite of this material, there is still a dearth of articles and books reviewing the application of this kind of technology to business and scientific problems. There are exceptions of course—the loom being the most obvious—but what role did counting devices have? What effects did these various inventions have on mathematics or accounting? To what uses, other than the loom, did people apply automata during the Industrial Revolution? To what extent where these devices deployed? Perhaps the answer to these questions is that automata and information-handling equipment were minor players hardly applied to the common daily problems of Europeans or Asians, but until the issues are researched and studied we do not know. Conflicting evidence still suggests a story that has yet to be told, because we have detailed biographies of key scientists working with automata, yet a sampling of general histories of mathematics hardly mentions these devices before Babbage's time. The same holds true for the history of science.[29]

On the other hand, there are a large number of general histories devoted to the description of automata, computers, and other devices beginning with ancient times and carrying the story to the present. Most are chronological narrations of a series of historical events linked together only by chronology rather than by cause and effect. Hardly any attempt is made to show how the work of one period influenced that of another. Even less effort is evident to set these developments within the context of scientific endeavor in general, particularly in the Western world. In other words, simplistic histories generally describe various devices well but as if each were invented in a vacuum with hardly any input from other scientific developments, economic conditions, or social and political impacts. Almost as much of a problem is the lack of discussion about the effect of such inventions on the world outside the scientist's laboratory. This second problem may become the harder of the two to resolve since we need first to know what influence the community had on the development of computing before we can appreciate to what uses such efforts were applied. These observations on general histories of computing are meant less as harsh criticisms than as a statement of opportunity.[30]

For an ideal model of what is needed, I suggest Henri-Jean Martin's large and comprehensive *History and Power of Writing* in which he discusses not only various languages and writing systems, but also how they were used, the consequences on society, and degree of deployment on a global basis. The book should become mandatory reading for anybody wanting to do research on the history of information processing.[31]

Anyone looking at the body of literature could easily suggest that histories of automata need not be written since dozens exist, when what we really have is a series of loosely connected stories of various devices which focus more on identifying their technical characteristics than upon their contributions (if any) to society at large. Now that we know so many of these devices existed and have easily obtainable descriptions of many of them, historians can push to a more sophisticated level by setting the efforts of a few into the broader context of scientific contributions to the societies from which they emerged. Thus in the years to come, following a pattern evident in the historiography of other technical developments including printing, we might see not simply an illustration of a counter, but perhaps a picture of someone using it. We would expect to see lengthy discussions on the impact of automata on mathematics, and their effect on the thinking of eighteenth-century *philosophes* rather than on the grinding of wheels and pegs. To do this the historian will have to be a specialist in the history of science, technology, and economics first and an expert on computing second. The role model should be historians of publishing and books who have figured out how to balance technical skills with a deep understanding of social and economic history.

The effort toward a broader analysis of computing history has, in fact, begun, for there are some good examples of what is required. The more specific an historical inquiry, the better the literature seems to be. For instance, H. W. Dickinson's biography of Sir Samuel Morland (1625–1695) provides an excellent review of this man's life and his inventions, and their applicability to the world in which he lived.[32] Additional monographs of this type are needed constantly, but less so for the period prior to 1800 than for the years after. The sheer passage of time has allowed historians to work on the centuries following the Middle Ages in more detail than on those of the past 200 years. These monographs can provide more material for broader surveys—like Martin's on writing illustrates—of automata than the general histories of counters and related equipment because the narrower studies have attacked the kinds of questions already raised herein.

Besides biographies, some authors have attempted the complicated yet necessary task of comparing the work done in one country to that of another. The use of comparative history is a proven vehicle for describing the relative impact of specific inventions on the mainstream of scientific developments. The study of correspondence between inventors, subscription lists of scientific journals, and the location of various devices and papers all contribute to our understanding of how information about inventions flowed and to whom. Two examples of comparative history on computing that can serve as models are articles. Heinz Zemanek wrote an article on the history of computing in Central Europe over a long period of time, showing by his work the impact of research accomplished by a variety of people. If there is a criticism to make of this article it is that the subject deserves a book-length treatment that shows in more detail the correlation of various activities to one another. A second example of the kind of work desperately needed for the period prior to 1800 is T. M. Smith's interpretive piece that argues the case for computation evolving as a series of inventions building on the experiences of earlier ones.[33] For a model of a general history of technology Trevor I. Williams's *A Short History of Twentieth Century Technology* is an excellent model.[34] Linkage, thus, is an historical phenomenon that has been inadequately recognized by writers on the history of computing but that is essential to our understanding of the subject.

Smith's logic is particularly important since it is consistent with what historians of science and technology have noted for other developments in all fields: physics, chemistry, weapons, and transportation to mention a few.[35]

A good example of how cause and effect for a variety of inventions impacted a particular series of developments is evident if we peak into the nineteenth century. Geoffrey D. Austrian's biography of Herman Hollerith clearly shows us how technical developments in a variety of fields—counters, electrical machines, and railroad cars—led to the development of punch card equipment. He carries the story further with detailed descriptions of their applications and the influence those uses had on the subsequent evolution of that technology.[36] This work reflects the kind of coverage needed for the period prior to 1800s, and in particular for the period from the early 1600s to the time of programmable looms in the late 1700s or early 1800s.

So our discussion leaves us with a list of opportunities for historical research on computing and information processing. For the period prior to 1800 a list of needed work might look like this:

- Additional biographies (articles and books) on inventors, particularly for those in France and all of Central Europe and around the Mediterranean are needed.

- Comparative analyses of work done in one period in various countries concurrently (e.g., counting systems of the Middle Ages everywhere and their devices).

- Histories of institutions such as monasteries, academies, universities, and government agencies involved in the development of related technologies. (Available histories of computing developments at the University of Manchester and for specific military projects during World War II illustrate what is needed for the earlier years, much along the same lines as historians did with the topic of Portuguese institutional support for explorations of African coastlines during the period of Henry the Navigator.)[37]

- Serious attempts at identifying the impact of computational devices and data management within the mainstream of scientific developments in Europe and America during
  the Industrial Revolution (more specifically from about 1720 through the 1800s). The
  material for such studies is readily available: books and articles, journals, and significant archival collections. Such an effort would tell us how important computing developments were, instead of leaving us with a large collection of historical descriptions
  that may have little importance and only satisfy our curiosity about mechanical exotica.[38]
- Applications of various devices and efforts as another lens through which to view the
  dim past of computation. How were counting devices and information-handling inventions used? What effect did they have on business and scientific work? What techniques
  were employed? Today we have fragmented hints of answers. While much material for
  such studies exists, very few tools to help the historian do. There are no massive
  bibliographies on the history of computing and data processing prior to the early
  1800s.[39]

There are no guides to archival collections devoted to the history of information processing and computation prior to 1800. Pockets of materials are buried within archival descriptions of various institutions (e.g., British Museum and
Library), but not by subject. Materials will have to be collected by information
processing subject in the years to come and archival guides on them prepared.
But until historians pay more attention to mechanical computing before 1800s,
there will be little incentive for librarians and archivists to step in and help. This
was a problem two decades ago and remains unchanged. The good news, however, is that the history of technology has come into its own, a closer relative
to the history of science than we thought before, so the situation could change.

NINETEENTH AND TWENTIETH CENTURIES (TO 1939)

Historians of technology "discovered" the nineteenth century during the
1980s and the early 1990s. Institutional histories, and others on devices, technologies, biographies, societal impacts, and just about anything else any historian would want for the eighteenth century, are being supplied.[40] So once the
historian moves past the 1700s the history of automata comes into its own along
with new uses and expansion in our knowledge of physics and mathematics.
Each field evolves, thereby contributing the essential technical and scientific
ingredients to the creation of a data processing industry. Better machines to
manipulate numbers, the need to handle large quantities of figures (as in large
national censuses), continued research into electricity and metals, and a greater
understanding of relationships between numbering systems and electricity (such
as binary notations) all created the required atmosphere by the end of the 1800s.
During this period a wide variety of mechanical and electrical devices for use
in the office and by businesses was developed. The most obvious ones were
cash registers and adding and calculating machines. Institutions were becoming
larger and more complex, creating the necessary conditions for new applications.
Railroads had massive record-keeping requirements for fares and freight hauling.

Government agencies needed better tools with which to generate statistics to influence policies and programs. Cash registers by the tens of thousands were sold to large and small stores where benefits in accounting for money was key. In the nineteenth century as in our own, the "technological imperative" that allowed new changes to come faster than before, resulting in refinements of inventions, picked up speed. This was especially the case after 1870 and has remained unabated to the present.

The net result of all these forces at work was varied. The one by-product of interest to us is that the evolution of devices, the expansion of our knowledge of mathematics and electricity, and the development of scientific prerequisites made possible the electronic computer during the early decades of the twentieth century. As we look at the history of the 1800s and its literature, it is a century dominated by Charles Babbage and later by Herman Hollerith, with a healthy cast of minor players doing their jobs very well in mathematics and in the design of adding machines and calculators, not to mention others who figured out how to manufacture these devices at a profit. Researchers have already focused considerable attention on the work of Babbage and Hollerith. The bibliographies on each are impressive. However, much remains to be done in concentric circles moving out from these two men, for neither worked without the influences of the outside world.

We know that the conditions that made possible technological developments in the nineteenth century turned out to be of greater importance than the work of one or two inventors. That is certainly true in the case of Babbage who had little tangible luck with his projects, while Hollerith got machines built and out doing productive work. During the 1980s and 1990s we learned a great deal about the circumstances influencing inventors in the 1800s, but we still have much to learn. It is as if we were just starting the research. What made the demand for information technology great enough to justify the inventions that came? Was Beniger right when he argued that it was the result of a need for control, or others when they argued that technology and costs came together? Hollerith's biographer thinks it was the technological innovations that made things possible. Robert V. Bruce argued the case for science and the American economic takeoff coming together. They are probably correct because their arguments have been validated for twentieth century activities. Our biggest gap of information still remains in the area of applications: to what use were all these devices specifically put and did the owners get their money's worth out of them? Applications is a subject that crosses over from technology to industry, biography, social and economic conditions, the impact of World War I and the acquisition of empires (for example, Cuba and Puerto Rico by the United States), and social and intellectual attitudes.

We know that many of the technological developments in computing in the 1940s and 1950s resulted from the immediate past. For the historian this means that scientific activities during the 1910s, 1920s, and 1930s must be understood. Yet many of the components were developed late in the 1800s (e.g., wiring boards) and at the turn of the century (e.g., radio parts such as tubes). Except for the scientific literature of the inter-war years, there has been inadequate examination of computing activities during these decades, particularly their application in business and government.[41] To get the job done right, historians will have to study technology on the one hand but on the other, its use.

The first trail must begin deep in the nineteenth century, decades before Hollerith's punch card equipment began arriving on the scene. The focus should be on equipment (technical considerations) and their use in offices. This latter point—applications—is of particular importance because it encouraged many to look for better ways to perform common counting and accounting functions. History is motivated by the same factors that motivate individuals: self-advantage, economics, economies of scale, politics, or necessity. We know almost nothing about specific users of most computational equipment. Who used the Thomas Arithmometer? Why? What about cash registers and adding machines—who were their users and what were the very earliest applications and benefits?

A second line of investigation must pursue those scientific developments in laboratories, particularly in the late nineteenth and early twentieth centuries, that made it possible within a few short years of World War II for engineers to piece together what became known as the electronic digital computer. In short, John von Neumann (1903–1957) did not pop out of nowhere, even though the historical literature today would lead readers to think so. He grew up in an environment rich in scientific possibilities. More important were the lives of all the radio and electrical engineers of the 1920s and 1930s who later built computers.[42]

But before additional research is done, a quick audit of progress to date will serve as a guide to tasks left undone. As already mentioned, Charles Babbage (1791–1871) and Hollerith have already attracted the attention of many writers. Austrian's biography of Hollerith fills a major gap in our understanding of the inventor, his machines, and to some extent the applications to which they were employed. Within months of publication another book appeared, this time a major biography of Babbage by Anthony Hyman. Since then a continuous stream of Babbage's papers and articles about him have appeared in print.[43] The number of articles on his engines can only be considered vast, only to be followed by the number of articles about his private life. No figure in the history of data processing has been so studied and yet so little did he actually build! It would seem that it is time to leave Mr. Babbage alone and move on to more substantive topics.

Another feature of the years from the end of the Napoleonic Wars to the start of World War II was the development of a large number of counting devices (some scientific and others commercially available) and the formation of major companies to market them. The most obvious include Hollerith's firm, and later those formed by James Powers and others. In the same period as Hollerith there existed the company formed by William S. Burroughs (1855–1898) and the National Cash Register Company (NCR). Many others, selling mechanical devices, came and went during this period, especially after Hollerith's patents ran out in Europe. The devices developed and manufactured by these firms have been described in considerable detail by historians.[44] During the years when such units were being sold and used, descriptions of a large variety of accounting machines appeared in print, ensuring that historians in the years to come will have adequate supplies of technical descriptions for many models.[45]

Some companies and people obviously received more attention than others. We have a good start on the history of NCR but we need a fully developed corporate history, while biographical material appears on IBM's founder, Thomas J. Watson, and too little on the Burroughs Corporation even though the Burroughs Archives is housed at the Charles Babbage Institute. Anyone who has written on early IBM has commented on cash registers, adding machines, and punch card technologies of the years prior to World War I. Yet we still do not have a corporate history of James Power's company, or of the Felt & Tarrant Company, manufacturer of the Comptometer, the most popular adding machine of the early 1900s after Burroughs.[46] The effort expended on describing the evolution of the office, particularly recent work on the role of women, has been helpful.[47] But the truth remains that the role of office equipment in offices has yet to be told. There are exceptions, of course, but what we first need are company-focused studies, one by one. Early users of information technology remain almost a blank area for us, although we know that banks and insurance companies were extensive users along with railroads and government agencies. Currently JoAnne Yates is the leading student of what these industries did with computing-like equipment in the early decades of the twentieth century.

In his history of computers—written a generation ago—Herman H. Goldstine clearly described lines of intellectual thought and the evolution of applications that made possible the development of computers; his thinking is just as useful today as when first written. One of his suggestions still requiring an historian is the definition of the role of military applications in the development of the computer. It is not enough just to say that the U.S. military funded research on computers in the 1940s and 1950s. Goldstine also addresses the nineteenth-century concern about mathematical tables, one that continued through World War II with firing tables for artillery and bombing. In the years surrounding World War II, however, focus should be on military needs because therein lies the justification for much of the work done at the Moore School, Bletcheley Park, and at other universities and research centers. Today we have pieces of the story, not a comprehensive review of technology and applications for the military. To a large extent the focus on military applications has been on combat-related affairs.[48] But just as important as dropping bombs and breaking secret codes are more civilian applications like paying solders, ordering supplies, and doing normal office accounting. That story has barely been touched. Goldstine also harped on familiar themes to historians, about the need to understand the institutional political activities that influenced or dominated the development of the data processing industry.

I have suggested that technological and scientific developments in the 1920s and 1930s certainly made possible the creation of the modern computer. Looking at the work of specific individuals is a very useful exercise. Vannevar Bush has been studied along with von Neumann, J. Presper Eckert, John Atanasoff, John Mauchly, and Jan Rajchman (although he still needs a full biographical treatment). We need to also understand what really occurred in the way of technological developments at RCA in the 1940s and 1950s when Rajchman was there—this is a huge void in our understanding of technological developments in the 1940s and 1950s. Scientific literature of the period is prolific on various developments which could serve as starting points for any historian.[49]

Although more will be said later in this book about archival holdings, beginning with the 1930s we move into the modern era of computing, one typified by the availability of a large quantity of personal and institutional records, not to mention a massive volume of articles and books concerning technical issues, historical analyses, and application briefs. The files of just Bell Laboratories, IBM, Burroughs, various U.S. and British government agencies, the University of Pennsylvania, Harvard University, and MIT, when added to the papers of key inventors, could keep historians busy for a long time. Thus it is possible to conduct thorough and important research on the history of computing since the end of World War I.[50] This is an important fact to remember since many historical projects are only undertaken when neat collections of papers are available, especially by graduate students in search of clearly defined dissertation topics. These young historians searching for a topic about which they can write their second book usually focus on narrow themes also often defined by the nature of existing documentation. Thus such collections should encourage considerable work in the years to come.

Some quick examples suggest the opportunity before us. In the early 1990s the Charles Babbage Institute began to receive the archives of the Burroughs Corporation, a major U.S. company and an important vendor in the office appliance and computer industry. Hundreds of cartons of papers, company publications, and illustrations came in covering the whole sweep of information processing and company history from the 1880s to the 1960s. To put it mildly, it is the most important new corporate archive to appear in a decade and it is about computers! The same Charles Babbage Institute has also been quietly acquiring a very large collection of corporate archives of Control Data Corporation (CDC), a clearly important player in the computer industry of the 1960s and 1970s. Personal papers of twentieth century computer pioneers come into the Institute on a steady basis. Meanwhile as you read these words, the U.S. National Archives continues to release to researchers agency files. Just about everything up to the end of World War II is now available. The same holds true for French and British collections.

Let us look at the period 1800 to 1939 from another perspective. The majority of the literature on computing for these years concentrates on work in the United States, Great Britain, and Germany. Dutch archives for the 1930s are rapidly becoming more available, and developments in Polish archival policies since the fall of the Soviet Union should lead to significant new sources on the 1930s, particularly for code breaking and university research. Also, as anyone familiar with the work of Leonardo Torres y Quevedo (1852–1936) could argue, important developments were taking place in the same period in other countries, as in Spain.[51] The growing body of literature on this Spaniard suggests that, in addition to businessmen and scientists, there are other people associated with institutions doing basic and applied research in Europe who should be studied. Although we are learning rapidly about the Machines Bull company in France and about the Dutch experience, Germany's substantial information processing heritage from 1800 to 1939 leaves much to be studied. In fact, Germany remains the single largest national opportunity for historians of the pre-World War II period.[52] Hints of developments in industrialized Japan prior to 1868 suggest another line of research.[53]

The issues for these various geographical areas and for the people and institutions involved are the same as those already explored by historians for the United States, Great Britain, France, and the Netherlands. Because of the highly institutionalized research channeled through organizations and royal scientific societies in Western and Eastern Europe, archival holdings of these well-established groups can shed considerable light on information processing. We already know that these societies encouraged development of computing devices from the sixteenth century onward in France and Spain, for example, and extensively during the 1800s in Great Britain, and the 1920s and 1930s in Poland. Having done research in several monastic and royal society archives in Europe, I can attest to the real possibility of other treasures waiting for the historian, because these institutions all corresponded with each other to compare research projects, and most monarchies in Europe sponsored scientific research, particularly on gadgets. As an inducement to the historian, most of these organizations have journals and publish books that we have barely heard of, since they were usually published in tiny editions with limited circulation—less than 500 copies! They represent little gold mines of material.

Covering the years 1800 to 1939, if one were to make a list for the historian of areas requiring work it should include the following:

- institutional histories of organizations doing research (e.g., royal societies, private individuals)

- universities (particularly Chicago, Wisconsin, Illinois, almost all of the California campuses, and most of the universities in continental Europe)

- government agencies (e.g., European census bureaus, post offices, and military, labor, and commerce departments)

- biographies of key scientists, businessmen, heads of government agencies, and institutions encouraging research

- applications, particularly for the period 1845–1939

- devices, particularly 1800 to 1875
- military by period or branch of service, particularly navies in the inter-war period (1920s–1930s)
- scientific research relevant to the origins of computing, particularly first half of the 1800s
- societal attitudes toward the introduction and use of new technologies and impact on scientific developments and change.

The good news is that the years from 1800 to 1939 are richly endowed with the archival and printed materials that are the grist for any historian. No period before or after has so much available now for immediate use by historians. No era has so wide a variety of topics in need of research. What about the years after 1945? They are very rich, too. While very significant, research on many topics of the latter period is hampered by the lack of open government and business archives, the paucity of organized private papers, and the protective prejudice of people still working in the information processing industry. These problems are simply less evident the further back in time one goes. Consequently, the years prior to the 1940s remain very fruitful today for the historian. Indeed, without a good appreciation of what happened in these years, we can hardly be expected to understand fully the explosion of developments that came so quickly after World War II. If there is one thing historians have learned about the past two decades, it is that many of these information technologies and their base sciences had very long gestation periods.[54]

BIRTH OF THE MODERN COMPUTER, 1939–1955

The period from 1939 to the mid-1950s marked the birth of the modern electronic digital computer and the wide acceptance of analog computing devices. With the arrival of commercially viable computers by the mid-1950s, the computer industry was born, witnessing the arrival of yet another information-handling technology into an industry that was by then about 75 years old. Prior to the mid-1950s, computers were not mass produced; they were one-of-a-kind devices, many constructed for government and military agencies. We measured them in the dozens, after the mid-1950s in the hundreds, and by the early 1960s thousands of copies per model. Hollerith and other accounting machinery remained widespread all through the 1930s and 1940s, slowly being displaced after the mid-1950s. But with the waning days of World War II a new situation radically different from what existed prior to 1939 was emerging.

In the years after 1950 the quantity of computer processing grew exponentially or, put in other words, the rate at which computer technology was installed and used grew as time passed, as addressed in Chapter 2. The variety of technological changes far surpassed that of earlier periods. One might add that the variety of applications for such technology also grew in the decades after the 1950s, as set forth in Chapter 5. Perched as of this writing (1996) late in the twentieth century, one could easily speak about major revolutions in information processing taking place every three to seven years. In fact, we have all become accustomed to using the term "generations" in discussing new technologies—at least four for mainframes and, depending on how one counts, two for personal computers.

While such terms as "revolution" and "generations" are dramatic and often misused and misleading, they are often the correct words to apply when describing what occurred to computing technology between 1939 and 1955, between 1939 and 1965 and, once again, after the arrival of various microcomputers in the late 1970s and early 1980s. At the dawn of personal computers (circa late 1970s) the home computer was costly, scarce, and primitive; today personal computers can be found in over one-third of U.S. homes, are inexpensive, have as much horsepower as $1 million computers did in the mid-1970s, and are responsible for driving nearly two percentage points of the Gross National Product of the United States! Thirty years ago IBM's customers were installing thousands of System 360 computer systems which today seem like museum objects and have less power than a laptop. And yet the introduction of the S/360 family of computers with common operating systems was a profound event in the history of this industry and in the life of IBM.

If we borrow from the business world the term "positioning," that is to say, the idea of placing oneself in a situation to take advantage of some circumstance, and apply it to the years from 1939 to the mid-1950s, we can better understand that era. For it was the activities in information processing in those years that made it possible for computers to become the important element that they are today. That perspective gives historical significance to what otherwise might be quiet years in the history of computing and information processing. After 1955, computers exploded on the business scene with a robustness almost unmatched by any other technology or product in the history of the modern world. What a statement to make! But it is true, and it carries with it an important obligation on the part of the historian of computing to understand developments in this period of gestation, one that computer pioneers considered exciting, active, and fraternal.

The circumstances of war shook nations out of depression and scientists and engineers into focused activity, and enabled science to make significant bounds forward. World War II created a sharp increase in demand for cryptographic work and expanded the requirement to analyze data faster and in greater quantities for such applications as anti-aircraft weaponry, bombing, and weather reporting. The technology that emerged made it possible for companies to be formed for the purpose of marketing computers to commercial customers. The most obvious example was the company formed by John W. Mauchly (1907–1980) and John Presper Eckert (1919–1995).[55] Companies already active in other fields, such as RCA, General Electric (GE), IBM, and Remington Rand, just to mention a few, also entered into the information processing field with computer products. General surveys of the Data Processing Industry (as it was known by the mid-1960s) give short, broad-brush surveys of most of these firms (except IBM, which continued to receive detailed treatment) for the 1960s, insulting

them with labels like "dwarfs." But these companies represent topics historians
will want to examine more closely in the years to come.[56] There was no guar-
antee in the years following World War II that IBM would be so important; it
could have been any of the others. All of these institutions will have to be
studied in detail to find out what they were doing in the 1940s and 1950s, and
why they were not the IBM of their time. Eventually, company files for most
of these firms will serve as the building blocks for solid historical monographs,
assuming the companies do not destroy some or all of their papers.[57]

Company histories are crucial for any understanding of the computer industry
because these institutions were the vendors and customers that built and used
this technology. The group which has almost virtually been ignored, however,
are the users. The reason why the information processing industry became so
important probably rests more with what was done with computers from the
1940s onward and less on the activities of one individual or firm. For the period
1939 to 1955, admittedly, there were fewer firms and people building computers
and thus the role of individuals is perhaps greater than in later years. Nonetheless, it is the demand for computing capability that provided the economic and
personal incentives to press on with new developments. The fact that users have
not been well studied does not mean that good solid technical histories of the
period were not written. They were.[58] Software and hardware have been continuously studied, perhaps because they represent neat, highly definable, and important topics. As a result, we know a great deal about the technical history of
the period.

The challenge to the historian, after these studies, is to go beyond such technical issues to study who used computers and why. It is only then that the
scholar will be "positioned" to analyze the effects of computing on business
in the post-1955 period and appreciate the effects such technology had on society. By this last point, one must take on the difficult task of identifying how
people lived and thought in the industrialized world as a result of computers—
not an easy task. It is understandable that on these two points the literature is
still slim, speculation and essays the bulk of the staple. In short, other than for
a few monographs on the World War II years and some post-war developments,
everything remains to be done, representing the same challenges to the historian
as the 1920s and 1930s.[59]

The complaint that everything has yet to be studied for this period reflects a
more obvious fact—namely, that the closer one gets to the present the less the
work that has been done by historians and the fuzzier the historical analysis
becomes. Documents, interviews, and so forth are simply not as abundant for
the historians because they are spending time on issues of earlier times. There
are some notable attempts being made to preserve the experiences of computer
"pioneers" through various interviewing programs that promise to expand our
oral history research materials. The Charles Babbage Institute, for example, has
conducted hundreds of such interviews; it is a major ongoing initiative of this
organization.[60] This project is filling in many technical details of the period and

has begun to include discussions with business leaders and users. More, however, desperately needs to be done. The editor of the *Annals of the History of Computing* during the early 1990s, J. A. N. Lee, supplemented the oral interviews by encouraging key figures to write down their memoirs, publishing many excerpts in the *Annals*.[61]

Archival activity for these years is pressing forward and, like oral history, the closer we get to the present the less significant the effort. Most archival holdings for the period after 1960 are still not available to historians. Some private papers related to such technical issues as programming languages (e.g., COBOL) are, however. Again, the leading source of both materials and leadership in building collections is the Charles Babbage Institute. Corporate archives continue to store up materials, but companies are reluctant to make them accessible to professional historians. The future is promising for historians: the sheer volume of material to be looked at will be daunting, for both the 1950s and beyond. To cite one simple example, IBM's internal bibliography of its own publications in 1983 was easily three feet thick, in 8.5-by-11-inch, double-column format in 8-point print![62] And that represents only one organization's publications on information processing! Today it is an online database.

The growth of information processing during the 1940s and 1950s made it possible for such technology to have a great influence on our lives in the last decades of this century. This simple fact gives great urgency to one important historical question: How did it all happen, and so quickly? One suspects that the answer lies in the years between 1939 and the late 1950s. It was in those years that the nature of computer architectures were thought out and then applied to the construction of computers by von Neumann and others,[63] and it was also in this period that the suppliers of such technology and its software made their initial contributions.[64] These were the years that saw the concept of operating systems and then their development accepted for the first time along with programming languages. As early as the mid-1940s the demand for computing emerged out of university laboratories and from government projects into the commercial world. The earlier experiences gained through automation of counting and accounting functions with Hollerith-type devices made the ground fertile for computers.

Surveying the literature of this important period presents a number of problems. To begin with, the number of technical papers and books published increased enormously over earlier times. As the number of new products arrived in the marketplace, so did the bulk of materials describing their use. Furthermore, people knowing little about information processing commented more frequently on computing in the public press, commenting, for example, about "giant brains." Serious thinkers and writers also focused inceased attention on computers in this period. While their views are important indicators of contemporaneous views, they clearly reflected an understandable innocence about this new technology. Yet hidden in the literature of these years are a number of materials which contribute to the history of information processing.

Quickly visited, a number of useful items appeared during those years and since on such subjects as Harvard's role in computing,[65] Bell Labs' innovations,[66] specialized computers such as the BINAC,[67] the Colossus project,[68] ENIAC,[69] EDSAC,[70] and the MANIAC.[71] A similar story can be told about software.[72] Surveys of hardware of the period are becoming more abundant as well, covering a wide variety of issues of historical interest. As the years passed, the literature on the now-identified "data processing" industry made it obvious that a collective conscience and awareness of a new order of things had begun to appear worthy of historical attention.[73] As with earlier periods, a chronic problem and hence a task ahead is the job of identifying who was using computers and how.[74] Biographies of the key people of this period do not exist except for a few pages here and there; most biographical treatments are obituaries or short encyclopedic biographies.[75]

Much of the detail on the bibliography of this period I have driven into the notes simply to avoid confusion or obfuscation in the discussion. The more important point to keep in mind is the areas of opportunity for future historians which are similar to those of earlier periods: institutional histories, biographies, technical reviews, and more than ever, information on the uses of such technologies, particulary by the business community after 1950. It is this last area that suggests the most complex yet significant line of investigation. As archives of various companies open up, it will become easier to write biographies of key data processing managers and histories of companies and their use of computers. The real difficulty will come later, in drawing all these studies together to understand the relative popularity in the use of computers and the impact they have had on society.

The economics of this industry suggests another line of research for historians. If we look at the economics of computing, we see that the cost of conducting transactions in a computer has dropped dramatically with each new generation of technology.[76] As this technology became easier to use, as better languages became available, and as pre-written application software became usable, the motivation for using more information processing technology increased. The story of each of these developments needs to be told, and certainly more thoroughly than has been done to date. The tale is complicated by the fact that the motivations for using this technology changed from the 1950s through the 1970s, providing different perspectives on what happened in the 1950s and early 1960s. For example, today it is clear that computers were usually used in the 1950s to automate highly defined tasks that could be done quicker by computers. Pure economics was involved. By the end of the 1970s, economics was not the only motivation; decision making and effectiveness also played key roles—topics difficult to quantify and define in comparison to what happened earlier. Thus, the extent of successful implementations in the 1950s led to the opening of an era of wide adoption of computing such that by the end of the 1970s, justification for computers also was being influenced by a mindset that knew no other way to accomplish tasks but with the use of these machines. Did such a mentality exist in earlier decades, particularly in companies that had been extensive users of tabulating equipment? What about the mindset of the scientific and engineering communities? To what extent had society (or at least those in it who adopted computers) in the industrialized world moved in the direction of a mechanistic view of itself and of its functions that made data processing almost inevitable? Although some writers flirted with these issues during the 1950s and 1960s,[77] no comprehensive studies have been completed to provide answers. These two decades are wide open for just about any kind of study along these lines.

In short, the challenge facing historians reviewing the 1940s and 1950s is extensive and cannot be denied. There are many published materials to plow through and untold mountains of archival matter locked away in the homes of scientists, engineers, and data processing managers, not to mention institutional collections. While we have many fine histories covering the technologies of the period, historians face a period in which more people were involved with information processing than in the 1920s and 1930s, using a greater variety of new technologies and for a broad and ever-growing list of applications. Perhaps most significant, when we reach the 1950s we can think of a data processing industry that recognizes itself to be a new entity, suggesting to historians the need for global surveys such as have been done for the textile, agricultural, publishing, pharmaceutical, automotive, and shipping industries.

ERA OF INFORMATION SYSTEMS, 1955–1980s

The middle of the 1950s and the early 1980s appears to be emerging as a discrete historical period in the history of computing. At the earlier end, it was marked by the beginning of wide acceptance of computers by the business community through the installation of large mainframe systems, while the latter as the period when wide adoption of microcomputers could be documented. In 1982, for example, more than a million personal computers were sold. While mainframes have continued to be installed down to the present, the periodization seems to be taking hold. From the perspective of applications, the chronology is very fuzzy—large batch jobs done in the 1950s and 1960s, with online systems coming on stream in the mid-1960s and widely in the 1970s. In the 1950s and 1960s we see a heavy concentration on efficiency applications that essentially reduced human labor content in work; in the 1970s and beyond the shift appears to be toward more decision-support and to applications that could not be done without the use of computers. So periodization remains difficult at best, although the historical tradition so far has been to take a machine-centric view of the technology and of its use, hence the period 1950s–1980s.

Now the events subsequent to the late 1950s, however, are more than simply current activities. They represent a mirror of society and what it values in its work and pleasure. The issues facing historians in earlier years are simply compounded in the 1960s and 1970s. Highlights of these years that will require

historical attention are varied but some examples might include IBM's introduction of the S/360 and S/370 computers[78]; emergence of user-friendly languages such as APL, BASIC, and Pascal,[79] bringing computing to many people;
and novel applications involving the space program, the war in Vietnam, some
home computing, and distributed information processing. Some of the work on
this period has begun, as in the case of the U.S. space program.[80] Neat, clean
topics exist across the entire economy of the industrialized world ready for
study.

The literature on the early history of a variety of programs and applications
is good considering that in some cases historical events are less than fifteen
years old. Today the best source of articles on the subject remains the *Annals
of the History of Computing*; books are appearing, but are more focused on
personal computer hardware and software companies about which we will have
more to say below. The paucity of book-length historical monographs on applications, however, remains despite the mountain of material that exists for use
by historians.[81] Artificial intelligence and robotics represent an exception in that
much of the contemporary literature does take an historical perspective, although
more descriptive than analytical in substance.[82]

IBM continues to be the subject of much attention by both observers of the
information processing industry and historians. They have focused primarily on
the actions and perspectives of IBM's executives and less on the use of their
products or on the impact of their actions. IBM's technology has been commented on in print, shedding a great deal of light on this subject.[83] Considerable
attention has been paid to the company, based on solid archival research, covering the historical period to the early 1960s, with more newspaper-like research
covering the era subsequent to the introduction of the S/360 in 1964. The files
that were generated by the various lawsuits of the 1970s promise, when studied,
to shed vast quantities of light on the industry and on IBM. Many of the legal
records are public, and large quantities are available at the Hagley Museum in
Delaware and at the Charles Babbage Institute at the University of Minnesota,
so historians do not have to rely on the beneficence of IBM to get started.

Other institutional studies have begun to appear, primarily memoir in nature
and narrow in scope. However, they represent a growing awareness on the part
of the scientists of this industry of the need to record their actions for history.
Very little of a similar nature has been written by users or executives of information processing companies.[84]

The American Federation of Information Processing Societies (AFIPS) and
CBI have provided an answer about what historians can do regarding the post-
1955 era. This latest period is less a time for writing about than for preserving
research materials. The role of historians, thus, should be one of assisting in
collecting printed documents, preserving raw files, and expanding oral history
projects. We could also use the usual collection of industry and institutional
studies taking the story into the 1980s. Nevertheless, the primary focus for these
years should be the collection of materials.

Interviews represent a real opportunity for historians to ask questions about how things were done and why and what the effects were on other decisions and events. There is an opportunity to discuss fundamental issues that may not necessarily be covered in future archival collections or publications. Of particular concern should be how new technologies came about and were introduced, the effects of business decisions, and the role of law and economics, not to mention the use of computers! Biographical treatments of key information processing personalities are also essential. Statistical data on the growth and nature of information processing work must be gathered. But the big job is to get to living participants of this industry. Death is claiming major figures of the 1950–1970 period. In each issue of the *Annals of the History of Computing*, for example, you can read obituaries of scientists. There is no comparable source for the thousands of information processing executives of the same period. Fortunately for the 1980s, most of the major lights are still very young (e.g., Bill Gates, age 39 in 1996).

Another job involves the collection of publications. Too many university libraries do not subscribe to or have back issues of the key publications, such as *Datamation* or *Computerworld*, let alone many company magazines or annual reports. The lack of such basic collections suggests that in the years to come there may be a severe problem for the researcher. That problem may have to be solved by libraries making available machine-readable copies of those publications—an expensive proposition for such logical host candidates as CBI. Private collections of publications, such as those housed in IBM's internal libraries worldwide, are always at risk. At IBM, for example, during its downsizing in the early 1990s, it closed libraries and dispersed or threw away some materials. So did many other companies across the industry. As a counterpoint, Microsoft actually established a corporate archive, an even more daunting task than simply running a company library!

Related to the problem of magazines and journals is the process of collecting industry-related publications by libraries at colleges and universities. In general, collections at both European and American academic libraries are very weak. A decade ago I described the situation as "appalling." The circumstance may actually be worse now because during the 1980s, in an attempt to obtain more shelf space without building additional libraries, many librarians weeded out their collections. Some of the victims were old books on computing which were considered to be outdated and therefore of little value (except to the historian). Since there were few historians working on computing in the 1980s, the number of people to defend these old volumes was low. Many of these publications found their way into secondhand bookstores. I, for one, have found such stores a greater source of reference materials than major university libraries. The practice of tossing out books has to be stopped. Second, historians of technology need to work with their libraries to increase awareness of the importance of these materials and then turn around and start collecting them.[85]

This is not to say that there are no good collections around. CBI's is an obvious one—driven as much by participants in the industry as by historians, not librarians—as are those at MIT, Harvard University, and Dartmouth College and at some of the technical universities in Western Europe. But, as with all good collections on any topic, the common thread is always that a local historian or collector worked with his or her library to build a collection over a long period of time. It is now the turn of computer and business historians and managers to do the same. And it is logical that they should because they are the only individuals, as a rule, who know what is worth preserving and collecting.

A WORLD OF PCS

Probably the biggest surprise in the history of information processing has been the speed at which, and extent to which, personal computing burst on the scene. This technology caught the industry off guard as well. The first widely available machines appeared in the middle to late 1970s and made their way into the hands of technologically oriented individuals—many of them in higher education—and then became products for use in schools and for some limited engineering projects. In the early 1980s, microcomputers worked their way into businesses in the United States and by the mid-1980s several million had been sold each year. By the end of the decade, annual installations routinely exceeded 10 million. In the early 1990s, the technology became ubiquitous with 65 million Americans familiar in part or better with these devices by 1995, and 35 million people around the world logged on to the Internet and other public access networks. Symptoms of the growth of this technology were becoming evident everywhere for the historian. For example, by the start of the 1990s there were more than 150 journals and magazines devoted to the subject of microcomputers worldwide. Thousands of user manuals and guidebooks to PCs were available. Major best sellers appeared routinely. For example, the IDG dummies series routinely sold millions of copies (e.g., *PCs for Dummies*, *Windows for Dummies*, and so on).[86] Microsoft, which so far only produces software products for microcomputers, was worth more than General Motors at the same time, while its delivery of Windows 95 operating system in August 1995 was one of the more sensational business events of the year, not just as an important one within the information processing industry. During the 1980s and 1990s some of the most volatile and lucrative (and riskiest) stocks worldwide were PC-related. Twenty-four-year-old millionaires came and went with each season. In short, microcomputers snuck up on all of us and pounced on the industrial world with an aggressive pattern hardly seen with any other technology, and with a massiveness that we are still trying to catalog. Clearly, microcomputers have come to absolutely dominate computing.

What happened? Past the shock, beyond the almost indescribable disbelief at the extent to which microcomputers have come into our lives, are the basic historical questions that will need to be answered by historians in the years to come. It should keep many of them busy for whole careers through the twenty-first century. The devices have come so fast, and with no end in sight for some stabilization, that historians are hardly in any position to comment on them. Business professors, sociologists, and economists are almost buried alive with the issues and the amount of data involved to let alone make access to the historian even reasonable. It appears that a similar scenario is currently being played out with the Internet, with usage rising much faster and across a larger audience than academics or businesses realize.

As with every other development in the field of information processing in the past century, microcomputers are leaving behind a trail of documentation that will delight historians for a long time. For one thing, as it became obvious that microcomputers were playing significant roles in our lives, journalists and other writers turned their attention to the topic. The result has been a long string of biographies of key industry players (e.g., Steve Jobs, Bill Gates.) and books about their companies and on minor participants as well.[87] Even how well established companies in the information processing industry have responded to this new computing tool have been studied, like IBM.[88] Historians can expect to see several new books and more than 1,000 articles per month on microcomputers for years to come. This body of literature may well come to represent the largest body of material on any one form of technology in the history of world, surpassing even agriculture, possibly medicine, and certainly automobiles. A trip to any bookstore in Latin America, Asia, Western Europe, and North America will demonstrate that nearly half the business-related books for sale concern microcomputing. Currently most of these are use manuals for various machines, software packages, and programming languages. The number of publications on applications for microcomputers appearing each year is approaching over a dozen per month. The point is, historians are going to have quite a task in front of them.

To a large extent, however, the topics of all these publications are similar to what has appeared on information processing for decades: descriptions of equipment and software; "how to use" books; analyses of the industry, key vendors, and biographies of luminaries; and eventually analysis is the worth and applications of these technologies. Already the sociologists, business professors, and consultants are documenting the effects of all this new technology.[89] Thus organizing this current material to facilitate historical research should not be difficult. The topics to be addressed will also mimic those we have discussed for the period 1939 to the 1980s. Indeed, the era of the microcomputer will probably be seen as a virulent extension of the earlier period insofar as computing issues are concerned.

THE PROBLEM OF ARCHIVES

So far we have reviewed problems and opportunities for research chronologically, concentrating primarily on developments in the United States, with some passing comments on Europe, and a few on Asia. The requirement to have access to adequate supplies of archival materials for historical research, however, cuts across all periods and continents. We have both a problem and some good news. Access to corporate archives globally for the period from the 1940s forward is usually a problem, as is the risk of corporate archival material being destroyed out of ignorance of its value, in an attempt to save expenses, or because lawyers do not want to leave a trail behind. As we move closer to the present, we have to ask the question: What are the chances of preserving corporate papers of small, high-tech companies that come and go, particularly small component shops, specialized software houses, and microcomputer vendors of the 1980s and 1990s, many of whom are run by managers barely out of their twenties or thirties and hence hardly have history on their minds?

The good news is that in the past decade, an outstanding amount of historically significant material that has been collected. The work that the IEEE, Smithsonian, British Science Museum, and CBI have done, for example, in collecting oral interviews is superb, resulting in hundreds of new sets of records properly organized. CBI scored a major coup with the acquisition of the Burroughs Papers in the 1990s. Duplicates of papers and publications are finding their way to CBI, the Hagley, the Smithsonian Institution, and to other archival centers. Some universities are now aware of the need to collect in this area. Models to be proud of include MIT and a raft of engineering schools.[90]

There are some major sources of material in addition to traditional documentation on companies and products. The anti-trust suit leveled against IBM by the U.S. government ensured that the giant corporation, the government, and several archives (Hagley and CBI for instance) would have a massive collection of documents relating to the history of information processing from the 1950s into the 1970s. IBM's archives on earlier decades are very impressive and well organized. More important, the company has been more cooperative with historians than some of its competitors. This is an industry that loves to sue, leading to mountains of useful materials as a by-product of its legal gymnastics. A careful analysis of this kind of material suggests that it addresses how products are designed, marketed, used, and supported; what the consequences of decisions and actions were, and who the key players were.[91] We have also seen recent evidence of corporations willing to permit serious historical analysis of their actions. The model for this kind of cooperation and access is the study about the breakup of AT&T done by Peter Temin and Louis Galambos.[92]

It is beginning to appear that corporate archives do shed light on how computers were used in banking, airlines, manufacturing, and insurance. Excellent archives exist in industries that have not been examined for the history of computing. The obvious candidates are railroads and major retailers. Institutional archives exist within the information processing industry ready to be looked at. Already mentioned were CDC and Burroughs at CBI, but also there are Remington Rand and Sperry Univac documents at the Hagley Museum and Library, and less accessible collections can be found at NCR, IBM, AT&T, RCA, and Honeywell, to mention a few. The experience of historians during the 1980s and 1990s has demonstrated that contrary to assumption, corporate archivists have increasingly been cooperative with scholars. The largest constraints for historians have usually been either denied access to legally sensitive materials or insufficient staff to facilitate access to papers. The legally sensitive material is no different from a national government archive denying access to historians for a period of 25 to 50 years. The British government, for example, imposes a minimum 50-year rule which it sometimes extends, while normally the U.S. National Archives tries to release material after 25 or 30 years. In both cases opening materials is less a question of censorship and more an issue of insufficient staff to make materials available.

We have a much larger problem, shared with historians on many topics of late twentieth-century life: machine-readable files. This is not the place to review this problem in detail; however, it should be pointed out that if critical files are on magnetic tape, circa 1960s, and we no longer have tape drives and systems plugged in that we can use to read this material, a real problem exists. The U.S. government has been struggling with this issue for a decade now, attempting to establish policies for its own records retention and for solving the access issue, with few results so far. Paper-based records are, in short, a minor problem in comparison to electronic-based ones.

Let us summarize the tasks that face historians when dealing with archives. First, we must continue to identify where papers and machine-readable records are today. Second, we must make sure that these are organized properly for research. Third, we must continue to maintain or implement programs to build up existing and new collections. This includes acquisition of contemporary printed materials, like user manuals. Fourth, we must spread news on archival developments in a more logical fashion. Today most news is spread through newsletters published by the IEEE, CBI, and other archives. We need articles and books cataloging and describing this material. It would also make sense to start moving that kind of information, along with bibliographies, to online databases, perhaps made available through the Internet, following CBI's lead onto a page. This four-point program should be open-ended, ideally partially supported by the industry that created the technology we are studying.

CONCLUSION

This chapter began with a plea that historians tackle the complex job of writing on the subject of information processing. That plea has been made at various times for scholars for over a decade. The good news is that more research on the topic is being done today than ever before. The prospect of that research being expanded is excellent. However, given the importance of computing in late twentieth-century society, the amount of current and anticipated research on the history of information processing remains inadequate both to the opportunity and to the need. The difficulties of looking at such a contemporary story are daunting, and access to material not as convenient as for earlier periods and more traditional topics. Tools for historians, economists, and sociologists have improved dramatically over the past decade, to the point where the field is competitive with other historical topics in terms of works of reference and organizations to assist in the research process. Yet after all is said and done, no subject in modern history remains so ripe for investigation—for publications in journals and by book publishers—as the history of information processing. The subject is acknowledged by all to be important; it simply must be pursued. It is a subject with a very long history. Now we need to give the subject a long line of historians.

NOTES

1. "Introduction," in James W. Cortada, *An Annotated Bibliography on the History of Data Processing* (Westport, Conn: Greenwood Press, 1983): ix–xlii.

2. To some extent that is my fault because I wrote a history of the origins of the computer industry that demonstrated the point that computers were not the only calculators in use. See James W. Cortada *Before the Computer* (Princeton, N.J.: Princeton University Press, 1993).

3. This statement is based on my research for three bibliographies on the history of computing published in 1990 and in 1996, and cited elsewhere in this chapter.

4. Thomas K. Landauer, *The Trouble with Computers: Usefulness, Usability, and Productivity* (Cambridge, Mass.: MIT Press, 1995): 15.

5. Robert W. Fogel, "The Limits of Quantitative Methods in History," *American Historical Review* 80 (April 1975): 342–343.

6. For some early examples see Edmund A. Bowles (ed.), *Computers in Humanistic Research: Readings and Perspectives* (Englewood Cliffs, N.J.: Prentice-Hall, 1967); and James W. Cortada, "Possible Uses of Computer Technology in the Study of Spanish History," *Cuadernos de Historia Económia de Cataluña* 16 (February 1977): 181–198.

7. For the bibliography involved see my *A Bibliographic Guide to the History of Computing, Computers, and the Information Processing Industry* (Westport, Conn.: Greenwood Press, 1990) and its sequel, *Second Bibliographic Guide to the History of Computing, Computers, and the Information Processing Industry* (Westport, Conn.: Greenwood Press, 1996).

8. An important guide to this literature is Bruce H. Bruemmer, *Resources for the History of Computing: A Guide to U.S. and Canadian Records* (Minneapolis: Charles Babbage Institute, 1987): 157, a list of bibliographic citations on oral history collections.

9. Cortada, *Before the Computer*, passim.

10. The literature on World War II is growing. Some of the key studies include Ralph Bennet's account of work at British locations, *Ultra in the West* (London: Hutchinson, 1979). On Allied espionage operations (including an analysis of Alan M. Turing and his work) see A. Cave Brown, *Bodyguard of Lies* (New York: Harper & Row, 1975). On German and British code breakers, see Josef Garlinski, *Intercept: Secrets of the Enigma War* (London: Dent, 1979), the well-done book by R. Lewin, *Ultra Goes to War: The Secret Story* (New York: McGraw-Hill, 1979), and F. H. Hinsley and Alan Stripp (eds.), *Codebreakers: The Inside Story of Bletchley Park* (New York: Oxford University Press, 1993).

11. On this industry see James J. Flink, *America Adopts the Automobile, 1895–1910* (Cambridge, Mass.: MIT Press, 1970); and for a good review of its mass use, see John B. Rae, *The Road and the Car in American Life* (Cambridge, Mass.: MIT Press, 1971).

12. Herman H. Goldstine, *The Computer from Pascal to von Neumann* (Princeton, N.J.: Princeton University Press, 1971) and Emerson W. Pugh, Lyle R. Johnson, and John H. Palmer, *IBM's 360 and Early 370 Systems* (Cambridge, Mass.: MIT Press, 1991).

13. The role of the historian-practitioner is almost nonexistent. Your author is of both worlds, an historian by training and mind-set, but also earning his bread and butter working for IBM in sales and consulting. The issue, however, is beginning to draw the attention of the traditional academic historian. For an example, see the entire issue of the *American Historical Review* 100, no. 3 (June 1995).

14. IBM, *It Was to Have Been the Nuclear Age. It Became the Computer Age: The Evolution of IBM Computers* (Armonk, N.Y.: IBM Corporation, 1976, 1979).

15. For some useful statistics see James Martin, *Telematic Society: A Challenge for Tomorrow* (Englewood Cliffs, N.J.: Prentice-Hall, 1978): 158–160; Landauer, *The Trouble with Computers*, 17–21; Kevin Maney, "Digital Age: PCs Power '90s Renaissance," *USA Today* (July 27, 1995): B1–2.

16. Alvin Toffler, *Future Shock* (New York: Random House, 1970) and *The Third Wave* (New York: Random House, 1980), and continuing with his other books and articles to the present.

17. See J. E. Sammet's important study, *Programming Languages: History and Fundamentals* (Englewood Cliffs, N.J.: Prentice-Hall, 1969); Richard L. Wexelblat (ed.), *History of Programming Languages* (New York: Academic Press, 1981); N. Metropolis et al., *A History of Computing in the Twentieth Century: A Collection of Essays* (New York: Academic Press, 1980); James L. McKenney, *Waves of Change: Business Evolution through Information Technology* (Cambridge, Mass.: Harvard Business School Press, 1995); and virtually each issue of the *Annals of the History of Computing* (Vol. 1, 1979, to present).

18. Some of the most important studies include the authorized biography of Thomas J. Watson by Thomas and Marva Belden, *The Lengthening Shadow* (Boston: Little, Brown and Company, 1962); the much better survey by William Rodgers, *Think: A Biography of the Watsons and IBM* (New York: Stein and Day, 1972); Robert Sobel, *IBM: Colossus in Transition* (New York: Times Books, 1981); Thomas J. Watson, Jr.'s excellent memoirs, written with Peter Petre, *Father, Son & Co: My Life at IBM and Beyond* (New York: Bantam, 1990), and the most recent history by Emerson Pugh, *Building IBM* (Cambridge, Mass.: MIT Press, 1995).

19. This growing body of publications is listed in *A Bibliographic Guide* (1990) and in *Second Bibliographic Guide* (1996).

20. My attempt to demonstrate that approach is *The Computer in the United States: From Laboratory to Market, 1930 to 1960* (Armonk, N.Y.: M. E. Sharpe, 1993).

21. Charles Babbage Institute *Newsletter* 4, no. 3 (October 1, 1982): 1.

22. For an excellent review of the pertinent literature, see W. W. Rostow, *The World Economy: History and Progress* (Austin, Tex.: University of Texas Press, 1978): 47–203. For a fascinating example of how distance in time is required to understand historical movements, see Massimo Livi-Bacci, *A Concise History of World Population* (Cambridge, Mass.: Blackwell, English trans., 1992): 100–130, in which he demonstrates the profound effects that the Industrial Revolution had on the growth of European populations.

23. Katharine Davis Fishman, *The Computer Establishment* (New York: Harper & Row, 1981), in which the author surveys briefly the role of major computer vendors, and hardly discusses the role of information processing in society, the technological developments accurately, or the applications.

24. See, for example, John Diebold (ed.), *The World of the Computer* (New York: Random House, 1973); John C. Dvorak, *Dvorak Predicts* (Berkeley, Calif.: Osborne McGraw-Hill, 1994).

25. This complex subject has generated an enormous body of literature. Some of the more useful introductions include the Hudson Institute, *The Next 200 Years* (New York: William Morrow, 1976); W. W. Rostow, *Politics and the Stages of Growth* (Cambridge: Cambridge University Press, 1971); Dennis L. Meadows et al., *The Dynamics of Growth in a Finite World* (Cambridge, Mass.: Wright-Allen Press, 1973); Stephen P. Bardley and Jerry A. Hausman, *Future Competition in Telecommunications* (Boston: Harvard Business School Press, 1989); and Norman Weizer et al., *The Arthur D. Little Forecast on Information Technology and Productivity: Making the Integrated Enterprise Work* (New York: John Wiley & Sons, 1991).

26. James R. Beniger, *The Control Revolution: Technological and Economic Origins of the Information Society* (Cambridge, Mass.: Harvard University Press, 1986).

27. JoAnne Yates, *Control through Communication: The Rise of System in American Management* (Baltimore: The Johns Hopkins University Press, 1989).

28. Most of the bibliography for these can be found in Cortada, *A Bibliographic Guide*, 47–65.

29. Based on W. W. Rouse Ball, *A History of the Study of Mathematics at Cambridge* (Cambridge: Cambridge University Press, 1889); Florian Cajori, *A History of Mathematics* (New York: Macmillan, 1919); Phillip J. Davis and Reuben Hersh, *The Mathematical Experience* (Boston: Birkhauser, 1981); Anton Glaser, *History of Binary and Other Nondecimal Numeration* (Los Angeles: Tomash, 1981); D. E. Smith, *History of Mathematics*, 2 vols (New York: Dover, 1923–1925); R. Taton, *Histoire du Calcul* (Paris: Presses Universitaires de France, 1969); and *Conference on Critical Problems and Research Frontiers in History of Science and History of Technology, 30 October–3 November 1991* (Madison, Wis.: University of Wisconsin, 1991). On looms, see C. Ballot, *L'Introduction du Machinisme dans l'Industrie Française* (Lille: O. Marquandt, 1923); A. Barlow, *History and Principles of Weaving by Hand and Power* (London: S. Low, Marsten, Searle and Rivington, 1878); and John Howard Brown (ed.), *Textile Industries of the United States* (Boston: James Lamb, 1911). We do need a more up-to-date history of programmable looms.

30. For example, J. Cohen, *Human Robots in Myth and Science* (London: Allen and Unwin, 1966); and M. Harmon, *Stretching Man's Mind: A History of Data Processing* (New York: Mason Charter, 1975).

31. Henri-Jean Martin, *The History and Power of Writing* (Chicago: University of Chicago Press, 1995).

32. H. W. Dickinson, *Sir Samuel Morland, Diplomat and Inventor, 1625–1695*. The Newcomen Society for the Study of the History of Engineering and Technology, Extra Publication no. 6 (Cambridge: Heffer and Sons, 1970).

33. Heinz Zemanek, "Central European Prehistory of Computing," in N. Metropolis et al. (eds.), *A History of Computing in the Twentieth Century* (New York: Academic Press, 1980): 587–609; T. M. Smith, "Some Perspectives on the Early History of Com-

puters,'' in Z. W. Pylyshyn (ed.), *Perspectives on the Computer Revolution* (Englewood Cliffs, N.J.: Prentice-Hall, 1970): 7–15.

34. Trevor I. Williams, *A Short History of Twentieth Century Technology* (New York: Oxford University Press, 1982). He is the editor of the massive multi-volume history of technology that Oxford has been releasing since the 1950s.

35. For examples of what is needed, see J. G. Crowther, *Discoveries and Inventions of the Twentieth Century* (New York: Dutton, 1966); editors of *Electronics, An Age of Innovation: The World of Electronics, 1930–2000* (New York: McGraw-Hill, 1981); Elting E. Morison, *From Know-How to Nowhere: The Development of American Technology* (New York: Basic Books, 1974); Duane H. Roller, *Perspectives in the History of Science and Technology* (Norman, Okla.: University of Oklahoma Press, 1971); George Basalla, *The Evolution of Technology* (Cambridge: Cambridge University Press, 1988); and Walter Vincenti, *What Engineers Know and How They Know It: Analytical Studies from Aeronautical History* (Baltimore: The Johns Hopkins University Press, 1990).

36. Geoffrey D. Austrian, *Herman Hollerith: The Forgotten Giant of Information Processing* (New York: Columbia University Press, 1982). I continued the story of punch cards in Cortada, *Before the Computer*, 44–63, 128–137, 149–157.

37. For example, S. Lavington, *A History of Manchester Computers* (Manchester: N.C.C. Publications, 1975) and his *Early British Computers* (Maynard, Mass.: Digital Press, 1980).

38. An example of the exotica approach is Gerard L'E. Turner, *Antique Scientific Instruments* (Poole, Dorset, U.K.: Blandford Press, 1980).

39. My two bibliographies hardly do justice to the topic, *A Bibliographic Guide*, 47–65; *Second Bibliographic Guide*, 15–32.

40. Two wonderful examples are the 1988 Pulitzer Prize winner by Robert V. Bruce, *The Launching of Modern American Science, 1846–1876* (Ithaca, N.Y.: Cornell University Press, 1987) and David A. Hounshell, *From the American System to Mass Production, 1800–1932* (Baltimore: The Johns Hopkins University Press, 1984); for a book straddling both centuries, see Steven Lubar, *Infoculture: The Smithsonian Book of Information Age Inventions* (Boston: Houghton Mifflin Co., 1993).

41. Arthur L. Norberg, ''High-Technology Calculation in the Early 20th Century: Punched Card Machinery in Business and Government,'' *Technology and Culture* 31, no. 4 (October 1990): 753–779.

42. While a regular stream of memoirs from this community has been appearing for years now both in book form and as articles in the *Annals of the History of Computing*, a major step forward was taken with the publication of hundreds of short biographies of these individuals by J. A. N. Lee, *Computer Pioneers* (Los Alamitos, Calif.: IEEE Computer Society Press, 1995).

43. Anthony Hyman, *Charles Babbage: Pioneer of the Computer* (Princeton, N.J.: Princeton University Press, 1982). For the recent bumper crop of publications, see Cortada, *A Bibliographic Guide*, 74–92; *Second Bibliographic Guide*, 18–21.

44. My favorite one-volume introduction to these machines is by Michael R. Williams, *A History of Computing Technology* (Englewood Cliffs, N.J.: Prentice-Hall, 1985); but do not overlook the accuracy and depth by two outstanding historians of computing devices, Peggy A. Kidwell and Paul E. Ceruzzi, *Landmarks in Digital Computing* (Washington, D.C.: Smithsonian Institution Press, 1994).

45. I have cataloged hundreds of titles, Cortada, *A Bibliographic Guide*, 142–186, *Second Bibliographic Guide*, 35–37.

46. Sadly, Felt & Tarrant's archives, which had been carefully put together for historians, were destroyed in the late 1980s by a successor company interested in saving the cost of renting warehouse space to store them. Some of the small companies that made machines, particularly typewriter and adding machine firms, have always run the risk of oblivian the same way. As of 1996, some major archival holdings were at risk. The Charles Babbage Institute was paying close attention to them in the event of a problem to avoid the kind of disaster as occurred with the Felt & Tarrant files.

47. The pioneering work and early role model is by Margery W. Davies, *Women's Place is at the Typewriter: Office Work and Office Workers, 1870–1930* (Philadelphia: Temple University Press, 1983).

48. For typical examples, see C. A. Deavours, "The Black Chamber," *Cryptologia* 4, no. 3 (July 1980): 129–132; Goldstine's ideas are in his *Computer from Pascal to von Neumann*, 84–121.

49. Key journals of the period include *Journal of the Optical Society of America, Proceedings of the Physical Society, Nature, Journal of the Franklin Institute, Bulletin of the American Mathematical Society, The Electrician, Journal of the Royal Statistical Society, Academie des Sciences du Paris, The Radio Review, Journal of American Statistical Association, American Mathematical Monthly* and *Scientific American*, among others. On von Neumann we now have two solid biographies: William Aspray, *John von Neumann and The Origins of Modern Computing* (Cambridge, Mass.: MIT Press, 1990) and Norman Macrae, *John von Neumann* (New York: Pantheon, 1992).

50. The best way to keep up with the growing archival materials is to read the *Newsletter* of the Charles Babbage Institute since it is the largest collector of information processing archives in the world. For an overview of major archival holdings and some bibliography, although beginning to become dated, see James. W. Cortada (ed.), *Archives of Data Processing History* (Westport, Conn.: Greenwood Press, 1990). Chief archivists for the major holdings in the United States comment on their holdings.

51. Materials on this Spanish inventor have appeared rapidly over the past quarter century. Some of the most useful include *Homenaje a D. Leonardo Torres Quevedo (1852–1936)* (Madrid: Centro de la Informática Tecnica y Material Administrativos, 1977); *Leonardo Torres Quevedo* (Madrid: Colegio de Ingenieros de Caminos, Canales y Puertos, 1978); and a useful biography by L. Alcalde Rodríguez, *Torres Quevedo y la Cibernética* (Madrid: Ediciones Cid., 1966), and a revised version, *Biografía de D. Leonardo Quevedo Torres* (Santander, Spain: C.S.I.C., 1974); yet the best biography continues to be José García Santesmases, *Obra é inventos de Torres Quevedo* (Madrid: Instituto de España, 1980).

52. For some extant literature on German events, see Cortada, *Second Bibliographic Guide*, passim.

53. Hidetosi Takahasi, *The Birth of Electronic Computers in Japan* (Tokyo: Chuockoronsha Publisher, 1972), in Japanese, is one of a small minority of publications, almost all in Japanese, on the subject. There is still no comprehensive history in English or any other European language on Japanese information processing. Yet we know, just from sales data of Burroughs, IBM, and NCR, that the Japanese have long been users of information processing equipment.

54. Williams, *A Short History of Twentieth Century Technology*, 1–194.

55. The best history of the early years is by Paul E. Ceruzzi, *Reckoners: The Prehistory*

of the Digital Computer, from Relays to the Stored Program Concept, 1935–1945 (Westport, Conn.: Greenwood Press, 1983). I have tried to take the account up to 1960 in *The Computer in the United States*.

56. For bibliography, see Cortada, *A Bibliographic Guide*, passim; *Second Bibliographic Guide*, passim.

57. A notorious example of lost archival collections consists of important files from GE destroyed by the company. The files of the Felt & Tarrant Company, important in an earlier era, suffered the same fate. Historians cannot assume that corporations will retain and protect their archives.

58. An excellent source on the scientists and engineers of this period is Lee, *Computer Pioneers*; another is Aspray's biography, *John von Neumann and the Origins of Modern Computing*.

59. Martin Campbell-Kelly, "The Development of Computer Programming in Britain (1945–1955)," *Annals of the History of Computing* 4, no. 2 (April 1982): 121–139; good examples on American affairs are Nancy Stern, "The BINAC: A Case Study in the History of Technology," *Ibid.*, 1, no. 1 (July 1979): 9–20; and Charles J. Bashe et al., *IBM's Early Computers* (Cambridge, Mass.: MIT Press, 1986).

60. Other important oral history projects can be found at the British Science Museum and the Smithsonian Institution.

61. All of these citations may be found in Cortada, *Second Bibliographic Guide*.

62. IBM, *Branch Office Information Sources (BOIS)* (White Plains, N.Y.: IBM Corporation, 1983).

63. See Aspray's biography, *John von Neumann and the origins of Modern Computing* and Nancy Stern, "John von Neumann's Influence on Electrical Digital Computing, 1944–1946," *Annals of the History of Computing* 2, no. 4 (October 1980): 349–362.

64. For a brief overview, see Fishman, *Computer Establishment*, 51–228.

65. H. H. Aiken, "Proposed Automatic Calculating Machine," *I.E.E.E. Spectrum* (August 1964): 62–69; A. G. Oettinger, "Howard Aiken," *Communications, ACM* 5, no. 6 (1962): 298–299, 359.

66. E. G. Andrews, "Telephone Switching and the Early Bell Laboratories Computers," *Annals of the History of Computing* 4, no. 1 (January 1982): 13–19; Ernest Braun and Stuart MacDonald, *Revolution in Miniature: The History and Impact of Semiconductor Electronics* (New York: Cambridge University Press, 1978); W. H. C. Higgins et al., "Defense Research at Bell Labs," *Annals of the History of Computing* 4, no. 3 (July 1982): 218–236; B. D. Holbrook, *Bell Laboratories and the Computer from the Late '30s to the Middle '60s* (Murray Hill, N.J.: Bell Labs, 1975), and one of many volumes published in the 1970s by Bell Labs on its history.

67. For bibliography, see Cortada, *A Bibliographic Guide*, 220; *Second Bibliographic Guide*, 43.

68. Brian Randell, "The COLOSSUS," in N. Metropolis et al., *History of Computing*, 47–92.

69. It continues to draw the attention of researchers. For the latest crop of publications, see Cortada, *Second Bibliographic Guide*, 51.

70. Ibid., 49–50.

71. Ibid., 60; The most frequent commentator on this system was N. Metropolis, see his "The MANIAC," in Metropolis et al., *History of Computing*, 457–464.

72. See, for example, F. E. Allen, "The History of Language Processor Technology at IBM," *IBM Journal of Research and Development* 25, no. 5 (September 1981): 535–

548; Robert W. Bemer, "A View of the History of COBOL," *Honeywell Computer Journal* 5, no. 3 (1971): 130–135; Adin D. Falkoff and K. E. Iverson, "The Evolution of APL," *ACM SIGPLAN Notices* 13, no. 8 (1978): 45–57; S. A. Greibach, "Formal Languages: Origins and Directions," *Annals of the History of Computing* 3, no. 1 (January 1981): 14–41; Sammet, *Programming Languages*; and Cortada, *Second Bibliographic Guide*, 269–270.

73. See, for examples from the period, American Management Association, *Advances in EDP and Information Systems* (New York: American Management Association, 1961); Jerry Rosenberg, *The Computer Prophets* (London: Macmillan, 1969); and M. V. Wilkes, *Automatic Digital Computers* (New York: John Wiley, 1956). Also look at Harry Wulforst, *Breakthrough to the Computer Age* (New York: Scribners, 1982).

74. A good introduction to the themes is McKenney, *Waves of Change*; see also for a European perspective, Dirk de Wit, *The Shaping of Automation: A Historical Analysis of the Interaction between Technology and Organization, 1950–1985* (Rotterdam: Hilversum, 1994). An early example of interest in the whole theme is Edmund J. Lias. "A History of General Purpose Computer Uses in the United States, 1954–1977" (unpublished Ph.D. dissertation, New York University, 1979).

75. For example, Lee, *Computer Pioneers*; and James W. Cortada, *Historical Dictionary of Data Processing: Biographies* (Westport, Conn.: Greenwood Press, 1987). All of the major obituaries are in the *Annals of the History of Computing*; hundreds of obituaries and short biographies are listed in Cortada, *A Bibliographic Guide*, and *Second Bibliographic Guide*.

76. See Chapter 2 for a detailed discussion of this issue.

77. Hubert L. Dreyfus, *What Computers Can't Do* (New York: Harper & Row, 1972); Norbert Wiener, *God and Golem, Inc.* (Cambridge, Mass.: MIT Press, 1966), and his *The Human Use of Human Beings* (New York: Avon, 1969); James Martin, *The Wired Society* (Englewood Cliffs, N.J.: Prentice-Hall, 1978), which addresses in part the mindset of the earlier period; E. A. Tomeski, *The Computer Revolution* (London: MacMillan, 1970); A. F. Westin (ed.), *Information Technology in a Democracy* (Cambridge, Mass.: Harvard University Press, 1971); John Naisbitt, *Megatrends: Ten New Directions Transforming Our Lives* (New York: Warner Books, 1982): 11–38; James W. Cortada, *Strategic Data Processing* (Englewood Cliffs, N.J.: Prentice-Hall, 1984).

78. With an excellent start already taken with a technical history by Emerson W. Pugh, Lyle R. Johnson, and John H. Palmer, *IBM's 360 and Early 370 Systems* (Cambridge, Mass.: MIT Press, 1991).

79. It has now been approximately fifteen years since the publication of the last major history of programming languages; we are due for a new revised and comprehensive survey. The last major study was a collection of papers edited by Richard L. Wexelblat, *History of Programming Languages* (New York: Academic Press, 1981), and the last monographic survey was by Sammet, *Programming Languages*.

80. W. von Braun and F. I. Ordway, *History of Rocketry and Space Travel*, 3rd ed. (New York: Thomas Y. Crowell, 1975); L. N. Ezell, *The Partnership: A History of the Apollo-Soyuz Test Project* (Washington, D.C.: NASA, 1978); Paul E. Ceruzzi, *Beyond the Limits: Flight Enters the Computer Age* (Cambridge, Mass.: MIT Press, 1989); S. E. James, "Evolution of Real-Time Computer Systems for Manned Spaceflight," *IBM Journal of Research and Development* 25, no. 5 (September 1981): 417–428; and the vast monographic literature on every major U.S. space program, such as spacelab, Gemini, Mercury, and so on.

81. I have put together an initial listing of over 2,500 examples in, Cortada, *A Bibliographic Guide to the History of Computer Applications, 1950–1990* (Westport, Conn.: Greenwood Press, 1996).

82. John Cohen, *Human Robots in Myth and Science* (London: Allen and Unwin, 1956), offers an early view in historical context; Edward A. Feigenbaum and Julian Feldman (eds.), *Computers and Thought* (New York: McGraw-Hill, 1963) talks about early attempts to model human thought. For a more contemporary analysis, see Howard Gardner, *The Mind's New Science: A History of the Cognitive Revolution* (New York: Basic Books, 1985); and for a history of early artificial intelligence, Steve J. Heims, *The Cybernetics Group* (Cambridge, Mass.: MIT Press, 1991). For an introduction to the history of robotics, see Jasia Reichart, *Robots: Fact, Fiction, and Prediction* (New York: Viking Press, 1978).

83. For a current history of the firm that lists much of the bibliography on the company, see Pugh, *Building IBM*.

84. There are some notable exceptions to this statement. See, Watson, *Father, Son & Co.*; the memoirs of IBM's highest European executive, Jacques Maisonrouge, *Inside IBM: A Personal Story* (New York: McGraw-Hill, 1985); and those of the CEO at Xerox, David T. Kearns, with David A. Nadler, *Prophets in the Dark: How Xerox Reinvented Itself and Beat Back the Japanese* (New York: Harper Business, 1992). For additional citations see Cortada, *A Bibliographic Guide*, 492–588, and *Second Bibliographic Guide*, 150–278.

85. A recent study of book collecting demonstrates clearly that librarians provide very little leadership as a rule in the collection of materials; it remains to the specialist and book collectors to gather up publications, manuscripts, and ephemera. For details, see Nicholas A. Babsbanes, *A Gentle Madness: Bibliophiles, Bibliomanes, and the Eternal Passion for Books* (New York: Henry Holt, 1995).

86. Dan Gookin and Andy Rathbone, *PCs for Dummies* (San Mateo, Cal.: IDG Books, 1994); and Andy Rathbone, *Windows for Dummies* (San Mateo, Cal.: IDG Books, 1992). Gookin also wrote the popular *DOS for Dummies* and *WordPerfect for Dummies*, also published by IDG in many editions and reprints during the 1990s. By the end of 1994, they had published nearly two dozen titles totaling over 10 million books in print!

87. Two examples of large, well-developed biographies include Jeffrey S. Young, *Steve Jobs: The Journey Is the Reward* (Glenview, Ill.: Scott, Foresman and Co., 1988) and Stephen Manes and Paul Andrews, *Gates* (New York: Doubleday, 1993)—both about young men. People barely get into new jobs and they publish memoirs, see for example Job's replacement at Apple Computer, John Sculley, *Odyssey* (New York: Harper & Row, 1988), like the other two references above, a best seller. Company histories, by mid-1995, totaled several dozen. For example, on Computerland, see Jonathan Littman, *Once Upon a Time in Computerland* (Los Angeles: Price Stern Sloan, 1987); on an early company, Osborne, see Adam Osborne and John Dvorak, *Hypergrowth: The Rise and Fall of Osborne Computer Corporation* (Berkeley, Cal.: Idthekkethan Publishing Co., 1984); and on GO Corporation, see Jerry Kaplan, *Startup: A Silicon Valley Adventure* (Boston: Houghton Mifflin Co., 1995). For an initial attempt to catalog some of the historically significant publications on microcomputers, see Cortada, *Second Bibliographic Guide*, 104–117. However, it should be noted, this list is sketchy at best.

88. James Chposky and Ted Leonsis, *Blue Magic: The People, Power and Politics Behind the IBM Personal Computer* (New York: Facts on File, 1988); Paul Carroll, *Big Blues: The Unmaking of IBM* (New York: Crown, 1993).

89. For a couple of very different examples of reacting to the availability of so much new technology in a business setting, see Sharon M. McKinnon and William J. Bruns, Jr., *The Information Mosaic* (Boston: Harvard Business School Press, 1992); James W. Cortada, *TQM for Information Systems Management: Quality Practices for Continuous Improvement* (New York: McGraw-Hill, 1995).

90. For a now outdated but still useful overview of archival conditions in the U.S., see the reports by archivists on their collections in Cortada, *Archives of Data-Processing History*. It includes a detailed bibliography of guides to archives published through 1989.

91. The best exploitation so far of the IBM antitrust material, suggesting its value for historians, is by Franklin M. Fisher, John J. McGowan, and Joen E. Greenwood, *Folded, Spindled, and Mutilated: Economic Analysis and U.S. v. IBM* (Cambridge, Mass.: MIT Press, 1983). For an example of a poorly conducted study using similar material but which drew a great deal of attention when it was published, see Richard Thomas De-Lamarter, *Big Blue: IBM's Use and Abuse of Power* (New York: Dodd, Mead, 1986).

92. Peter Temin and Louis Galambos, *The Fall of the Bell System: A Study in Prices and Politics* (Cambridge: Cambridge University Press, 1987). Perhaps the best role model for this kind of study using friendly access to corporate materials comes from another industry, David A. Hounshell and John Kenly Smith, Jr., *Science and Corporate Strategy: Du Pont R&D, 1902–1980* (Cambridge: Cambridge University Press, 1988). See also D. Quinn Mills and G. Bruce Friesen, *Broken Promises: An Unconventional View of What Went Wrong at IBM* (Boston: Harvard Business School Press, 1996).

I

The Industry's Structure

The history of information processing and computers over the past century has increasingly been seen as the study of business history, not simply of science and technology, although there is a great deal of that involved, too. Most recently, sociologists, economists, and business professors have concluded that computers are an integral part of what late twentieth century society is about. So if anything, over time the history of computing has become broader in scope, spilling over into many fields.

Part I of this book of essays deals with computing as a business topic. That approach was already demonstrated in Chapter 1. Here we delve into more detail. Chapter 2 examines the broad outlines of what we have come to call the computer or information processing industry in the second half of the twentieth century. It addresses the question of how the computer went from laboratory to marketable product: Who did it, why, and what were the results.

Chapter 3 argues that long before the computer there were other information processing products being used in the economies of the industrialized world. In this chapter I demonstrate that some patterns of technological evolution and business practices were honed long before the arrival of the computer. I also will show that the application of technology in the development of products follows a pattern that transcends many decades and, of course, goes back farther than the computer. That is not to say things did not change, they did. But it is important to recognize that the business side of the history of computing has a history too, and quite an important one. To a large extent Part I is the vendor side of the story; that of the end user of this technology is the subject of Part II.

2

An Introduction to the History of the Information Processing Industry

The information processing industry did not come into existence as we know it today—dominated by the computer—until the 1950s when digital electronic computers were widely distributed to commercial and government agencies for the first time. Equipment has been used to process data for a much longer period, with most such devices (e.g., cash registers, adding and billing machines, and calculators) invented in the quarter century beginning around 1870–1875. The issue of when the sellers and users of such devices finally constituted an industry has been resolved.[1] Continental Europe and East Asia (Japan in particular) still await their historians. However, what we have learned is that a collection of similar economic activities can be described as an industry when a series of services or products lend themselves to a collective identity. An industry is also characterized by a set of dependencies among its members. Thus, for example, a dependency might include makers of components that go into a computer, then the actual manufacturer, and finally the data center that uses it. The act of identification is initially the result of the recognition that certain efforts represent a common set of actions. In the next phase, economists or historians name a cluster of economic entities as an industry.

This is an important discussion to have when looking at high technology-based industries, because they are often new and put historians in the bind of having to identify when they do become industries. The problem is an ongoing one. For example, in 1993–1994, we also witnessed what may turn out to be a new industry being born in the United States as telecommunication companies, cable TV firms, and entertainment empires (e.g., TV and movies) bought each other, merged, and formed alliances in anticipation of delivering a combination of voice, data, and video to home users and businesses in the late 1990s and beyond. In 1994–1995, the role of Internet simply called attention to the same process continuing. The point is, new industries are born, old ones never go away; they are there for historians to study and for economists to criticize. My research, and the work of many historians of American business in particular, has been informed by the pioneering work of a business professor, Michael Porter, on the nature of competition. He is not an historian. However, in 1980, he published *Competitive Strategy: Techniques for Analyzing Industries and Competitors.*[2] While it became instantly popular with executives for the lessons it taught about competition, it is equally useful to business historians for helping to define what constitutes an industry, and then how to conduct research on it. It is very relevant to the issue of the information processing industry, about which Porter commented in this and in all his other books.[3]

Looking at information processing as constituting an industry once it had suppliers and customers, we can then say that the era of modern data processing (that is, based on the use of digital computers) began in a very crude way in the late 1940s but became measurable and obvious in the 1950s. The pre-data processing era, then, can be defined as any time prior to the implementation of modern punch card technologies in the 1880s. The use of Herman Hollerith's cards marked the transition between an era when little technology was employed to manipulate data and one that relied increasingly on the use of electronic components. The great era of punched cards lasted from the 1880s through the mid-1950s, with little competition from other input/output gear when the processing involved very large batches of data not suitable for adding machines and calculators. Punch cards remained an important medium for input/output in computers in the 1950s and 1960s, although beginning in the early 1960s we can document the decline in the use of this medium steadily through the end of the 1970s and early 1980s. In short, cards were used for a century.

THE PRE-COMPUTER GENEOLOGY OF THE
INFORMATION PROCESSING INDUSTRY

Long before the arrival of the computer, people were gathering, manipulating, and using data to run their lives and affairs. In short, the computer comes from a long line of distinguished ancestors which traveled with humankind from the dawn of what we call civilization. Lessons learned before the dawn of modern data processing influenced the early development of the new industry. For example, the gathering and manipulation of data had been going on for centuries. Scribes and artists left humankind's written records on the walls of caves. At the dawn of ''recorded history'' (circa 10,000 B.C.) languages together with writing came into being, with writing becoming a more formal set of disciplines within a couple thousand years reflecting the growth in societal structures, complexity of human interactions (particularly in business dealings), and the need to manage precisely larger bodies of information. These various developments displaced human memory as the primary repository of information, allowing larger quantities of data to be gathered and used. The ancient Egyptians improved writing instruments, with their use of papyrus signaling a new level of technological innovation. China's introduction of paper allowed new levels of price/performance in the handling of data, and the development of movable printing presses during the Renaissance rapidly and radically changed information management. In net terms, the amount of information that could be recorded and used exploded exponentially within two generations. The number of people who could now access data also grew, particularly in Europe and China. Books fundamentally altered the very nature of thinking and attitudes. But why reach back so far when describing the computer industry? The answer in a simple phrase is that computers simply represent the latest in a very long chain of devices and techniques for the handling of information. Every previous tool inevitably led to the creation of an industry devoted to the manufacture, sale, and use of such tools.[4]

These changes directly paralleled the history of information processing in the twentieth century. For example, like books, computers allowed greater amounts of information to be gathered, stored, manipulated, and ultimately used. The role of pencils, paper, and books was very instructive to historians who were studying data processing use patterns and the sociological and philosophical implications of such technologies.[5] Books were easier and quicker to produce and less expensive than hand-copied manuscripts. Information became a symbol and source of power in society, unleashing economic and political forces that helped speed up the rate of change in the Western World. Information (some scholars use the term "knowledge") molded a society and economy that became increasingly dependent on information.[6] By the 1970s, some writers were speaking about an information-based economy, in the 1980s, learning organizations, and then in 1990s, on the strategic necessity for businesses to produce information-based learning products.[7] As a by-product of the Industrial Revolution, pressure grew for better or more information. The correlation between major changes in society and the growth in information was direct and obvious. Historians now have the task of defining and describing this correlation, set into a broader context than merely the past five decades; try the past five centuries!

In the 1800s the most important impetus for better data management came from the need to manipulate increasing quantities of numbers. By the early 1800s, navigational tables were being corrected and enhanced, encouraging such individuals as Charles Babbage to design machinery to do the work. During the middle decades of the nineteenth century, insurance companies, railroads, and governments found the need to gather rapidly growing mountains of information, doing it manually at a time when their operations were both growing in complexity and volume, and when they needed timely information with which to function. The need to speed up this process, improve accuracy, and reduce costs became the bedrock source of motivation for a host of technological innovations in the last quarter of the nineteenth century. By the 1880s, information handling machines were turning up in offices all over the world. Pencils and pens spread rapidly, along with adding machines, calculators, and cash registers.

The telegraph, which had existed since before the American Civil War, was used to transmit information in ever-increasing amounts, and, of course, the telephone made its initial appearance in the 1870s.[8] New printing technologies were developed throughout the century, causing publishing costs to drop and literacy rates to rise.[9] By the end of the century, the typewriter had become a common instrument, and by 1910 almost a commodity.[10] The rate at which technology evolved and penetrated the economy was higher in the United States than in Europe, a pattern evident to the present. For example, microcomputers became widespread in the United States in the 1980s, in Western Europe in the 1990s. An earlier example: In 1919, at the end of World War I, only Washington's diplomatic delegation in Paris used typewriters.

By 1880 the belief was widespread that mechanical devices could handle many traditional office tasks. By 1890 that attitude was also dominant in factories. The time was ripe for changes in the application of technology to the manipulation of data. At this point punch card equipment became available. Herman Hollerith's collection of tabulating equipment created a new sub-industry within a generation. When various adding and calculating devices are joined to the business selling typewriters, we see a new industry begin to take definition by the end of the first decade of the twentieth century. This new industry was variously called office products, office automation, office equipment, tabulating industry, and the card punch business. By the end of World War I an identifiable sector of the economy used punch cards and related equipment to manipulate information. Increased reliance on such technology during the 1920s and 1930s motivated many to graduate to more powerful technologies in the 1940s.[11]

The growing demand for better ways to manipulate data on cards coincided with the development of what would become computers in the late 1930s and early 1940s. After World War II, one would think that the technology developed for war-related projects would next be applied to the civilian manipulation of information. The facts prove otherwise. In the mid-1940s there was concern about whether the market was large enough to justify the investments necessary to develop computers. Questions concerning demand for such technology were raised at International Business Machines Corporation (IBM) and National Cash Register Company (NCR), as well as within well-established electronics firms like General Electric (GE) and Raytheon. Only those who had worked on government projects during World War II and were close to the early devices showed faith in computers. This group took the first steps to build commercial machines and to demonstrate that data processing equipment could profitably displace card-tabulating and sorting products.[12] The use of data processing increased dramatically during the 1960s as a result of sharply declining costs for computing, better technology, and increased ease of use. By the 1970s computer technology was an important influence on the industrialized world's economy, and by the 1980s on the culture of some nations, especially the United States.[13]

FROM HOLLERITH'S CARDS TO A COMPUTER INDUSTRY

The following discussion about information processing centers on the United States because most developments in data processing industry have taken place there.

Modern information processing is rooted in punch card technology as a method for recording and manipulating data. Although its origin is traditionally ascribed to the work of Herman Hollerith in the late 1800s, in fact various Americans and Europeans had been developing cards with punched holes and equipment to trap or manipulate information since the early to mid-1700s. This is an often-told story about cards and tabulators and for good reason, because it represents a direct lineage to the computer. The story becomes critically important when we reach the late 1870s, however, because it was then that the possibility of using cards was sufficiently understood to help launch a new set of economic opportunities, and eventually an industry. The modern punch card came into being thanks to the work of the American, Herman Hollerith. Hollerith came to Washington, D.C., in 1879 to begin work at the U.S. Bureau of the Census to help with the following year's count of the nation's population. The census was taken primarily without the help of data-handling equipment. The information collected that year was barely analyzed and final reports completed before it was time to take another census in 1890. It was becoming obvious that with the United States' phenomenal growth in population, more advanced census methods would be required.

In 1884 Hollerith obtained patents for equipment to punch and read holes in cards, each hole representing one piece of information. The punched cards—which would remain in use for more than 100 years—provided a portable, yet standard, medium for interchanging and recording data. Thus, information could be processed and shuffled into various categories, enabling a wide variety of tabulating applications to emerge over the next half-century. Hollerith also used electrical power for what otherwise were Jackquard-like devices of the past to process these cards.

During the 1880s Hollerith convinced various organizations to use his equipment in gathering statistics. The city of Baltimore, for example, used his devices in 1886 to collect data on health conditions, making this government body perhaps the first user of punch card equipment in information processing. Hollerith's major breakthrough came when the U.S. Bureau of the Census adopted his equipment for the Census of 1890. It was to be a complicated census, for the agency now planned to obtain information on 235 topics per person versus 215 in 1880 and only 5 in 1870. Furthermore, the population had grown; both greater and quicker number counts were required than in 1880. His equipment proved a complete success. On December 12, 1890, the government announced that the U.S. population totaled 62,622,250, and it completed its analysis of various data elements within a couple of years. Hollerith's equipment saved the government over $5 million in expenses. During the 1890s governments in Russia, France, and several other countries used his equipment to conduct their census studies of population and agriculture. Railroad companies and insurance firms were also persuaded to rent his gear and to buy cards from Hollerith's company. In short, by the early 1900s Hollerith and several other vendors (fewer than four) were operating tabulating companies in the United States and Europe. And as would happen in the 1940s and 1950s, various government agencies were sponsoring research and development of improved versions of such technology.

Hollerith's successes suggest how greatly this sector of the information processing world had grown. In 1896 he established the Tabulating Machine Company, capitalized at $1 million. For the census of 1900 he rented 311 tabulating machines, 20 automatic sorters, and 1,021 punches to the federal government. Revenues that year exceeded a half million dollars. In 1911 the company had assets of over $2.3 million. That year it was reorganized into Computing-Tabulating-Recording Company (C-T-R) and sold. In 1914 the firm acquired a new general manager, Thomas J. Watson (1874–1976). It was he who converted the little company into IBM.[14]

In 1912 net profits for the firm reached $541,000, with equipment installed in both commercial and government accounts. During World War I, as in all twentieth-century wars, the need for information processing increased sharply and companies that sold data-handling equipment did well. C-T-R had sales of $4.2 million in 1914, and in 1917, $8.3 million, with earnings that year approaching $1.6 million. In 1918 the company was renting 1,400 tabulators and 1,000 sorters scattered across 650 accounts. The largest customers were still railroads and insurance companies, and government agencies. It had only one competitor, James Power, but he was not a significant threat, and thus the industry's size can be measured by studying C-T-R.[15]

The 1920s held great promise of prosperity for firms in the office equipment market, as it was then known. The market defined itself as including typewriters, adding machines (such as Burroughs), cash registers (such as NCR), and tabulating equipment (such as IBM). Coin changers, spiral notebooks, and forms were sometimes also counted in this group. Although the decade started with an economic recession that hurt C-T-R, the environment seemed favorable for the long term. The gross national product of the United States went from $69 billion in 1921 to $103 billion in 1929. Per capita income also rose, increasing from $641 in 1921 to $847 in 1929, fulfilling the promise of the little industry at the start of the decade. During the 1920s Americans confirmed the faith in new gadgets and machines, buying radios, refrigerators, and cars in record numbers. America became more urbanized and talked on more phones than ever before. The demand for typewriters, accounting devices, bookkeeping equipment, and tabulating gear rose steadily during the decade until the Great Depression.

IBM typifies the pattern of behavior within the office equipment industry during this era. In 1922 IBM's revenues totaled $10.7 million and hit a high of

$20.3 million in 1931. During the 1930s revenues declined (as did those of most companies) to $31.7 million in 1937, yet closed out the decade with $46.3 million. Other major suppliers during the inter-war period included Burroughs Corporation and NCR. Remington Rand became a major supplier of office equipment and office supplies at the end of the 1920s and all through the 1930s and 1940s. Other major firms included the aging Powers Accounting Machine Corporation in the 1920s and which became the core of the office equipment arm of Remington Rand, and Underwood Elliott Fisher, a well-established type-writer vendor. These few companies came to dominate the market and accounted for about $180 million in business by the end of 1928, the lion's share of the total.[16]

The sale of cards suggests the size and scope of the punch card part of the business. IBM dominated in this area. By the mid-1930s the firm sold more than 4 million cards per year. At a price of $1.05 per thousand, they generated an income of $4.2 million, which remained fairly steady throughout the decade. Yet in 1938 cards generated $5 million in revenues out of the company's total of $34.7 million. Throughout the 1930s demand for machine-readable data increased, despite the raging economic depression which resulted in nearly a third of the workforce being unemployed. Demand was particularly high within the New Deal government agencies. The largest user was the Social Security Administration. IBM's rental income from keypunches (used to convert data into holes in cards) grew from $743,000 in 1929 to $1.4 million in 1931. In 1933, the first year of the new Roosevelt administration, revenues climbed to $1.8 million. Thus, when these revenues along with the role of cards are considered, it is apparent that the need for information was growing. One other lesson for the historian lies here as well: IBM learned the value of doing business with the U.S. government, one that it never lost sight of for the rest of the century. While IBM was drawing closer to the U.S. government, the American economy was shifting rapidly from agriculture to manufacturing, from farm labor to factory and office work—natural markets for information processing technology. IBM ended the decade as the largest supplier of office equipment. Yet the industry continued to be dominated by the same companies as at the start of the decade: Burroughs, IBM, NCR, Remington Rand, and Underwood Elliott Fisher. This leads to another historical observation: While companies came and went in this industry, all through the twentieth century a small handful of companies dominated the industry. Just as we could speak of a handful in the 1930s, there were just another handful selling mainframes in the 1960s, and dominating the supply of personal computers and operating systems for them in the 1990s.

World War II had a profound impact on the information processing industry. The war was the leading cause of the conversion from office tabulating equipment to data processing. All electronics firms, as well as office equipment manufacturers, devoted much attention to war-related projects. Some firms, such as IBM, Burroughs, and NCR, made weapons and office equipment. Others helped develop sophisticated electronics to handle range-firing equipment and radar.

But in the rush to discuss war-related applications, almost all historians forget the obvious—that government agencies, including the military services, had normal accounting to do. The bulk of data processing during World War II was exactly the same as in the 1920s and 1930s, a story that has yet to be fully told.[17]

The majority of military-oriented research was done at American universities. One important activity involved the study of electronics at universities to build large calculating devices to prepare tables for ballistics, such as artillery range-firing charts, and to do calculations essential for the development of the atomic bomb. Major projects that had begun before the war (such as at MIT) or during the fighting for specific military purposes (as at the Moore School of Electrical Engineering at the University of Pennsylvania) led to the construction of the first digital computers by 1944–1946. All of these machines were unique. Yet they proved so successful that government agencies ordered more of them following the war and supported research and development related to the construction of newer devices. The developments of World War II were not exclusively an American story. Others, particularly the British, built equipment designed to break enemy communication codes. As a consequence, Britain's knowledge of computational equipment was quite high at the end of the war. Yet the dominant field of activity in the area of computers remained overwhelmingly in the United States.[18]

The industry grew on the basis of that expertise. On the one hand, American government agencies were willing to buy computers and to support research leading to their construction. On the other, individuals who had worked on such devices began to establish their own firms to satisfy that demand. Finally, the traditional electronics firms such as GE, and the major office equipment firms, such as IBM, had the potential to participate from the start in what would become the data processing industry.[19]

Events moved very quickly in the late 1940s as government-sponsored research at companies and universities progressed, resulting in the development of new computers from a variety of sources by 1950. Machines were constructed at over twenty locations at U.S. universities and research institutes. In Great Britain nearly ten such projects were underway by the early 1950s. Among American projects were those at the Universities of California at Berkeley and Los Angeles, Harvard, the University of Michigan, the University of Pennsylvania (home of the ENIAC, the first operational electronic digital computer), the Institute for Advanced Study in Princeton, New Jersey, the Los Alamos Scientific Laboratory, the National Bureau of Standards, the U.S. Naval Research Laboratory, and the RAND Corporation. Thus, by the early 1950s considerable expertise existed on how to make workable stored-program electronic digital processors. Those with technical knowledge and ability to obtain a contract from the U.S. government were potential participants in the nascent data processing industry.

THE DATA PROCESSING OR COMPUTER INDUSTRY

Demand for these expensive pieces of equipment grew sharply during the early 1950s, far in excess of what had been experienced in the late 1940s. Yet in the beginning the primary customers were universities and government agencies. As I will demonstrate in Chapter 5, that was about to change with the arrival of commercial customers for this technology. While a number of small start-up firms took advantage of the growing demand for computational devices to get started, at the end of the 1950s the large office machine manufacturing firms dominated the market. Also participating were some electronics companies. New firms that appeared in the 1940s and 1950s included the Engineering Research Associates (ERA) and the Eckert-Mauchly Company—EMC—(which Remington Rand later acquired, makers of the UNIVAC using the talent at EMC). IBM moved into computers by the early 1950s along with Burroughs, NCR, and Radio Corporation of America (RCA).

Yet all through these years, while special projects generated considerable amounts of revenue, these firms still sold punch card equipment, adding and calculating machines, and a variety of other office appliances. Several statistics suggest the volumes involved. In 1953—when, many historians argue, all activity in the development of computers was for the government—U.S. firms manufactured nearly $90 million worth of adding machines, an additional $61 million in calculating machines, and nearly $90 million in cash registers, for a total of about $241 million. In 1956, the year most historians argue commercial computing real took off, total production of adding machines, calculators and cash registers in the U.S. reached $200 million, no small number.[20]

By the mid-1950s IBM was struggling with the issue of whether or not to relinquish its hold on the tabulating market in favor of computers. It, together with others with a stake in an existing market, finally opted to lead customers from punch card gear to electronically based calculators, to stored program computers, and to data storage first on tape and later on disk drives. Specific decisions were made, but in general companies evolved through circumstances into a greater reliance on computers for their revenue streams as the 1950s progressed. The insights were more related to the recognition that computers represented a growing market and that to participate, and not be shut out, would require substantial investments and commitments.[21] What the computer vendors were finding out, too, was that each new generation of computers had to provide additional efficiencies and capacity, and perform its functions at always lower costs.

So as new technical and economic dynamics began to make themselves known, a problem of language did also. What do you call this new business, this new industry? Office appliances? Punch card tabulating? By the 1970s the common term was usually "computer industry". In the mid-1960s the phrase "electronic data processing industry" had gained currency. The term "computer industry" more aptly described the new world of data processing during the

1950s. This was an industry made up of organizations that either manufactured computers or provided computer-related services and supplies. Throughout the 1950s equipment was consciously developed which was directed at satisfying the need for more information in machine-readable form. And while the term "calculators" was used widely at the start of the decade, by mid-decade the word "computer" was solidly in place, along with its role as the centerpiece of a new data processing industry.

It is not difficult to understand the economic and social bases for this phenomenon. The traditional shift in the workforce in America offers a quick insight. Between 1880 (when Hollerith was busy inventing tabulating equipment) and 1955, the percentage of the total U.S. workforce in agriculture decreased from approximately 45 percent to 37 percent. By 1980 it was below 25 percent and a decade later below 10 percent. The industrial workforce grew in the late 1800s and then declined as a percentage of the total working population in the same period. Thus, that sector in 1880 accounted for about 27 to 28 percent of all workers but by 1955 had dropped below 15 percent and, by 1980 to less than half that share. The most important change apparently occurred in the service sector, which represented just over 25 percent of the workforce from 1880 to World War II, over 35 percent in 1955, and nearly 50 percent in 1980.

Equally impressive were the trends in the information sector of the economy. In 1880 that group comprised less than 10 percent of the workforce, grew steadily in proportion over the next 60 years to nearly 25 percent in the late 1940s, and experienced a modest decline in the 1940s and early 1950s as the service sector grew sharply. Then it experienced a steady, even extensive, growth beginning in the second half of the 1950s. It passed the 30 percent mark by the early 1980s. Although many definitions were developed to define the information-based workforce, thereby resulting in different statistics, the trends were consistent. They all showed that the office-bound worker had become an increasingly prevalent force in the economy and had become more dependent on handling data and information. In other words, the percentage of their work requiring manipulation of data had risen.

The underlying reasons for these changes whereby the economy shifted from one that first grew food, then made goods, and finally manipulated information will be argued for decades to come. However, some incentives for change are readily discernible. For one thing, as a managerial class rose within the U.S. economy after the early 1840s, becoming the "visible hand" so aptly described by Alfred D. Chandler, information was needed with which to manage (control) companies. Recorded data proved more valuable than memory.[22]

Second, the cost of gathering, manipulating, and using data through mechanical and electronic means kept declining over the preceeding 100 years. Nowhere was this trend more evident than with computers. For example, multiplying two numbers on a computer cost nearly $1.50 in the early 1950s but declined to a miniscule fraction of a penny by the late 1970s, and its cost has continued to go down. One megabyte of memory on a large mainframe as late as 1979 cost

Table 2.1
Earnings for Selected Companies, 1928 (Millions of Dollars)

Company	Earnings
Burroughs Corporation	8.3
International Business Machines	5.3
National Cash Register Company	7.8
Remington Rand	6.0
Underwood Elliott Fisher	4.9

Source: Moody's Industrial Manual, 1930.

about $110,000 and occupied the same space as a very large Samsonite suitcase. In 1995, that memory cost less than $100 and could be carried in your wallet. Such decreases made the use of computers practical in business, government, universities, and many other applications. By the 1980s commentators on industrial society had concluded that information processing had taken on a life of its own that transcended simple economics, becoming a fundamental feature of developed societies.[23]

The definition of the data processing industry (as it was known for the greatest period of time) remained relatively uncontroversial and constant from the 1950s until at least the early 1980s. Collectively and individually, participants in data processing defined industry participants as those who manufactured, sold, and serviced computers, peripheral equipment, software, and related services. By the early 1960s the growing community of users of computers no longer thought of themselves as simply scientists or engineers but as members of the data processing world. This phenomenon can be traced by studying the growth of various associations within this industry during this decade, such as the Data Processing Management Association (DPMA), the Association for Computing Machinery (ACM), and the American Federation of Information Processing Societies (AFIPS).

DOLLARS, ECONOMICS, AND COSTS OF HARDWARE, 1950s–1970s

Measuring the revenues of data processing suppliers suggests the extent to which the data processing industry had grown. As Table 2.1 illustrates, the industry was worth just less than $1 billion in the mid–1950s but over $28 billion by the late 1970s. A similar trend was evident for the industry worldwide; it stood at over $40 billion by the end of the 1970s. These statistics account only for the total shipment of products and services. Historically, these dollars represented between 20 and 40 percent of all expenditures for data processing. The other costs went toward salaries for users of computers or for the facilities in which they were housed. The data presented in Table 2.1 reflect only the earnings of American companies. They do not take into account the activities of European or Asian firms. However, by the early 1990s, we had a $300 billion industry (suppliers of goods and services only), and the world was spending closer to one $1 trillion per year (e.g., programmers, staff, etc.). Going back just to software and boxes, cumulative investments in computing technology was hovering at some $4 trillion.[24]

Over 50 percent of all revenues for the period 1952–1982 came from hardware. Percentages changed over time, however. Thus, for example, in 1955 over 80 percent of all shipments of products by U.S. firms (as measured in dollars) went toward hardware. The percentage dipped into the mid-70s percentile during the 1960s and into the 60s range during the 1970s. It leveled at about 50 percent by the early 1980s. During the same period, the percentage of contribution to the total hardware expenditures made by computers themselves dropped even more sharply, especially after 1970 as expenditures for peripheral equipment rose, along with the demand for more machine-readable data. Although these percentages shifted, the actual amount of money spent on data processing increased. The use of more peripheral equipment per data system (each included at least one computer) became a boom subset of the data processing world because between 1968 and 1978, for example, those who sold such equipment grew on average by 25 percent annually.

Several other trends should be noted. First, the number of computer systems in use within the United States grew slowly during the ten years from 1955 to 1965 and then exponentially from 1965 to the early 1970s, slowed during a recession then continued a steady expansion all through the second half of the 1970s and into the 1980s. By the late 1980s demand stabilized again, but the data were mixed because during this period millions of personal computers were acquired, driving up the number of dollars invested in computing, although not reflected in statistics dependent on mainframe expenditures. Measuring the total number of computers in use by the thousands, there were fewer than 1,000 at the start of the 1950s, 100,000 by the early 1970s, nearly 300,000 by 1975, and beyond 450,000 at the end of the 1970s. Large mainframes drove up the number of dollars expended until the mid-1970s, when their absolute number remained steady. What changed was the fact that general processors individually grew in size and value, accounting for the continued surge in the overall expenditure of dollars on computers since 1965. Measuring the total value of computer systems over that era of mainframe dominance suggests the extent of the phenomenon (Table 2.2).

Hardware accounted for many capital dollars within the industry and obviously was the topic of much discussion. In the 1950s the single most expensive component of a system was the computer. The mainframe's percentage of dominance, measured in dollars, declined steadily after the 1960s, while other de-

Table 2.2

Value of Computer Systems in the United States, 1965–1979, Selected Years (Billions of Dollars)

Year	General Purpose	Minis
1965	5.0	0
1970	18.0	1.0
1975	30.0	5.0
1979	50.0	7.0

Source: Extracted from Montgomery Phister, Jr., "Computer Industry," in Anthony Ralston and Edwin D. Reilly, Jr. (eds.), *Encyclopedia of Computer Science and Engineering* (New York: Van Nostrand Reinhold, 1983): 337.

Table 2.3

Relative Price Performance for Selected IBM Mainframes, 1953–1979

Computer	Relative Price to Execute 1 instruction per second	Relative Speed/Price
650 (1953)	1	1
360/30 (1964	43	1,700
370/135 (1971)	214	19,000
4341 (1979)	1,143	1,143,000

vices, disk drives, and terminals began consuming an ever-larger portion of money spent on hardware. As Tables 2.3 and 2.4 show, the value of mainframes in thousands of dollars declined in the 1950s and 1960s and rose in absolute terms in the late 1970s. Terminals rose steadily along with the cost of peripherals during the entire period. As the price per byte of memory improved, mainframes' relative value in absolute dollars remained flat, with very moderate increases over time.

The extensive growth in expenditures and, consequently, the value of peripherals over the past 30 years were dramatic. Online information storage sharply rose in value as the cost per byte declined. The amount of online storage nearly doubled each year from 1974 to the present. The total amount spent on tape drives declined as disks replaced them. Printers were very expensive when they first appeared, dropped in cost by nearly half during the 1960s and 1970s, and then rose again as impact printers were slowly replaced with laser-based tech-

Table 2.4
Relative Price Performance for Selected IBM Computers, 1950–1979

Computer	Relative Speed/Price
650 (1950)	1
370 (1970)	150,000
4341 (1979/80)	1,000,000

Table 2.5
Value of Keypunches and Verifiers versus Keyboard Data Entry in the United States, 1950–1980 (Billions of Dollars)

Year	Keypunches and Verifiers	Keyboard Data Entry
1950	4	0
1960	4	.1
1970	3.4	1.1
1975	2.8	2.5
1980	1.9	2.6

Source: Extracted from Montgomery Phister, Jr., "Computer Industry," in Anthony Ralston and Edwin D. Reilly, Jr. (eds.), *Encyclopedia of Computer Science and Engineering* (New York: Van Nostrand Reinhold, 1983): 339.

nologies that could handle hundreds of times more volume than earlier machines for mainframe systems. As usage of terminals and magnetic storage media for input/output equipment rose, beginning in the early 1960s, the value of punch card equipment declined gently (see Table 2.5). Throughout most of this period, data entry equipment never exceeded 5 percent of the overall value of computing gear, whereas computers always took more than half.

The cost per transaction executed in digital computers has declined steadily over the entire period of their existence (see Table 2.6). Thus, between 1954 and 1979, for example, for a given number of dollars, processing speed increased by a factor of over 1,000. We would see similarly dramatic improvements in the 1980s and 1990s with personal computers. Put in nontechnical terms, the number of answers obtained from a mainframe computer of that period for the same amount of money rose by over 1,000 times. The second most dramatic change came with computer memories. The price of disk storage declined by a factor of 100 between the mid-1950s and the late 1970s. Shifts in economics, as well as in the quantity and speed of technologies, were also evident. For example, in 1956 it was far cheaper to have data on magnetic tape than on disk

Table 2.6
Cost of Processing One Million Instructions, 1955–1985, Selected Years

Year	$ Cost/Million Instructions
1955	40.0
1961	2.0
1965	0.40
1971	0.11
1977	0.08
1981	0.02
1985	0.004

and so batch applications continued to dominate. But by the early 1980s the reverse was true, accounting for the sharp rise in online applications and direct access of data. Montgomery Phister, who has collected more data on costs for the period 1950–1970s than anyone else, notes that when inflation is taken into account, the change in costs of storage were profound and informative. According to Phister, a penny in 1955 had the purchasing power of 2.5 cents in 1979. Using that baseline, he discovered that the cost of storage on disk per byte went from 2.5 cents in the mid-1950s to 0.006 cent, using 1979 cents. Thus, while in absolute numbers costs for storage had declined by a factor of 167 to 1, when recalculated to take inflation into account it was actually 417 to 1. A similar tale could be told for memories and processors. The only constant was punch card equipment which had essentially the same value throughout the entire period.[25]

Although data on the characteristics of each decade are presented below, it is instructive to study the value of hardware by several groups over time. Among the earliest users computers were U.S. government agencies. As Table 2.7 suggests, during the short period from 1962 to 1974, the number of computers owned by the federal government grew fourfold. Taking into account raw dollars expended from 1954 through 1973 by all users for computers and related equipment in the United States, the growth in expenditures was one of the most significant trends within the industry. Table 2.8 presents a reliable set of statistics suggesting the magnitude of growth. The information processing industry grew, for example, by over 27 percent per year during the 1960s and frequently between 11 and 17 percent during the 1970s. It was slower during the 1950s and 1980s. Growth rates picked up in the 1990s, driven as much by incremental technological innovations as by a healthy economy, suggestive of the pattern evident in the 1970s.

Worldwide revenues generated by the sale of computer-related equipment between 1965—the year third-generation computers were sold in quantity—and 1981 also grew sharply. As Table 2.9 indicates, the second half of the 1960s

Table 2.7
Number of Computers Owned by the U.S. Government, 1962–1975,
Selected Years

Year	Number
1962	1,030
1964	1,862
1966	3,007
1968	4,232
1970	5,277
1972	6,731
1974	7,830
1975	8,649

Source: General Services Administration, *Inventory of Automatic Data Processing Equipment in the United States Government* (Washington, D.C.: U.S. Government Printing Office, 1975): 2.

Table 2.8
Expenditures for Computer Hardware in the United States, 1954–1973,
Selected Years

Year	Millions of Dollars
1954	10
1958	250
1963	1,500
1968	4,500
1973	7,000

Source: EDP Industry Report (Waltham, Mass.: International Data Corporation, August 1974): 2.

witnessed a growth matched by no other major sector of the U.S. economy, and while it slowed during the early 1970s—a period of economic recession in the United States—it nonetheless grew and experienced another takeoff in the late 1970s. Another way to measure the size of the industry is to determine the number of people employed by manufacturers of computers in the United States. Table 2.10, covering the period of 1967–1972, when sales grew rapidly and then declined after the economic recession, showed a range of 145,000 to 190,000 jobs that did not exist a decade earlier. Tables 2.11 and 2.12 reconfirm the trends described earlier. Information processing enjoyed a similar, if smaller, experience in Europe during the same period.[26]

Table 2.9
**Worldwide Data Processing (DP) and Business Equipment (BE) Industry
Revenues, 1965–1981, Selected Years (Billions of Dollars)**

Description of Revenue	1965	1970	1975	1980	1981
Total	4.5	20.5	46.2	90.6	101.6
Total DP Equipment	2.4	10.5	29.9	55.1	61.8
Application Software	.2	2.5	6.5	18.0	21.0
Total BE Equipment	3.5	6.0	9.3	13.5	14.7
Business Forms	.9	1.5	2.5	4.0	4.1

Source: U.S. Department of Commerce, International Trade Administration, *The Computer Industry* (Washington, D.C.: U.S. Government Printing Office, April 1983): 52.

Table 2.10
U.S. Employment by Computer Manufacturers, 1967–1972, Selected Years

Yearly Average	Employment
1967	145,100
1968	160,600
1969	182,700
1970	190,300
1971	170,100
1972	172,300

Source: U.S. Department of Labor as reported in Bruce Gilchrist and Richard E. Weber (eds.), *The State of the Computer Industry in the United States* (Montvale, N.J.: AFIPS, 1973): 23.

SERVICES AND SOFTWARE IN THE INFORMATION PROCESSING INDUSTRY, 1950s–1970s

In addition to the sale and service of hardware within the data processing industry, there were other sectors. One such sector consisted of service bureaus. These bureaus were individuals or companies that would either turn data into machine-readable form and produce reports for clients or make computing power available to their customers. In the early 1900s companies were formed that owned or leased tabulating equipment used to punch data into cards and process

Table 2.11
Growth Rates of Revenues of U.S. Firms from World Operations, 1961–1971

Period	General Purpose	Mini and Specialized	Services	Leasing	Supplies
1961-65	31.5	37.5	20.3	-----	7.7
1965-69	24.3	34.3	28.9	84.5	10.3
1969-71	8.2	-6.0	20.5	6.4	3.9
1961-71	23.0	27.5	23.8	58.5*	8.0

*For the period 1965–1971.
Source: International Data Corp., as reported by Bruce Gilchrist and Richard E. Weber (eds.), *The State of the Computer Industry in the United States* (Montvale, N.J.: AFIPS, 1973): 21.

Table 2.12
Annual Exports and Imports of Computer Equipment in the U.S. Market, 1967–1971 (Millions of Dollars)

Exports/Imports	1967	1968	1969	1970	1971
Exports	475	530	786	1,237	1,262
Imports*	20	18	37	60	119
Net Exports	455	512	749	1,177	1,143

*Parts not included.
Source: Bruce Gilchrist and Richard E. Weber (eds.), *The State of the Computer Industry in the United States* (Montvale, N.J.: AFIPS, 1973): 21.

them for clients with no such equipment. By the 1930s that kind of service had become an important subset of the office machine equipment environment. Some of these companies and others that were founded later bought some of the first commercially available stored-program digital computers to provide services to customers who knew nothing about data processing and did not own computers. By the end of 1976, just within the U.S. economy, there were more than 1,500 such companies, perhaps the most important of which was Automatic Data Processing (ADP), still providing payroll and many other accounting services in the mid-1990s as a leading member of this sub-section of the information processing industry.

At first, batch processing dominated, with, for example, weekly reports prepared and mailed to customers. In the 1960s telecommunications made it pos-

Table 2.13
Estimated Growth in Service Sector of Information Processing Industry,
1960–1980, Selected Years

Year	Percentage of Revenue (U.S. Market)
1960	12.5
1965	11.0
1970	18.0
1975	18.5
1980	20.0

Source: Anthony Ralston and Edwin D. Reilly, Jr. (eds.), *Encyclopedia of Computer Science and Engineering* (New York: Van Nostrand Reinhold, 1983): 342.

sible to transmit information back to a customer over a telephone line to a specialized terminal or printer, starting a 30-year trend in how information was delivered. During the 1970s one could begin to access a service bureau computer via a terminal, an approach to computing that had first appeared at the Massachusetts Institute of Technology (MIT) in the 1950s, and later in the 1960s across the entire U.S. economy. One simply paid for either "x" amount of time attached to a computer or a fixed rate for output. As Table 2.13 indicates, service industry sales grew from 12 percent of all nonhardware revenues in 1960 to over 20 percent by 1980. Measured in billions of dollars, revenues grew almost as rapidly as expenditures for hardware during the same period (see Table 2.14).

Until the early 1980s, software, although important, had been neglected by economists and historians. The large vendors in the industry did not focus on this market until the 1980s, even though they had led the entire industry in manufacturing programs for decades. But like economists and historians, the executives of these firms as a rule thought of software as ancillary to hardware. By the mid-1980s all that began to change. The first to take software seriously were executives of manufacturing firms within the information processing industry who recognized that programming represented an untapped, multibillion-dollar opportunity. Understanding this segment of the industry proved difficult because historically 85 percent of all expenditures on software went toward salaries of employees to write programs. This situation stood in sharp contrast with hardware because users typically did not build their own computers; they leased or bought them from manufacturing firms such as IBM or Honeywell.

Despite this belated acknowledgment of the value of software, observations are not as solidly grounded in data as they are for hardware. Nonetheless, some obvious patterns are evident.

In addition to the 85 percent spent on salaries for programmers and systems

Table 2.14
Estimated Revenues from Service Sector of Information Processing Industry,
1955–1979, Selected Years (Billions of Dollars)

Year	Total
1955	0.3
1960	0.4-0.5
1965	0.5-0.7
1970	1.1
1975	3.2
1979	5.5

Source: Data collected by Montgomery Phister, Jr., "Computer Industry," in Anthony Ralston and
   Edwin D. Reilly, Jr. (eds.), *Encyclopedia of Computer Science and Engineering* (New York:
   Van Nostrand Reinhold, 1983): 342–343.

analysts, another 5 percent went to cover the costs of program development by
software manufacturing firms. The remaining 10 percent was used to rent or
buy software packages or services. Most of the data available about expenditures
on software concern this 10 percent. The portion of software expense associated
with packages constituted the software industry or subset of the information
processing industry, and the greatest amount of data has become available for
it over the past decade.

Vendors first emerged in the late 1940s and early 1950s, primarily as con-
tractors servicing government-supported projects, usually concerning defense
systems. Software was made to order during this period. By the mid-1950s,
companies were developing application packages that organizations with specific
types of computers could use. Programming languages, for example, came into
their own, along with accounting, financial, and inventory control programs.
During the 1960s this trend continued, keeping up with new developments in
hardware. In the early 1970s database management systems flourished along
with thousands of new application packages. By the early 1980s, for the IBM
Personal Computer alone there were more than 3,000 software packages on the
market. That number skyrocketed through the 1980s and 1990s. As Table 2.15
demonstrates, the software community expanded into an important segment of
the industry after the announcement of the IBM S/360 family of mainframe
computers in 1964. Revenues in the United States went from several hundred
million dollars to over $2 billion by the late 1970s, and by the mid-1980s had
doubled again. In the decade 1985–1995, software sales continued to grow both
in dollar volume and as a percent of total information technology expenses. To
a growing extent, obviously, software sales shifted to personal computer platforms.[27]

Table 2.15
Estimated Software Revenues, 1964–1980, Selected Years (Millions of Dollars)

Year	Total
1964	175-275
1968	400
1972	500
1976	1,100
1980	2,100

Source: These data were collected by Montgomery Phister, Jr., "Computer Industry," in Anthony Ralston and Edwin D. Reilly, Jr. (eds.), *Encyclopedia of Computer Science and Engineering* (New York: Van Nostrand Reinhold, 1983): 343; additional qualification of data in James W. Cortada, *Strategic Data Processing: Considerations for Management* (Englewood Cliffs, N.J.: Prentice-Hall, 1984): 37–46.

The dynamics of software business received little attention in the literature until the second half of the 1980s, nearly 30 years after its arrival. But several factors that influenced this segment are identifiable and have started to influence the study of software. First, in the 1950s there were too few people who knew about information processing and thus were forced to turn to specialized companies. Computer manufacturers such as IBM wrote all the systems control programs (SCPs) necessary to operate equipment and frequently the compilers necessary to use such major languages as COBOL, FORTRAN, BASIC, and APL. Industry groups also participated or defined the architecture for specific languages (such as for COBOL in the United States and ALGOL in Europe). The number of lines of programming written in each decade is not known, but the statistics would be massive because they ran into millions of lines per data center, billions for very large applications. Citing one small example to illustrate the issue, just for one SCP, IBM wrote over 5 million lines of code for the operating system of the S/360 in 1968, and that statistic does not include application software. By the early 1970s many minicomputers had 500,000 to 700,000 lines of code. A major purchasing application package might have a similar amount of programming. To put that size and quantity of code into greater perspective, in the 1970s it was estimated that one line of code cost $10 to write.[28]

Another element was IBM's unbundling of software in 1969. In midyear, IBM announced that it would no longer "bundle" together software and hardware for one price. Rather, it would now break the two apart, with the exception of operating systems and other basic utilities. Hence, firms that sought to compete against IBM (as well as competitors who also unbundled) could do so by providing packages for applications, sort/merge utilities, and competitive database managers. Such a policy change did more to encourage the growth of a software industry than any other factor. Sales statistics for that segment suggest a correlation between unbundling and the growth of revenues. By the end of 1975 standard software packages exceeded customized programming in value. The balance has remained tipped in favor of commercial packages over ''roll-your-own'' software for both mainframe and personal computing ever since.[29]

Issues of historical interest have influenced the use of software. During the 1950s and early 1960s, programming languages were complex and usable only by people with extensive information processing backgrounds. As the number of mainframe computers installed increased, so, too, did the demand for programmers to write more applications. By the early 1970s the entire industry was experiencing a shortage of qualified programmers. By then, the effective use of information processing could mean life or death for many organizations. As the cost of computing dropped, demand for more application software rose, often far ahead of price improvements in software. With the introduction of microcomputers in the late 1970s, the need for more software that could be used and maintained by individuals with little or no background in data processing began reaching crisis proportions and existed side-by-side with the great programmer famine which was decried by industry experts all through the 1980s, even into the 1990s. The information processing industry simply could not train enough programmers in the Western World.[30]

A couple of responses emerged. First, pressure increased to develop software faster, better, and with decreasing amounts of technical expertise by writers. Many techniques were developed for the design and creation of software applications. Architectures and methodologies became fashionable and were no sooner introduced before they were replaced with supposedly even better ones. Second, at the same time, the industry searched for better ways to make existing programmers more productive—hence, the introduction of database managers, code generators, macros, and decision-support packages. Third, by the end of the 1980s, large pools of new programmers were becoming available. One group consisted of programmers in third world countries, such as India, which rapidly became one of the world's largest source of new programmers.[31] In addition, many people learned to do some programming through their interaction with personal computers, making it possible to write applications for those machines that never ran on mainframes, even though some of the languages they used also were available for large systems (e.g., BASIC). Quite possibly, then, once the history of programming is properly understood from the point of view of users of software, historians will have a firmer grasp of why and how the industry was so rapidly accepted in about 1965. Software functions will be part of the answer.

In addition to the dynamics of companies manufacturing hardware and their impact on the industry as a whole—together with software vendors and programming—there is a third major component of the information processing industry: those who make and sell the consumables of the industry. These are primarily the media in which data are stored in machine-readable form. We will only discuss paper briefly, although the paper industry attributed a significant part of its successes of the 1980s to the demand for paper to feed computer-driven printers. The electronic media included computer cards, paper, disk packs, magnetic tape, and diskettes, and, as a subset of the industry, existed from the day Hollerith decided to sell cards while leasing tabulators to the present. An internal IBM study of the early 1980s suggested how important this segment continued to be. The IBM study demonstrated that the ''average'' personal computer user typically spent an additional sum on supplies for that machine (along with some upgrades) in the first year of ownership to the tune of 40 percent of the original purchase price of the computer system. Historically, supplies for mainframe systems were always far less costly although the absolute monetary amounts were higher.

Looking at the period from the 1950s through the early 1980s—that is to say, the period prior to the arrival of the personal computer—points to some identifiable trends. First, the cost of computer paper rose sharply, especially since the 1960s. Second, computer cards remained essentially flat in terms of both price and quantity used since the 1970s. Third, a similar pattern is evident with tape, the only exception being in the 1950s when this was the medium of choice over disk. Fourth, disk packs (hardly sold after 1980 since disk drives came with a built-in disk) made up the smallest portion of the media community and declined sharply in the 1980s. Diskettes (which look like 45-rpm records or smaller, and by the early 1980s were used primarily with personal computers) have not been around long enough to characterize generally. However, overall this medium has not been an inconsequential component of the information processing industry; from the 1960s onward annual sales of electronic media (e.g., disk packs, tape, diskettes) increased from a low of a few million dollars to volumes of hundreds of millions of dollars by the late 1970s. By the early 1980s, the volumes were exceeding $2 billion annually just in the United States. Paper products overwhelmingly were continuous forms and paper, while card stock grew only slightly but continuously in volumes during the 1970s and basically dropped off the radar screen in the 1980s.

Function and price played complementary roles. In the early 1950s the medium of choice were cards because people understood them and you could hold them in your hands. As magnetic tape became increasingly available and cost competitive with cards, an enormous debate took place within the industry about the benefits and risks of this new medium. Fear that one could not get to data was offset by the convenience of manipulating large volumes of information quickly and with less space. By the end of the 1950s tape had won a place in a data center's operations, used side-by-side with cards. By the late 1950s disk drives appeared and once again a debate took place. Disks were attractive for the same reasons as tape—convenience, space compression, speed, and eventually cost. They also had the unique capability of allowing people to access a file directly without having to read all files prior to the one desired, as in tape, thus making online systems possible. By the mid-1960s, therefore, you could see all three mediums in concurrent use: cards, tape, and disk. In the 1970s, cards began to retire, tape was used for large batch jobs (e.g., billing) and by the end of the decade, for cheap backup of disk files. In the 1980s, tape remained for backup and a vast migration to disk was completed. Personal computers always began with diskettes, and one could not widely find tape drives for these machines until the late 1980s, and even then were rarely used. In the 1990s one was hard put to find someone with a tape drive—diskettes were reliable, cheap, and convenient. So more convenient forms always won the day.[32]

But price performance was always a factor. Electronic media were very expensive in the 1950s, and while less so in the 1960s still expensive, particularly disk technology. Vendors were able to deliver the greatest improvements in price/performance in the 1970s since the birth of the computer, and built on that economic momentum through significant improvements in performance, reliability, capacity, and miniaturization in the 1980s and 1990s on the same base technologies. Looking at the 1970s, we can see the degree of price/performance improvements that increasingly became the norm. Magnetic tape in 2,400-foot reels (the standard length), for example, went from $13 each in 1971 to just under $10 in 1979. Disk packs were widely used in that decade and declined in price from about $1,000 to $500 (for those used on the IBM 3330—the industry standard). The cost of paper, usually continuous forms and often with multiple copies and ribbons, however, soared in the 1970s by 125 percent. But that price increase affected all users of paper—newspapers, book publishers, and vendors of office supplies—as well as information processing. Finally, the cards that IBM sold in the 1930s for just over $1.00 per thousand dipped to just under $1.00 in 1971 but in 1978 reached $2.30 per thousand. Interestingly, IBM, which had so carefully guarded its ability to sell this product for nearly seven decades, discontinued their manufacture during the 1980s.[33]

The only other major segment of the information processing industry was telecommunications, which involved transmissions and specialized equipment. As a subset, this segment came into its own in the 1970s and by the early 1980s attained a value of over $2 billion just within the United States. Companies that sold computers entered the telecommunications field (IBM, for example), while those strictly in telephone and telecommunications sold computers, American Telephone and Telegraph (AT&T), for example. The breakup of AT&T in the United States in the early 1980s began a historic process in which the world of telecommunications fundamentally changed. Computer companies expanded their involvement in telecommunications, telephone companies started selling computers, and, by the early 1990s, we see entertainment companies, cable providers, and electric and gas utilities becoming involved. In short, the picture became increasingly unclear and complex in the 1980s and desperately awaits its historians. Like the history of software after 1960, the subject remains poorly understood as a segment of the history of information processing.[34]

THE INDUSTRY IN THE 1950s

The single most persuasive feature of the 1950s was the attempt to commercialize computers. The major companies of this period were Remington Rand which was the premier company in the first half of the decade, particularly after acquiring Univac and later IBM when it outsold and outdelivered by overwhelming volumes, more systems than the rest of the industry put together in the second half of the decade. Other players in the industry included GE, Burroughs, NCR, and Honeywell. The first computer built in a factory (as opposed to within a user's data center or in a special laboratory) was the IBM 701, which was announced in May 1952 and which signaled the company's commitment to participate extensively in the world of commercial computers. The next major announcement from IBM was the 650, introduced in 1953 and first shipped in 1954. That product propelled IBM into the mainstream of the new computer market. Over 1,800 of these systems were sold—a phenomenal number by the standards of the day. In contrast, the highly publicized Univac computers shipped only by the dozen. The 650 was likened to the Model-T of computing because it was the first mass-produced computer.[35]

Such changes in the configuration and construction of computer systems drove down costs and helped standardize the introduction of new technologies. By the end of 1954, the two dominant vendors of mainframe systems were Remington Rand with its UNIVAC I (also brought out in the early 1950s) and IBM. In addition, 23 other companies either manufactured computers or declared their intention to do so that year.

The industry in the 1950s offered computers for rent that had limited capacities and suffered from an equally limited knowledge of computing by potential customers. Everyone was a first-time user forced to invest a great deal of money in quasi-reliable technologies. There was real concern about quantifying the benefits of such expenditures. The confidence which would be so much in evidence a decade later was nowhere in sight. Vendors had to teach customers why they should use equipment and how to operate it, while trying to justify costs. At the same time, vendors rushed to improve reliability and capacity, particularly the speed and size of computer memories. Major suppliers provided software, education, maintenance, and encouragement. Those tactics continued throughout the 1950s and 1960s.[36]

The rivalry between IBM and Remington Rand was finally resolved by 1956–1957 with IBM the clear winner. Along the way certain technical milestones were achieved which in turn spurred the use of information processing technology. SAGE, a defense system sponsored by the U.S. government, generated a great deal of new technology which emerged by the late 1950s in various computers, especially those introduced by IBM. In the mid-1950s just over half of IBM's data processing revenues in the United States came from SAGE. The development of a high-level programming language called FORTRAN, beginning in 1957, began the long process of making programming easier. Before then, almost all programming was done by using a machine-level code that required significant technical expertise by a programmer. With high-level languages, productivity increased because it took less knowledge of how computers were coded to use them. Programs could be written quicker, and commands could be articulated with few instructions. Thus, for example, at General Motors, FORTRAN cut the time it took to write a program by a factor of five. By 1956 IBM had also made the critical decision to begin retiring its long-profitable tabulating business and commit itself fully to computers. There would be no turning back. During the rest of the decade, it brought out a variety of computers and introduced the disk drive, making it possible during the 1960s to develop large online files and direct accessing of information by commercial users for the first time.[37]

Applications, about which we will have more to say in Chapter 5, fell into two categories. At the beginning of the decade, scientific users dominated computing, particularly at universities and at government-managed research facilities. The U.S. and British governments had their own applications covering a wide range of issues: the census, weather, atomic bombs, real-time computing for defense, inventory control, and payroll. By the second half the same could be said of computing in France and in the Soviet Union. Also in the second half, commercial users began to weigh in heavily as they sought to reduce clerical expenses and cut the number of employees doing tasks computers could perform. At first applications included traditional accounting (accounts receivable, accounts payable, general ledger, and so on), followed by payroll and inventory control. Analog computers were used for process control in manufacturing, at chemical plants, and at oil refineries. Almost all work was batch with minor exceptions, usually at universities. MIT was one of the leading centers in the United States for innovations and home for some of the earliest uses of real-time systems and cathode ray terminals. British universities, such as Cambridge and Manchester, had been very innovative with hardware technology in the 1940s and early 1950s but by the end of the decade had lost that lead to the better-staffed and better-funded American universities.

Remington Rand's activities in this decade were historically important. The company began the 1950s in a better position than just about any other firm to dominate the development and sale of computers. It had the UNIVAC which was synonymous with the word "computer" during the first half of the decade—what a wonderful marketing and management position to be in! We would not see that situation again until the late 1960s or early 1970s when Xerox and its copiers gave us the phrase "to xerox" a document. By the late 1980s, IBM gave us the personal computer as the phrase of choice to describe microcomputers, and yet it was the official name for the company's small-end product. But back to Remington Rand; it did not effectively exploit its early lead. The root of its problem was that the company's senior management failed to commit themselves as totally to data processing as it needed to in order to compete profitably in the decade. Management in the Univac Division complained about this problem continuously to no avail; Remington was in too many lines of business. Further, its UNIVACs came out late when newer technologies were driving costs and hence profits per unit down for all vendors. This applied both to the Model I and the Model II—the company's two major computer systems of the decade. During the winter of 1954–1955 IBM gained the technical lead and kept it for the rest of the decade. Honeywell played a minor role, delivering its first computer in 1958 and selling only about ten machines. GE built one machine and did not attempt to play an important role until the 1960s. NCR did not deliver computers between 1954 and 1959, and RCA produced only six. More specialized firms also delivered a few devices. Most firms had failed to recognize the potential of computers early enough, and thus the industry as a whole remained small.

The advent of a second generation of computers in the late 1950s signaled increased attention and activity. IBM profited enormously from its STRETCH project, which caused so much new technology to become available for use in products in the late 1950s and early 1960s. The SABRE system, providing the first online reservation system in the world, was launched with American Airlines. That project gave IBM a wealth of technology which it applied in the years ahead. The airline set a standard with SABRE which the industry copied, and the application was still an integral part of the company's operations in the mid-1980s. The number of computers sold increased, suggesting that a new era was at hand while quantifying its size. IBM brought out the 1401 in October 1959 and rented almost 20,000 of them. To put that accomplishment in perspective, in the United States alone in 1960 only 6,000 general-purpose computers were installed from all vendors. In short, the information processing industry began its enormous and rapid growth at the dawn of the new decade. The period from the end of the 1950s to April 1964 is an historical era. It was the time of second-generation equipment, modest expansion in applications, and introduction of many new technologies, most notably the use of the transistor, with the silicon chip poised to appear. As Table 2.16 illustrates, the worldwide population of computers grew sharply by the end of 1962, with the United States dominating what was then well known as the data processing industry.[38]

THE INDUSTRY IN THE 1960s

By the early 1960s the story of information processing could no longer be told solely through the discussion of rivalry between IBM and Sperry Rand Corporation (the old Remington Rand), as is normally done by industry historians of the 1950s. The analogy of these two companies shooting it out as if in an old Western movie had to be modified to account for more—and more skilled—gunfighters because many new vendors entered the fray. As measured

Table 2.16
Number of Installed Computers, Worldwide, 1962

United States	9,337
Germany	472
Great Britain	389
Other Nations	761
Total	10,959

Source: Montgomery Phister, Jr., *Data Processing Technology and Economics* (Santa Monica,
    Calif.: Santa Monica Publishing Co., 1976): 32–34.

in terms of data processing revenues only (citing 1963's data since it was the
highwater mark of second-generation systems), IBM was number one ($1.2 bil-
lion) but shared sales with, among others, Sperry Rand ($145.5 million), AT&T
($97 million), Control Data Corporation (CDC) ($84.6 million), Philco ($73.9
million), Burroughs ($42.1 million), GE ($38.6 million), NCR ($30.7 million),
and Honeywell ($27 million). IBM retained its dominance by concentrating on
data processing markets, unlike other firms which were also interested in other
products (such as RCA with television). It built its own in-house technical expertise and risked its corporate health on new technical ventures that did well.
No other company was willing to invest proportionally as much on data processing, and so IBM prospered in the years before its announcement of the
S/360, despite its own perception that the successful products of the past (e.g.,
1401) were aging.[39]
    The most dramatic industry event of the 1960s clearly was IBM's announce-
ment in April 1964 of the S/360 family of computers. One could argue that it
was one of the most successful products in the history of American industry; it
certainly was for information processing in the era of the mainframe (pre-late
1980s). Under its blue metal covers it gathered the latest technology packaged
in sensible ways that made use easier and at costs impressively lower than in
the past. The largeness of the announcement far exceeded anything seen in the
nearly hundred-year-old office products industry: more than 150 separate products. Historians have yet to fully realize the stunning quality of this product
announcement, although for any data processing professional who lived through
the 1960s and 1970s, it was the most important computer event of their career.
They talk about their experiences with the S/360 the way veterans would speak
about theirs in World War II. IBM's "Blue Letters" (which were product announcements), and later name plates off these machines, became almost holy
relics in the industry. Even in the spring and summer of 1964, the announcement
startled the entire industry. By the end of the decade, IBM had doubled in size,

and, overall, the industry had grown each year at averages in excess of 27 percent. By 1968, 15 percent of all computers in the world were S/360s and by the end of the 1970s, the majority were either IBM or IBM-compatible (read as compatible with S/360-S/370 system using IBM's operating systems). Historians would have a difficult time overestimating the significance of this family of products on the industry or on the history of computing.[40]

What happened? Briefly, this family of compatible systems, software, and peripherals provided less conversion efforts for users moving from one size machine to another, standardized operating systems for all members of the computer's family which drove down operating costs, and improved reliability, which encouraged people to "rely" on computers more than before. To be certain, the introduction did not go smoothly in its entirety; for example, problems with operating systems plagued IBM for several years. But after all is said and done, in effect S/360 ushered in the third generation of computers: All other vendors were now forced to scrap old products and bring out new, better, faster machines and in greater quantities.

Why was the S/360 necessary? Changing configurations of whole product lines, with real threats to existing streams of revenue, is not how companies like to operate. If anything, the problem is that they are too risk adverse, regardless of what decade you look at or to which business experts you turn. So again, why such a change, especially since senior executives at IBM realized that the answer would be some form of significant leap into uncertainty? A task force commissioned within the company produced the SPREAD report which argued that competition would eventually destroy IBM's ability to market what was already an aging set of computer products. To maintain and expand growth, IBM had to bring out better machines which took advantage of new technologies, some of which had not yet been tried in lower-risk products. The company's management agreed with the general conclusions of the report, in the early 1960s poured increasing amounts of resources and eventually just about all available resources into the project, and, in effect, built the giant that became IBM of the computer era. At the time, managers and engineers knew that they needed to refurbish the entire product line with something new; that was the bold part of the initial effort. The result went far beyond what they originally anticipated (that is, the 150 products), and the consequences were not anticipated (that IBM would quickly double in size and reset the technical standards of the industry). But that is what happened. After the introduction of the S/360, for example, every major vendor responded by lowering prices on their existing products while scrambling to introduce new ones that had many of the technical characteristics and functions of IBM's new equipment. Furthermore, IBM became the target or benchmark against which great segments of the industry measured themselves. The decade ended with IBM's announcement (followed by that of other vendors) that software would be unbundled, in itself a change in support so different from what support had been for decades first with tabulators and later with computers, that historians might some day conclude was almost as profound a move as the new product announcements of the day.

Competition heated up sufficiently in the decade to drive both GE and RCA out of the computer business. In May 1970 GE announced that it had sold off its data processing business to Honeywell. In contrast to GE, which built computers different from IBM's, RCA manufactured computers (Spectra series) compatible with IBM's and marketed against the giant's installed base. In 1971 RCA made the most surprising announcements that it was withdrawing from the information processing industry. Sperry Univac survived the 1960s and entered the 1970s as an important force within the industry.

During the late 1960s Burroughs Corporation converted fully into a data processing vendor. NCR introduced a few products, all of which were successful. CDC was one of the fastest growing companies between 1963 and 1969, with revenues increasing from $85 million to $570 million in that period. CDC prospered because it was practical and had many cost-effective products. Smaller firms with specialized knowledge were acquired and then integrated into the overall operations of a parent company, whose sole business was information processing. This pattern would be repeated many times within other organizations throughout the 1960s and 1970s, and to a lesser extent in the 1980s, picking up with small high-technology companies again in the 1990s.

The industry of the 1960s was characterized by features different from those evident in the 1950s. The first of these were manufacturers of plug-compatible equipment (called PCMs). Vendors, recognizing that IBM's equipment had set the standards for the industry in terms of technology, functionality, and a level of cost, built computers and peripherals that used IBM's operating systems or that could be attached to systems made up of its equipment. The plug-compatibles competed by offering similar products at lower prices, often with more flexible terms and conditions. PCMs competed aggressively, primarily against IBM throughout the decade, first in the offices of potential customers and later with less success in the courtrooms of America. Some of the important PCM vendors were Telex, Ampex, Memorex, Information Storage Systems, and CalComp. They usually sold their look-alike products for between 10 and 15 percent below IBM's prices.[41]

Leasing companies came into their own in this period. They would buy a vendor's product, such as IBM's S/360s, and then lease them to customers over a longer period of time than would the manufacturer, thereby enabling reduced monthly costs for customers. This strategy also inhibited manufacturers such as IBM from displacing these kinds of products as soon as it wanted with newer ones. Between 1961 and 1965 leasing companies bought between $10 and $20 million worth of IBM equipment. Cumulatively, they had acquired $2.5 billion worth of IBM products by 1969. Thirty-three percent of all S/360s purchased in 1966 were owned by leasing companies. That year there were 92 leasing companies; by 1970 the number had grown to 250 in the United States. Many also operated in Europe. Some of the major leasing firms of the period included

Greyhound, Boothe Computer Corporation, and Itel. Their stocks did well until the 1970s when IBM and other major vendors brought out less expensive equipment to compete against purchased third-party hardware. Competing against leasing parties continued to influence profoundly the mainframe and peripheral product strategies of the key manufacturers all through the 1970s and 1980s.

Service bureaus did well in the 1960s. The Association of Data Processing Service Organizations proudly announced that, between 1965 and 1966, the revenues of the average firm grew by some 50 percent. In 1966 there were 700 service bureaus, and they generated $500 million in revenues. Some of the more important members of that community included McDonnell Automation, ADP, and Tymshare.[42]

Software firms were also thriving. By 1965 between 40 and 50 independent software companies were operating in the United States, and they did 30 to 50 percent of all the systems software development work done in the United States for third-generation computers (many of them S/360s). Computer Sciences Corporation (CSC) was particularly successful. By 1969, only ten years after its founding, its U.S. revenues reached $67.2 million. Informatics, Inc., established in 1962, ended the decade with revenues of $19.9 million. ADP, founded in 1959, also prospered and became an important supplier during the 1970s. In 1968 there were more than 2,800 companies in this sector of the economy. Contract programming the following year approached $600 million; software products generated another $20 to $25 million in revenues just in the United States. Users spent an estimated $200 million writing their own software in 1960; $3 to $4 billion in 1965; and $8 billion in 1970. Five years later the volume had grown to $12 billion.[43]

All of these various numeric citations lead us to the observation that in the 1960s, data processing enjoyed a prosperity unrivaled by any industry in any period in American history. In particular, America's large companies, and many others in Europe, had fully embraced the use of computers and did not hesitate to invest vast sums in this technology. Only some 6,000 computers had been installed by the end of 1960, but by the end of 1968 the number had grown to more than 67,000, one full order of magnitude! The market had climbed to a value of $7.2 billion, reflecting a demand that continued to grow impressively during the 1970s, despite a slowdown in the United States at the start of the decade due to an economic recession. In 1972, despite a recession, total data processing revenues exceeded $6 billion. Of 618 firms in business in 1972, only 9 had existed in 1952, 75 in 1960, and 188 in 1964. Revenues in these years were $39.5 million, $1.3 billion, and $3.2 billion, respectively. The group in 1972 generated $12.8 billion. Although historians and economists generally accept growth rates of over 27 percent in this industry, the above statistics suggest a compounded growth rate for the period that was closer to 33.5 percent. Regardless of which percent you use, the rate and speed of adoption of computer technology was profound to say the least. Of course, it also took place in a period when capital was readily available. By the end of the 1960s, vendors and bankers had learned that this is a capital-intensive industry and that its fortunes in the future would be increasingly tied to the strength of the capital funds market. The events of the 1970s and 1980s bore witness to that reality.

When you speak of growth in an industry's performance, you also are talking about expanding demand, which is another way of looking at an industry. The demand for computing set the pace, a requirement never saturated throughout the period. Even colleges and universities, which historically have had less money to invest in leading-edge technologies, exhibited an impressive demand on manufacturers consistent with the huge response from American and European industry as a whole. In 1957 higher education institutions had only 47 computers in the United States; in 1959 that number jumped to 105 and the following year to 142. But then the takeoff came: 186 in 1961, 248 in 1962, and 329 in 1963. And IBM had not yet announced the S/360, a system as popular in colleges and universities as in business and government, and for the same reasons.

Demand could also be measured by the increase in the number of organizations using computers, creating a very large base that continued to add data processing equipment to their inventories during the 1970s. The concept of the "installed base" as it was called in marketing circles of the day is crucial to understanding how the engine of growth was fueled in the 1970s and 1980s. Most manufacturers of computer hardware and software expanded their revenues by selling new, additional, or replacement products to existing customers. Thus the bigger the installed base you had, the greater the opportunity to sell more products. New customers were always celebrated, but you could not fuel the flow of revenues that were enjoyed by IBM and others just with new customers. From time-to-time, new products made it easier to expand the customer base, such as happened when IBM introduced the 4331 and 4341 systems at the end of the 1970s, which made it possible to buy market share from some competitors and to install computers for the first time in medium-size companies. Thus historians need to pay attention to what was going on with installed bases of customers, because many machines were being installed and used in new ways. The biggest customer of them all, the U.S. government, had only 5 computers in 1952, but 531 in 1960 and 1,862 in 1964, and closed out 1970 with 5,277. And, like corporate users, old machines were continuously swapped for newer ones all through the 1960s–1990s.

There are very few reliable statistics on applications or usages in the private sector, although what there is we look at in Chapter 5. But the previously cited statistics on the number of devices sold and leased, the volume of dollars generated, and the improvement in price/performance ratios were all dramatic, if indirect, descriptions of what happened during the 1960s in the growth of applications. While in Chapter 5 we discuss the kinds of applications implemented, the above numbers hint at the extent of deployment. Next, historians will have to slice the data by industry because the rate of adoption varied widely from one industry to another and from decade to another. The patterns of adoption remain unclear.

THE INDUSTRY IN THE 1970s

During the 1970s the information processing industry built on the momentum of the second half of the 1960s, expanding rapidly and deeply within the U.S. economy, and while to a lesser extent nonetheless significantly in both Western Europe and East Asia. The economic data for the United States are the most complete and document the extent. Data from 1972 are suggestive of the scope involved. Some 5,000 firms supplied products to the data processing industry (as it was still known throughout this decade). Nearly 700 of these companies made hardware; 500 made supplies of various types. The others produced a wide gamut of services. In 1971 the total value of hardware installed was $30.9 billion. To suggest what the future would hold, the investment in hardware worldwide reached over $4 trillion by around 1994! But back in 1971 there were 54,470 general-purpose systems in existence, of which only a third were very large (that is, leased for over $40,000 per month). Yet this top third accounted for 75 percent of the total value of the installed base of computers. Minicomputers accounted for nearly 30 percent of all installed computers.

Shipments to customers outside the United States indicate that during the 1970s, other countries experienced what the United States had in the 1960s. In 1971 nearly 45 percent of all U.S.-made computers went outside the United States for a total value of $3.3 billion. As of December 1971 approximately 57,800 systems of all types and sizes were installed outside the United States (communist countries were excluded from this census), with a value of $18.4 billion.[44]

Another way of measuring the size of the industry at the start of the decade involves looking at how many people were employed in it. One study sponsored by the American Federation of Information Processing Societies placed the total population in August 1972 at 172,300 but included only those employed in the actual manufacture of computers. The total industry (including all data processing professionals) was several times larger, easily over 300,000. In 1971, American users of information processing expended about $8.3 billion in salaries, another $10.3 billion in goods and services, and probably another $5 billion in miscellaneous overhead, according to AFIPS. Put another way, in 1971 the data processing industry may have had a $23.6 billion, or 2 percent, share of the Gross National Product (GNP).

The decade began with some 24,000 organizations operating one or more computers apiece; perhaps an equal number used service bureaus. Measured per $100 of national income in 1971, banking devoted 6.5 percent of its workforce to data processing. Ironically, railroads, which had been such a major user of tabulating equipment in the early years of the twentieth century, now spent only 0.7 percent of their labor on information processing, followed in descending order by banking and insurance. If measured by percentage of employees devoted to data processing, the breakdown was: banking (16.4 percent), insurance (3.5 percent), aerospace and defense (2.3 percent), utilities (2.2 percent), airlines

Table 2.17
Value of Installed Computers as Percent of Gross National Product, 1973

Country	% of GNP	Country	% of GNP
Japan	1.44	Belgium	0.87
West Germany	1.29	Brazil	0.66
United Kingdom	2.13	Spain	0.64
France	1.36	South Africa	1.22
Soviet Union	0.40	Austria	0.79
Canada	1.48	Mexico	0.38
Italy	1.13	Norway	0.88
Australia	1.22	Yugoslavia	0.57
Netherlands	1.28	All other countries	0.16
Switzerland	1.63	United States	2.59
Sweden	1.05	Total international	0.32
Denmark	1.71	Total Worldwide	1.29

Source: U.S. Department of State, *Bureau of Intelligence and Research Reports* (Washington, D.C.: GPO, 1974): passim.

(1.5 percent), electronics (1.4 percent), and chemicals (1.2 percent), while each of the other sectors dropped below 1 percent. The total number of data processing professionals in 1971 had already reached 1 million in the United States—a useful yardstick by which to measure the growth of the industry even in the late 1960s.

The role of information outside the United States increased sharply during the 1970s. As Table 2.17 illustrates, by examining the percentage of GNP devoted to information processing, one quickly realizes that the industry had become important to the United States (about 2.59 percent) and United Kingdom (2.13 percent), and was growing in significance in Denmark (1.71 percent), Switzerland (1.63 percent), and Canada (1.48 percent). Japan followed closely behind with 1.44 of GNP. The industry in the Soviet Union hovered at 0.40 percent, which suggests that it had not yet realized the significance of information processing to the local economy. Percentages of GNP should be used with caution because the definition of an industry varies from country to country and thus can influence statistical evidence. The broader the definition, the higher the GNP that would be cited. Because various government agencies and private researchers gather together such data, conflicting statistics on the size of the industry remain common, particularly from about 1972 to the present. However, GNP data suggest a relative presence within a particular national economy and are consistent in terms of relative size to internal marketing intelligence reports from such vendors as Burroughs and IBM.

As early as 1969, the United States had 57 percent of all computer installations in the world, as compared to Japan and Germany which had 8 percent each. By the end of 1972 Japan had the second highest number of computer installations in the world. Japan had around 45,000 general-purpose computers in 1970, 75,000 five years later, and 125,000 in 1980. The number of special-purpose computers increased from 25,000 in 1970 to 575,000 in 1980. In 1975 the United States had 86,499 mainframes, up 350 percent since 1965. The U.S. Department of Defense used 5,027 of these systems, making it the largest single user of computers within the government. Federal use of computers grew steadily through the remaining years of the decade, continuing to make the U.S. government the largest processor of data in North America, a distinction it had held in each decade since before Hollerith came along with his punch cards.

The 1970s witnessed technological innovations which led to continued decreases in cost and improved reliability. The major advances were the use of monolithic semiconductors with large-scale integration, major advances in telecommunications, wide use of time-sharing services, and the installation of minicomputers. High-speed printers, large storage and memory units, many new programming languages, and more usable operating systems rich in function also characterized the period. By 1979 Americans were living in the computer age. Alvin Toffler's *Future Shock* was not simply the title of a best-selling book forecasting the future and increased use of computers, it flirted with what some saw as reality then. Readers were already aware of the nearly ubiquitous nature of computers. Surveys and interviews of the time suggested that Americans sensed that they were experiencing its predictions daily. Almost all of their bills and paychecks were generated by computers, and credit checking via computer had become a reality for over half the entire population.[45]

Like other vendors, IBM replaced its third-generation equipment with fourth-generation computers which were essentially sophisticated refinements of the basic technologies and architectures which appeared in the S/360. These newer systems included the S/370 (a direct replacement for S/360) and, in 1979, the 4300 series which represented an important repackaging of technology. IBM had already started to replace large S/370s with 308X machines.

Computer wars now characterized the entire industry. Much of the fighting took place in courtrooms, with most lawsuits directed against IBM in an attempt to charge it with monopolistic practices. The list of litigants read like a *Who's Who* of the industry: Greyhound filed against IBM in 1969, Telex in 1972, CalComp, Hudson, Marshall, Memorex, and Transamerica in 1973, Forro and Memory Tech in 1974, and Sanders in 1975. They all lost. But the giant lawsuit was *U.S. v. IBM*, which was filed in January 1969 and lasted until the government dropped it in January 1982. It was the largest and longest antitrust suit in American history. The government failed to build a case against IBM despite a heroic attempt costing hundreds of millions of dollars. But the case was important, not just as a legal precedent, but also because it influenced the actions of vendors throughout this and subsequent decades. As this is being written (1996), the giant software vendor Microsoft is having difficulties with the same agency of the U.S. government that came after IBM, as had AT&T in the 1970s and early 1980s, IBM and AT&T in the 1950s, IBM and Remington Rand in the 1930s, and NCR just before the start of World War I. One of the great research projects waiting for historians is to study and understand the effects of U.S. antitrust suits against these companies. With the passage of time, for example in the IBM case, IBM employees can look back and see that the suit was very exhausting, and caused IBM to take its eye off some emerging markets, to back off from others, and to reorganize in ways to protect the company from the government but that did not optimize its ability to do what companies are supposed to: sell products and make profits. The one benefit of this terribly long legal ordeal was that it made public several billion documents on the entire data processing industry from sources scattered and hard to come by across the entire industry. That means the day can be expected when historians will have carefully mapped out the history of information processing in the United States from the 1950s through the 1970s, based on a mountain of excellent research.[46]

Although it is easy to think lawsuits acquired their own life-forms and came to dominate events in this industry, nothing could be further from the truth when you look at what occurred daily on the street. While lawsuits continued, vendors competed in the marketplace. These included IBM, Burroughs, Control Data, NCR, Sperry Rand, Digital, Honeywell, and even Xerox for a while. PCMs were very active, again targeting their efforts largely at IBM's S/360 and S/370 customers. Telex, Storage Technology, Memorex, and Advanced Memory Systems were active throughout the decade. As IBM introduced new computers or disk drives, for example, these vendors brought out similar products but at lower prices within eighteen months, often coinciding with first shipments of IBM products, most of which were announced a year to eighteen months earlier.

Leasing companies gained importance in the 1960s but faced a difficult period in the 1970s, despite the fact that by then their presence affected pricing and buying strategies of vendors and customers, respectively. Leasing companies particularly faced a difficult time in the second half of the decade. They had been placing their equipment on depreciation schedules that were longer than, say, IBM's, usually seven to ten years, based on their conviction that IBM in particular would not announce replacement products before then. To their surprise, IBM brought out new products faster than it had in the 1960s, but closer to the announcement cycle of the late 1950s, which reduced the residual values of leasing companies' machines faster than they were prepared to handle. They had no choice, therefore, but to depreciate faster, taking losses in order to continue financing inventories.

Another feature of the 1970s was the introduction of widespread use of minicomputers. Although they had been around since the early 1960s, not until the 1970s did they come into their own as departmental systems or as small, high-function application machines widely marketed by such firms as Data General Corporation, Hewlett-Packard, Prime Computer, Perkin-Elmer, Harris Corporation, Wang Laboratories, Tandem, and Datapoint. These vendors did so well during the 1970s that the industry could no longer be discussed simply in terms of large mainframe manufacturers. That historians, economists, and journalists have continued to be mainframe focused in dealing with the 1970s is an error that will be corrected in time. At the time, however, the arrival of the minicomputer was well understood by reporters at such key publications as *Computerworld* and *Datamation*, and by customers, particularly engineering departments, the original core set of customers for such systems.

Plug-compatible large mainframes added competitive spice, particularly after 1975, when Amdahl Corporation introduced its first product to sell directly against IBM's S/370s, especially the larger models. They all did well during the mid-1970s, but with new introductions from IBM in the last years of the decade they experienced slowdowns in sales.

Software firms continued to thrive. In 1975 about 1,000 such companies with more than 3,000 products in their sales kits had been established. When combined with contract programming, their revenues in 1975 amounted to $1.3 billion. Service bureaus also grew; ADP (21 years old in 1970) expanded into one of the most important of these. By 1979 it had more than 75,000 users generating revenues of $371 million.

IBM continued to be an important force in the market. According to data submitted in the government's lawsuit against the giant, IBM's share of data processing revenues in 1973 was 33 percent of all money raised in the industry, down from 49 percent in 1963. That company's domestic revenues during 1976 reached 44 percent of the total, but by the end of 1979 had settled down to 34 percent. The market expanded, but IBM did not grow as quickly, which led management to launch an aggressive program introducing new products and spending over $17 billion in modernizing plants between the late 1970s and early 1980s. The results were spectacular during the early 1980s, but they were not evident in the late 1970s. Nonetheless, the company continued to prosper, though not with the growth rates it had experienced during the 1960s. The outstanding news for the company was the settlement of almost all private lawsuits against it, including the one filed by the U.S. Department of Justice.

An enormous variety of competition now typified the industry. Several tens of thousands of vendors which had not been in business at the start of the 1970s, let alone in the 1960s, were now operating in the industry around the world. Thousands alone functioned in the United States, including almost all the largest vendors in the world. The use of information technology expanded to the point where the average medium-to-large company spent between 1 and 2 percent of its budget on it. Nor did technological change slow down. It was during this period, for example, that the desktop computer was born (late 1970s) which so profoundly influenced access to computers in the 1980s. It did nothing less than democratize computers.

During the 1970s it became easier to use computers, easier, that is, than it had been in the 1950s or 1960s, but still complicated enough that users continue to complain about usability issues. Getting computers to do one's bidding by wiring boards in the 1950s or writing in complex languages in the 1960s was nothing compared to the ease that came with terminals and online applications in the 1970s increasingly using English-like instructions, a trend that continued into the 1980s. Terminals came into their own as the most widely used method for getting to computing power. More than 200 vendors sold these, primarily cathode ray terminals (CRTs). In the United States alone, *Computerworld* reported that at the end of 1976, more than 58,000 CRTs were installed along with 294,500 other terminals. The first 100,000 terminals sold in the United States went into data centers, but soon after they began appearing on desks in end-user departments, used by people who knew little or nothing about information processing. Whereas at the start of the decade the ratio of terminals to workers exceeded 1:100, by the end of the decade it was less than 1:10 and by the mid-1980s, 1:4, and headed rapidly toward closer ratios.

In 1978 revenues of U.S. companies in the data processing industry accounted for approximately 1.5 percent of total GNP. It took the industry 27 years to reach that point. To put that growth into perspective, factory sales of automobiles reached that percentage of GNP in about 15 years and the telephone in 44 years. Television sales reached 0.05 percent in less than a decade and remained at that level. Automobile sales varied between 1 and 3 percent of GNP and telephones at about 2.3 percent, while data processing (or information landing, depending on whose statistics and definitions were used) exceeded 1 percent by the end of the decade.

The volume of revenues generated by the industry made it a critical component of the U.S. economy by the early 1980s. As in the 1970s, dominance of world sales by U.S. firms ranged between 70 and 80 percent, generating a trade surplus of $6.84 billion in 1982, despite challenges from Japanese vendors. The entire market was valued at $65 billion worldwide in 1982. Growth in the industry during the 1970s averaged 18.1 percent and closer to 21.3 percent during the first three years of the 1980s. In 1976 worldwide production of U.S. computer companies was worth $23.4 billion, but by 1981 had grown to $56 billion. The faster growth came in software and services, which went from $5.2 billion to $14.9 billion. Mainframes nearly tripled in worth, from $6.2 billion to $17.2 billion, whereas minicomputers quadrupled to $8.8 billion. Only peripherals experienced slow growth, going from $10 billion to $13.9 billion.[47]

The rate of growth in production by country also suggests the size and source of goods and services. Between 1978 and 1981, U.S. production grew by 23.2 percent, yielding a world market share of 57.7 percent; in second place was Japan with rates of 17.5 and 13.1 percent, respectively; and in third place was France with 18.1 percent and 9.5 percent, respectively. All other nations became less important except for Italy, whose market grew 30.4 percent, apparently suggesting that it was catching up with other industrialized countries, particularly its peers in the European Market. Italy's world share was only 2.3 percent, proof that most of its production was for internal consumption. When comparing

Table 2.18
**Sales of Major Information Processing Firms in Japan, 1976–1981, Selected Years
(Millions of Dollars)**

Company	1976	1979	1981	Growth Rate Percentages 1976-1981
Fujitsu	1086.5	1481.9	2033.3	13.4
NEC	516.9	810.1	1507.7	23.9
Hitachi	643.9	979.5	1305.9	15.2
Oki	219.0	284.8	494.7	17.7
Toshiba	268.4	228.5	430.8	9.9
Mitsubishi	145.1	240.3	331.0	17.9
Subtotal	2879.0	4125.1	6103.4	16.2
IBM Japan	1248.8	1470.1	1944.9	9.3
Nippon Univac	320.1	333.7	412.2	5.2
Total U.S. Affiliates	1568.9	1803.8	2357.1	8.5

Source: Japan Economic Journal (June 9, 1981; June 8, 1982), Bureau of Industrial Economics, as
tabulated and presented in U.S. Department of Commerce, *The Computer Industry* (Washington, D.C.: GPO, 1983): 25.

worldwide manufacturing and buying patterns from one decade to another, during the 1980s Japanese data processing exports rose an average of 78 percent to nearly $700 million in value. Table 2.18 presents some of the financial characteristics of the Japanese information processing industry.[48]

The end of the 1970s also brought to a close a quarter century of computing in which we could conjure up images of big boxey computers with dials and lights. The 1980s, while a decade in which large computers were used in vast quantities, was overshadowed by the widespread distribution of personal computers, a new technology which, as of this writing (1996), held the promise of coming to dominate some of the key ways in which computing was sold and used.

THE INDUSTRY IN THE 1980s

The information processing world underwent profound changes in the 1980s at the same time it kept many of its traditional institutional structures. The central event of the decade was the broad deployment of microcomputers in businesses, government agencies, and even schools. In fact, PCs grabbed many of the headlines, particularly as new companies became important, such as Microsoft, the provider of DOS—the operating system for most PCs and Apple, the favorite vendor of microcomputers for the K–12 community. But alongside microcomputers was the continuation of mainframe and minicomputer businesses. IBM was more than just selling PCs, it was still delivering large mainframes. Digital Equipment Corporation (DEC) continued to serve its market niche.

During the 1980s a series of economic problems affected all of American industry, not just information processing, caused largely by worldwide competitive pressures. Recession, inflation, competition, and the start of the downsizing, restructuring, and "rightsizing" that would dramatically influence large corporations in the 1990s began in the mid-1980s, while the economy expanded nicely in the second half of the decade. But that fact did not alter the reality that large American corporations faced fundamental structural changes. For example, IBM deployed its first early retirement program that anyone could remember in 1986.[49] By the end of 1994, IBM's employee population had gone from a high of 404,000 down to just over 230,000. Almost all of the other major players in the industry also downsized.

The industry entered the decade with good prospects for growth. From 1981 through 1984, total outlays for computing products grew at an average of over 30 percent annually. In 1984 growth in revenues dropped to 15 percent and in 1986 to 5–6 percent. Yet sales of equipment and software in 1986 approached $300 billion. In the first four years of the decade, shipments of mainframes continued to grow, but flattened in the rest of the decade. Minicomputers grew steadily in volume all through the decade as businesses bought departmental systems. In aggregate, by the mid-decade the computer business had become sluggish in the United States yet continued to grow overseas. One could see the effects of sluggishness on the employment picture. In 1985, computer manufacturers in the United States lowered their overall employee population by 9 percent and in 1986 by another 7 percent. Production workers fell by 18 percent in 1985 and another 12 percent the following year. Software sales continued to grow, however, in this period. In 1986, for example, U.S. suppliers of software experienced a 22 percent increase in sales, with revenues totaling $22 billion.[50]

The real expansion was in microcomputers, however. These small, portable computers could easily be placed on a desk at the office or at home. They first appeared in the late 1970s and in a few years had become a major product. The growth in the volume of microcomputers and patterns of usage for the early years of the decade are shown in Tables 2.19, 2.20, and 2.21. The democratization of computing became evident as these little devices appeared in classrooms, college dormitories, and church rectories.

Homemakers kept recipes on them, children played games with their PCs, while uses in business and science made the traditional terminal an antique. Sales from 1978 to 1983 jumped from $15 million to nearly $500 million (Tables 2.22 and 2.23).

In those years computers could be placed on a desk at a cost of less than $2,000, providing computing power that would have cost over $1 million in the

Table 2.19
Number of Microcomputers Shipped to Businesses, 1981–1985

Year	Volume
1981	344,000
1982	926,000
1983	1,538,000
1984	2,384,000
1985	3,290,000

Source: Dunn & Bradstreet Corporation as reported in *USA Today*, June 16, 1985, p. 5.

Table 2.20
Size of Companies versus Percent Using PCs, 1985

Number of Employees	Percentages of Companies
1-19	23.9
20-99	36.3
100-499	47.2
500-999	71.8
1,000 or more	85.4

Source: Dunn & Bradstreet Corporation as reported in *USA Today*, June 16, 1985, p. 5.

late 1960s. Decision making increasingly relied on the modeling capabilities of such machines and their associated, relatively easy-to-use software, especially spreadsheet programs. Social commentators began arguing that the way people thought and talked was being restructured to conform to the systematized approach of information processing.[51]

Table 2.24 suggests the percent of company budgets that were being spent in these years on computing. While it is no surprise that the amounts varied by industry—largely a function of the applicability of computers from industry to industry—what is interesting is the enormous volumes. Distribution of expenditures across industries remained relatively in the same proportions through the majority of the 1980s, although in mid-decade demand for computing products softened across all industries in response to the start of restructuring, competitive pressures, and budget cutbacks.

Technological improvements also relentlessly pushed down prices of equipment, making the support of previous revenue streams always a challenge. By

Table 2.21
Business Uses of PCs, 1983 and 1985

Application	% in 1983	% in 1985
Accounting	61.3	72.5
Financial analysis	68.7	65.2
Word processing	48.4	56.8
Database management	34.6	38.3
Inventory control	30.5	31.5
Purchasing	14.1	22.8
Credit analysis of customers	20.3	14.2
Other	8.5	78.0

Source: Dunn & Bradstreet Corporation as reported in *USA Today*, June 16, 1985, p. 5. All data are from a U.S. survey; respondents could fill in more than one category.

Table 2.22
Personal Computer Sales in the United States, 1978–1983 (Millions of Dollars)

1978	15
1979	30
1980	85
1982	180
1983	300-500

Data for 1981 not provided in the original charts.

Source: A.D. Little, Inc., published in Ulric Weil, *Information Systems in the 80's: Products, Markets, and Vendors* (Englewood Cliffs, N.J.: Prentice-Hall, 1982): 214.

the end of the decade, for example, the industry's improvements in microcomputer technology every 18 months doubled the amount of power one could buy for a dollar. By the end of 1991, these kinds of price/performance improvements had resulted in the industry's net income being cropped from 6.5 percent of revenues in 1986 to −0.12 percent.[52] In other words, profit margins had become razor thin, a condition that would affect even large profit items (e.g., mainframes) in a similar way in the 1990s. Lower prices drove demand, particularly for PCs, in the second half of the decade to the point where annual shipments of 10 million or more became the rule.

The industry experienced significant restructuring as niche players became more predominant than the more traditional fully integrated providers (e.g., IBM). Minicomputer vendors, others specializing in microcomputers, still others

Table 2.23
Personal Computer Systems in the United States, 1978–1983 (Thousands of Units)

Year	Annual	Installed
1978	20	30
1979	20	50
1980	70	120
1982	120	240
1983	600-1,000	1,600-2,000

Data for 1981 not provided in the original charts.

Source: A.D. Little, Inc., reported in Ulric Weil, *Information Systems in the 80's: Products, Markets, and Vendors* (Englewood Cliffs, N.J.: Prentice-Hall, 1982): 214.

Table 2.24
"Official" Budgets Dedicated to Information Systems as Percent of Revenue by Industry, 1987

Industry	Percent of Revenue
Banking and Finance	4.5
Electronics	3.7
Food and Beverage	1.6
Health Care and Pharmaceuticals	0.6
Industrial and Automotive	2.7
Insurance	1.7
Metal and Metal Products	1.1
Petroleum and Petrochemicals	1.3
Process	1.6
Retail	0.2
Transportation	1.3
Utilities	1.0

Source: Data presented in "Industry by Industry IS Survey," *Datamation* (September 1, 1987): 46–48; but see also 58, 78.

that made machines and software for a particular industry (e.g., ATMs for banking) became the norm. Revenue sources shifted as a consequence. Worldwide sales of personal computers went from $30 billion in 1986 upward steadily in the second half of the decade, ending 1990 at over $80 billion. With profits declining, thanks to competition and technological innovations, employment in the industry continued to decline steadily all through the 1980s and into the 1990s, down by more than 100,000 just in the second half of the 1980s. The effects on computer stocks were obvious: While the S&P generally grew through the period 1987 to 1992, computer stocks generally shrank to nearly half their value.[53]

As in previous decades companies experienced rising and falling fortunes and new players appeared. For example, IBM's fortunes began to suffer while Unisys (the company that resulted from the merger of Burroughs and Sperry Rand in 1986) momentarily appeared to thrive by the end of the decade, despite a tough time in mid-decade. Sun, which produced high-function workstations, became the darling of Wall Street, grabbing significant market share from engineering workstation vendors like IBM and DEC. Microsoft and Apple were in their glory (usually), although this market segment became ferociously competitive in the 1980s. Table 2.25 attempts to answer the question, so how did the key players do? Using 1986 and then 1991 data demonstrates what happened during the period. What the data demonstrate are changes that occurred in who did well and who did not, a level of churn not seen in the industry since it expanded dramatically in the 1960s. Thus while strong interest in computing products continued in the 1980s despite various ups and downturns due to the vagaries of the economy, the real churn occurred in the kinds of computing of interest to customers.

Because computing had become such a large part of what businesses did in the United States, the ups and downs of the industry and its products (especially microcomputers) drew much attention. Every major newspaper and news magazine covered the industry in detail. Widely read books appeared describing this company or that, or industry trends. Microcomputer usage sensitized millions of users to industry-related issues as well. Until the mid-1980s, the information processing industry and its customers had been a relatively closed world, at once limited to those with knowledge of the technology.[54] But in this decade two things fundamentally changed. First, microcomputers made it possible for end users to appreciate how computing could help them in their work, and the cost was low enough that they could go and buy these devices without involving the computer establishment in their companies. That practice threatened the near strangle-hold that the MIS community had held over all computing. Second, by the end of the decade, a new generation of middle and young executives had emerged knowledgeable about computing issues, asking tough questions about how MIS was being run, and challenging the value they were receiving.[55]

In large corporations, MIS directors would conduct surveys to understand the extent of microcomputer and minicomputer deployment, often to be horrified to find out that computing power and dollars invested in these equaled or surpassed the "glass house" information processing budget. The data in Table 2.24 are drawn just from the IS budgets, not the underground expenditures which often were coded as "test equipment" or some other name. Centralized information

Table 2.25
Financial Performance Key Industry Players, 1987 and 1991 (Revenue in Millions of Dollars)

Company	1987 Revenue	1991 Revenue
Unisys	9,732	8,696
CDC	3,366	1,525
Prime	961	1,382
Wang	2,837	2,091
DEC	9,389	13,911
AT&T/NCR	5,641	N/A
Data General	1,274	1,229
HP	8,090	14,494
Motorola	6,727	11,341
Compaq	1,224	3,271
AMD	997	1,227
LSI Logic	262	698
Cypress	77	287
Lotus	396	829
WordPerfect	100	640
Borland	38	227
Chips & Tech.	80	225
Apple	2,661	6,309
Intel	1,907	4,779
Sun	538	3,221
Microsoft	346	1,843
Novell	222	640
Adobe	39	230
IBM	55,598	64,766

Source: Charles H. Ferguson and Charles R. Morris present a series of tables with this kind of data in addition to other financial information in *Computer Wars* (New York: Times Books, 1993): 214–220; on IBM, see Emerson W. Pugh, *Building IBM* (Cambridge, Mass.: MIT Press, 1995): 324.

processing departments resisted the arrival of minis and micros through most of the decade, seeing these as political, budgetary, and technical threats to their role. By about 1987, however, centralized computing organizations had lost the war of control over acquisition decisions. The PC-based end users had won. What did they win? They caused MIS organizations to start facilitating the further acquisition of micros (e.g., through quantity discount purchases from IBM and other vendors), and then to begin the process of networking the devices, a trend still underway. Volumes spent on computing rose continuously but without the disciplined purchasing and cost justification practices of the 1960s and 1970s with the result that, at least for historians, we have a great deal of work to do to find out who used computing, for what, why, and to answer questions about possible benefits received. MIS increasingly became demystified as an additional by-product, about which I will have more to say in Chapter 6.

The rise of a new cadre of middle and upper management increasingly savvy about computers also had its consequences. MIS managers improved their careers, rising from middle managers usually in financial organizations to full members of senior management with their own large organizations and even divisions. But they also had to begin answering tough questions about productivity. Business consultants and economists began to challenge the wisdom of blind investments in computing. Until about 1973 many new applications were simply replacements for highly defined yet labor-intensive work, so justification was fairly straightforward. If you could replace 1,000 clerks with a software package that required only 10 clerks, you could calculate the benefits quickly. But after 1973, new applications that could not have been performed without computers or which were intended to facilitate management decision making became more common, and these were very, very difficult to cost justify.

In the mid-1980s, an ex-Xerox MIS executive, Paul A. Strassmann, went public with this concern in a book called *Information Payoff*. While he argued how benefits would accrue, he exposed the fact that benefits had not yet accrued. It was one of the first studies to point out problems with technology along with its potential benefits. Excessive E-mail, new levels of complexity, unjustified use of computing, and so on, needed to be understood in addition to the potential benefits for improving productivity. Like the child in the fairy story about the emperor who had no clothes, Strassmann pointed to the industry and said "Not enough is known about what works and what does not work to make automation decisions with confidence."[56] He was simply echoing what many executives were beginning to believe. In 1990, Strassmann published a far more detailed, even massive, study, *The Business Value of Computers*, in which he presented an enormous amount of information in support of his thesis that "there is no relationship between expenses for computers and business profitability."[57] While this is not the place to review this mountain of material, it is, however, important to point out that the concerns he raised—be they true or false—were challenges posed to the MIS community. The questions raised would also engage the interests of economists in the 1980s and 1990s.

For the historian of the 1980s, there is more to be done than simply write about rivalries among companies, new technological innovations, or the continued spread of computing. The issue of productivity and impact on organizations—Strassmann's concerns—will require careful analysis equal in complexity to any other issue concerning the history of computing. The role of the information worker—the view of Fritz Machlup, for example— (he was one of the first scholars to identify "knowledge-producing" workers as a major group in the U.S. economy) will simply complicate the analysis. But such studies will address fundamental concerns about technology. Historians of technology generally agree both that needs cause new tools to be developed and that new tools cause new uses. Certainly, the experience with computers would validate this perspective. However, with the challenges to productivity being raised, we also have to ask ourselves other questions:

• Do people use information-handling tools differently than other technologies because of how the human brain functions? If so, how?
• Do computers allow us to do things that are so new and effective that our problem is that traditional ways of measuring efficiency and effectiveness no longer are useful benchmarks of computers? Why? How can that insight influence how we apply this technology?
• Why did so many people buy so many computers without formal cost justifications? Are we a species of toy players?
• How did the rapid proliferation of computers in the 1980s begin to change society?

The last question should be, after all, the bottom line concern of historians of computing.

The challenge is large. Almost all the literature of the 1980s continued the hype evident about the topic from the 1940s forward: giant brains, Age of Computers. Even in the 1990s the hype continues. *USA Today* in its July 27, 1995, issue had as its cover story ''Digital Age: PCs Power '90s Renaissance.'' The reporter, Kevin Maney, argued that ''high-tech could change society as autos did.''[58] As historians, we, too, are not immune to the experiences of our age. The hype can distort our thinking if we are not careful. So for the 1980s, the volume of work and the importance of the issues involved, make the study of the history of computing extraordinarily complicated and vital. If we can think of the 1950s as picking up speed, the 1960s as a great takeoff in computing, and the 1970s as a continuum, what are we to say about the 1980s? My sense is that in the second half of the decade, we began to experience the start of a new historical era in computing that may be still starting.[59]

THE INDUSTRY IN THE 1990s

Four trends of crucial historical importance were evident in the first half of the 1990s:

1. The continued and increased deployment of microcomputers.
2. The shift from centralized to network-centric computing.
3. The decline and rise of IBM.
4. The reconfiguration of the industry to include voice, data, and video.

We could argue for other trends: the ebbs and flows of business volumes, investment and deinvestments in new technologies, miniaturization of all devices, the demise and birth of major vendors. Those are the bread-and-butter issues of industry history, but I think historians will look back and say that in addition to those topics, there are at least the four listed above.

Microcomputing continued to expand unabated through the first half of the 1990s, regardless of recession in the United States and the Persian Gulf War, softness in the Japanese and European economies, and hard times at IBM. American corporations shed hundreds of thousands of jobs in the 1990s and yet microcomputers were being sold by the tens of millions. Industry observers suggested that perhaps, finally, the consequences of all the investments in computing made in the 1970s and 1980s had arrived in the form of flatter organizations, and process reengineering which always has a high information technology content. Also the consequences of price/performance perhaps had arrived at some magical level.[60] If the largest provider of PC software was to have a Golden Age–Microsoft—it was the early to mid-1990s. In 1995, Microsoft could sell a million copies of a new operating system and have it be the business news event of the year! IBM publicly committed to turn itself into a network centric (read, PC vendor) of choice for the world, pushing into the background its mainframe heritage. Compaq and Apple continued to be important American nameplate corporations, both providing microcomputing products.

The move to network-centric strategies for the use and deployment of microcomputing and information processing is a development that is growing out of the dispersion of microcomputers in general but also the further miniaturization of technologies. The process started in the 1980s when users of microcomputers began to look for ways to share information from one machine to another, leading to the creation of a variety of software and telecommunications tools in the late 1980s and early 1990s to facilitate the process. That trend increased in intensity as the 1990s aged, to the point where central computer operations were increasingly being seen as large switching points for data from one micro to another.[61] The move to network-centric strategies had dramatic effects that were almost immediately visible. For example, the number of office workers who could function outside their offices increased dramatically. Laptops came into their own, equipped with modems, fax function, and the usual assortment of PC software available in the 1980s.

While customers and vendors were increasing usage of communications technology while also linking phones and PCs, regulatory changes in the United States presaged profound changes in all forms of telecommunications. American telecommunications laws dated from the 1930s and had not been changed in the intervening decades; yet technology had gone from distinctly different forms (e.g., radio, telephone, telegraph, and later television) to more merged configurations, increasing pressure to revisit existing regulatory programs. In February 1996, after years of debate within regulatory agencies and across a wide variety of technology-based industries (e.g., computing/information processing, telephone, television, radio, cable, and movies), the U.S. Congress passed a new set of regulations that led technologists to realize that the next decade would see profound changes in how whole technology-based industries would operate, what products and services they would provide, and how consumers (businesses and individuals) would respond.

Essentially, the new law made it possible for television, telephone, and information processing industries to sell products and services in each other's markets. Up to that time companies could not do this. The fact that it passed in the U.S. Congress with overwhelming support (414 to 16 in the House, 91 to 5 in the Senate) suggests the significance of the change. This revision of the Communications Act of 1935 allows local and long distance telephone companies and cable providers to compete against each other with similar services. Cable rates (which years earlier had been fixed by law in the United States) were deregulated, while media corporations could expand their holdings in various types of communications companies across the nation and increase their market shares within specific geographies through acquisitions. To give one a sense of the order of change involved, the law covers the activities of the $700 billion telecommunications industry. This industry accounts for approximately one-sixth of the U.S. gross national product. Since all telecommunications providers and almost all vendors of information and electronically delivered entertainment expect to be immediately and profoundly affected by this law, historians will have to understand how various technologies influenced the changes in the law and how the new regulations affected the types of technology, products, and services that became available as a result. The same will apply to economic historians looking at the U.S. economy and its industries in the early years of the twenty-first century. Since information processing is an industry that is used to having its history written almost as rapidly as it occurs, historians will not have to wait long before they are tempted to document the effects of this new law.

Miniaturization of technology facilitated the process of profound change in technology which occurred in the 1980s and 1990s. Portable phones that used to be carried in bags about the size of car batteries now fold up into units the size of packs of cigarettes. Laptop computers weigh less than six pounds and are still on a weight diet. Phones and PCs are being packaged into one product. Miniaturization is also being coupled with growth in reliability and capacity, a process expected to continue unabated throughout the decade. One consequence is further mobility of workers and their application of technology to perform duties that were not effectively possible before; for example, distance learning for students away from campuses.

IBM's history in the 1990s will concern historians for a long time. Historians of the industry have gotten into the habit of treating this company much like a huge oil tanker in a small harbor. Whenever it moved all the other boats bounced up and down in its wake. Often the industry was defined and described in context of IBM circumstances. This began as early as the 1930s when looking at the office machine market. So that perspective has a long history of its own. Then in the late 1980s and early 1990s, the company experienced a severe downturn in business on the order of magnitude experienced by the U.S. automotive industry in the late 1970s and early 1980s, and Xerox in the 1980s. It would not be an exaggeration to argue that in 1992 IBM was slowly going out of business, just based on the data presented in its annual reports of the period. The company identified what markets it needed to be in and downsized its employee population by some 40 percent while preserving its revenue streams at rates similar to those of the 1980s. By the end of 1994, the financial data suggested the company had turned the corner. It made a profit, introduced new products that were well received, the U.S. economy entered a period of growth, and the company's expenses had been brought under reasonable control relative to its competitors. 1995 was a second good year for the company, further evidence that the bottom had been reached and recovery was well underway.

IBM's experiences profoundly influenced the information processing industry in ways not yet clear. PC vendors obviously thrived; Microsoft boomed. The number of niches and vendors in the industry gave the impression to customers that the stability provided in the past by the existence of only a few great providers of computing products was gone, making acquisition and setting of strategic technology directions now far more complicated. In short, we possibly are left with the need to redefine the major components of what was once called the computer, data processing, or information processing industry all within the context of growing demand for such technologies. The one historical certainty in this scenario is that IBM will continue to be a very large ship in an expanding harbor.

The harbor of information processing is also changing in shape. Already mentioned is the creation of new alliances inside and outside the industry for the delivery of information in ways not done before, largely driven by technical capabilities and government deregulations. Telephone companies in the United States were not allowed to distribute information over its lines until after 1993. Electrical utility companies, which were laying thousands of miles of fiberglass cables, had as a consequence the capability of delivering billions of bytes of data cost effectively to millions of homes, making these companies attractive to movie makers, cable companies, and telecommunications firms. The regional bell companies began forming alliances with movie makers, television broadcasters, and utilities. Movie moguls and cable companies began partnering. By the end of 1994, we began to see some very large clusters of capabilities under single corporate umbrellas that could deliver information electronically to millions of people through existing infrastructures (utilities, phone, or cable) with product produced by movie makers or television stations. ABC, CBS, NBC, Turner, Disney, TCI, Ameritch, AT&T, IBM, and so on were names we read about in the newspapers in new ways. Then came the U.S. Telecommunications Act of 1996, already discussed above. Was a new information processing industry being born?

It would seem that the world discovered Internet in the 1990s. Beginning in the 1940s, the U.S. government had supported the expansion of a data telecommunications network designed to facilitate research and communications vital to the nation's defense. Access to the network grew through universities and then around the world. By the early 1990s, the information processing industry and the public at large in North America, East Asia, and Europe began to realize that here was an "information highway" on which anyone with a PC, modem, and an "access ramp" could travel. This unregulated, almost chaotic infrastructure grew faster than more traditional forms of communications. For example, in the early to mid-1990s, the number of new cellular phone users in the United States increased monthly by about 125,000—an impressive number and an example of how useful and inexpensive technology increases demand—but the number of new Internet users far exceeded that figure. By the end of 1995, there were over 35 million users of the Internet around the world. Forecasts of users suggested that this number would continue rising rapidly all through the 1990s. All the key access providers for online systems available on PCs were already offering Internet access and search capabilities by 1994, and in 1995 were touting these as additional reasons to buy microcomputers and a variety of software products. Cautious forecasters could even see a third of the American public on Internet by the early years of the twenty-first century. One major new source of users consisted of university students who rapidly were moving onto the "net" in the mid-1990s as their campuses rushed to increased access to E-mail and other distance-learning tools as a means of improving productivity.

A quick example of the generational shift illustrates what is happening. The University of Wisconsin at Madison had embraced the use of computer technology earlier than many other institutions of higher learning in the late 1980s and early 1990s. In the school year 1994–1995, a survey of the student body suggested that over 80 percent had used the campus E-mail system. In the fall of 1995, 55 percent of the student body owned their own personal computers, up from 38 percent the previous school year. Everyone had access to computing. A hardware survey at the time indicated that there was one personal computer on campus for every 2 individuals (students, faculty, administration).[62]

CONCLUSION

The information processing industry, born in the nineteenth century, grew to importance in the post-World War II period, ending the century as a major segment of the world's economy. This industry was driven by innovations in technology that occurred over the course of a century plus that were dramatic to say the least. Yet this industry is part of a mosaic of human interest in tools that facilitate the use of information, from cave drawings to the use of language, papyrus, paper, books, television, and telephone. Computers can simply be seen as an extension of humankind's use of information-handling tools. But on a more complicated plane, the influence of computers holds the potential to be far more profound than, say, the book, maybe even as important at the creation of language because computers augment and have the potential of performing thinking functions.

Given this enormous importance to which scholars and users, vendors, and inventors have all attributed to the computer, the case for historical analysis is enormous. But the great surprise is the speed with which this technology became important and of our realization of how important it was to society. As historians we are scrambling to define this industry. We can barely describe its features from the 1950s to the present. We barely understand its roots prior to the 1950s and can hardly explain its consequences to any group or society. One could argue that this situation is appalling. More realistically, this situation represents perhaps the single largest research opportunity for the next several generations of historians worldwide. To come even close to identifying other research opportunities of this order of magnitude you have to go to far narrower topics like the history of the old Soviet Union now that Russian archives are opening up along with those in many East European nations, and the history of China since the mid-nineteenth century and then only grudgingly, since many archives remain closed. Where are the historic opportunities of this order of magnitude?

As we finally enter a period in which we can correctly say it is an age of information, we need to understand more than ever before what computers do for a society. How have they affected us so far? What has been the evolution of that technology and what influence have we, the users, had on its evolution? Are there some lessons we can learn that can influence national policies and economic realities in the twenty-first century? George Santayana's often quoted axiom that those who do not understand history are doomed to repeat it is only partially borne out by our experience with computers. I think his idea is more relevant if we think of computers as teaching us about other technologies, such as genetic engineering, biological-based technologies and products, or space travel. In the final analysis, the computer, and information processing in general, may be the first of a new wave of sophisticated enhancements to human activity beyond the wildest imagination of a science fiction writer.

Looking at computers and information processing through the eyes of an industry perspective is a very practical approach to the study of the subject, because it is through industry structures that new technologies and their subsequent innovations are channeled in a way that delivers value and consequences to a society. No technology is important until it is important. TV was not important when invented in the 1920s; it was profoundly important beginning in the 1950s and life today is unimaginable without it. Industries are the economic organization of invention, product development and manufacture, delivery and implementation, and the harvest of benefits and problems. Industries bring together those who invent/make products with users of these. It is the facilitative structures in society that make it possible for a TV to be invented and then made ubiquitous and hence important. That is why a good first step in the study of any technology is to document and understand the industry that facilitates its arrival.

It turns out that in reality historians like to study the technology first and its industry second. The first is easier to research, so the second waits. We are at a point, however, where historians know how to study industries and indeed have done a substantial amount on information processing, particularly for the 1950s and 1960s; they simply have to broaden their studies and bring them closer to the present. The good news is that there is a great amount of available research materials and many people interested in what the historians have to say. Historians, are these Giant Brains? Are they taking over? Tell us what we need to know.

NOTES

1. For the precomputer period in the United States, I addressed the issue of industry definition in *Before the Computer* (Princeton, N.J.: Princeton University Press, 1993) and for the first decade in the commercial availability of the computer in *The Computer in the United States* (Armonk, N.Y.: M. E. Sharpe, 1993); Martin Campbell-Kelly did the same for the British environment in *ICL: A Business and Technical History* (Oxford: Oxford University Press, 1989).

2. Michael E. Porter, *Competitive Strategy: Techniques for Analyzing Industries and Competitors* (New York: Free Press, 1980).

3. His two other most influential books are *Competitive Advantage: Creating and Sustaining Superior Performance* (New York: Free Press, 1985) and *The Competitive Advantage of Nations* (New York: Free Press, 1990).

4. My perspective has been profoundly influenced by the research of Henri-Jean Martin, *The History and Power of Writing* (Chicago: University of Chicago Press, 1995), and his earlier book with Lucien Febvre, *The Coming of the Book: The Impact of Printing 1450–1800* (London: NLB, 1976). Perhaps the most significant study of the effects of printing and books was written by Elizabeth L. Eisenstein, *The Printing Press as an Agent of Change*, 2 vols. (Cambridge: Cambridge University Press, 1979).

5. Even the humble pencil is important. There is a wonderful history of this writing instrument, replete with analysis of its effects on information handling and the societies in which it was used, Henry Petroski, *The Pencil: A History of Design and Circumstance* (New York: Knopf, 1992).

6. Perhaps nobody did as much to call to our attention the extent to which modern work is information handling than the late Fritz Machlup, who, in a series of books, cataloged in detail information-handling actions across all sectors of the economy, beginning with *The Production and Distribution of Knowledge in the United States* (Princeton, N.J.: Princeton University Press, 1962), and continuing into the 1980s, culminating in his *Knowledge: Its Creation, Distribution, and Economic Significance*, vol. 3: *The Economics of Information and Human Capital* (Princeton, N.J.: Princeton University Press, 1984). Vol. 1 was *Knowledge and Knowledge Production* (1981) and Vol. 2 *The Branches of Learning* (1982).

7. For this latest thinking see the wonderfully readable and informed book by Stan Davis and Jim Botkin, *The Monster Under the Bed: How Business is Mastering the Opportunity of Knowledge for Profit* (New York: Simon and Schuster, 1994).

8. James R. Beniger, *The Control Revolution: Technological and Economic Origins of the Information Society* (Cambridge, Mass.: Harvard University Press, 1986): 426–436.

9. James Moran, *Printing Presses: History and Development from the 15th Century to Modern Times* (Berkeley: University of California Press, 1973): 49–218.

10. The literature on the history of typewriters is extensive; a convenient source is W. A. Beeching, *Century of the Typewriter* (New York: St. Martin's Press, 1974).

11. The creation of the office appliance industry in the years prior to World War II is the heart of what I described in *Before the Computer*.

12. Paul E. Ceruzzi, *Reckoners: The Prehistory of the Digital Computer, from Relays to the Stored Program Concept, 1935–1945* (Westport, Conn.: Greenwood Press, 1983): 131–152; Cortada, *The Computer in the United States*, 12–63.

13. Gary W. Loveman, "An Assessment of the Productivity Impact of Information Technologies," in Thomas J. Allen and Michael S. Scott Morton (eds.), *Information Technology and the Corporation of the 1990s: Research Studies* (New York: Oxford University Press, 1994): 84–110.

14. My version of Hollerith's story is derived from his key biographer, Geoffrey D. Austrian, *Herman Hollerith: Forgotten Giant of Information Processing* (New York: Columbia University Press, 1982). For a good introduction to the same story, see Emerson W. Pugh, *Building IBM: Shaping an Industry and Its Technology* (Cambridge, Mass.: MIT Press, 1995): 1–18, and on the origins of IBM, 19–28.

15. Ibid., 323–325; Robert Sobel, *IBM: Colossus in Transition* (New York: Times Books, 1981): 75.

16. Cortada, *Before the Computer*, 89–170.

17. My own research on World War II suggested that bread-and-butter applications remained the heart and soul of this industry, Cortada, *Before the Computer*, 189–221.

18. Kenneth Flamm, *Creating the Computer: Government, Industry, and High Technology* (Washington, D.C.: Brookings Institution, 1988): 29–79. Flamm's account of government support in the 1940s and 1950s remains the best analysis, see Flamm, *Targeting the Computer: Government Support and International Competition* (Washington, D.C.: Smithsonian Institution, 1987): 42–92.

19. Franklin M. Fisher, James W. McKie, and Richard B. Mancke, *IBM and the U.S. Data Processing Industry: An Economic History* (New York: Praeger, 1983): 3–100.

20. U.S. Department of Commerce, *World Trade in Adding Machines, Calculators, Cash Registers* (Washington, D.C.: U.S. Government Printing Office, 1960): 8. For a survey of business volumes in this postwar period, see Cortada, *Before the Computer*, 222–263.

21. Thomas Watson, Jr., was at the heart of IBM's transformation into a computer company, and in his memoirs he provides a fascinating account of that process, see *Father, Son & Co.: My Life at IBM and Beyond* (New York: Bantam, 1990): 194–197, 215–222, 241–283.

22. Alfred D. Chandler, *The Visible Hand: The Managerial Revolution in American Business* (Cambridge, Mass.: Harvard University Press, 1977): 1–14.

23. See, for example, Tom Forester, *High-Tech Society* (Cambridge, Mass.: MIT Press, 1987) and John Naisbitt, *Megatrends: Ten New Directions Transforming Our Lives* (New York: Warner Books, 1982).

24. The literature on industry numbers is vast. For some idea of this documentation, see Thomas K. Landauer, *The Trouble with Computers: Usefulness, Usability, and Productivity* (Cambridge, Mass.: MIT Press, 1995): 9–46.

25. Montgomery Phister, Jr., "Computer Industry," in Anthony Ralston and Edwin

D. Reilly, Jr. (eds.), *Encyclopedia of Computer Science and Engineering* (New York: Van Nostrand Reinhold, 1983): 332–350.

26. The literature on this industry is extensive, see Cortada, *Second Bibliographic Guide*, 158–190.

27. These kind of data are most conveniently found in Bruce Gilchrist and Richard E. Weber (eds.), *The State of the Computer Industry in the United States* (Montvale, N.J.: AFIPS, 1973) and in U.S. Department of Commerce, International Trade Administration, *The Computer Industry* (Washington, D.C.: U.S. Government Printing Office, 1983).

28. An early study on the business of PC software was by Robert T. Fertig, *The Software Revolution: Trends, Players, Market Dynamics in Personal Computer Software* (New York: North-Holland, 1985).

29. Fisher, *IBM and the U.S. Data Processing Industry*, 176–177.

30. The subject of programmer availability and economics is well reviewed by Edward Yourdon, *Decline and Fall of the American Programmer* (Englewood Cliffs, N.J.: Yourdon Press/Prentice-Hall, 1992).

31. Ibid., 279–312 for the best account available on Indian programmers.

32. Norman Weizer et al., *The Arthur D. Little Forecast on Information Technology and Productivity* (New York: John Wiley & Sons, 1991), provides a contemporary and informed introduction to hardware trends. These kinds of books were published in each decade; this one happens to be one of the most useful.

33. The gold mine of information of this sort is Montgomery Phister, Jr., *Data Processing Technology and Economics* (Santa Monica, Calif.: The Santa Monica Publishing Co., 1979).

34. But to learn how to approach the subject a good place to start is with Peter Temin and Louis Galambos, *The Fall of the Bell System* (Cambridge: Cambridge University Press, 1987), and for some easier reading, Steve Coll, *The Breakup of AT&T* (New York: Atheneum, 1986).

35. Bashe, *IBM's Early Computers*, 165–172.

36. Cortada, *The Computer in the United States*, 102–124.

37. The exciting memoir of the period is by Emerson W. Pugh, *Memories that Shaped an Industry: Decisions Leading to IBM System/360* (Cambridge, Mass.: MIT Press, 1984).

38. This account is drawn from the good, but now slightly dated, Fisher, *IBM and the U.S. Data Processing Industry*, 3–100.

39. Ibid., 101–364.

40. For a recent account of the product and its effects, see Pugh, *Building IBM*, 263–277.

41. Historians have yet to study this segment, and very little good analysis of this sector is available, but see Robert P. Gandossy, *Bad Business: The OPM Scandal and the Seduction of the Establishment* (New York: Basic Books, 1985).

42. Fisher, *IBM and the U.S. Data Processing Industry*, 316–321.

43. Phister, *Data Processing Technology and Economics*, passim.

44. The U.S. government constantly surveyed for this kind of data, see Cortada, *A Bibliographic Guide*, 517–535.

45. For this sense of the time see John Diebold (ed.), *The World of the Computer* (New York: Random House, 1973).

46. For a brief discussion of these records, see Michael Nash, ''The Hagley Museum

and Library,'' in James W. Cortada (ed.), *Archives of Data-Processing History: A Guide to Major U.S. Collections* (Westport, Conn.: Greenwood Press, 1990): 117–118.

47. Fisher, *IBM and the U.S. Data Processing Industry*, 365–449 is the primary source for the previous several paragraphs.

48. For an excellent look inside the Japanese computer industry, see Marie Anchordoguy, *Computers Inc.: Japan's Challenge to IBM* (Cambridge, Mass.: Council on East Asian Studies, Harvard University, 1989) and Robert Sobel, *IBM vs. Japan: The Struggle for the Future* (New York: Stein and Day, 1986).

49. IBM had a well-publicized full employment practice that dated from the earliest days of the company. The last downsizing of any consequence occurred at the heart of the Great Depression in the 1930s but even that one was very selective. An equally small one occurred just after World War I as the economy of the United States readjusted from a wartime to a peacetime footing. For an excellent description of IBM's personnel practices, see D. Quinn Mills, *The IBM Lesson: The Profitable Art of Full Employment* (New York: Times Books, 1988). Ironically, this book was published on the eve of IBM's extensive downsizing during which the company abandoned full employment, a practice it did not restore after restructuring.

50. ''The Computer Slump Why Now? How Long?'' *Business Week* (June 24, 1985): 74–80; ''Computers: When Will the Slump End?'' *Business Week* (April 21, 1986): 58–61. The 1985 article reported results of a survey of why people were not buying computers: 40 percent due to cutbacks in capital budgets, 37 percent waiting for a new generation of less expensive equipment, 31 percent having more than enough hardware.

51. The effects of computers had long been studied much the same way cultural anthropologists studied primitive tribes. In the 1980s that process was taken to a new level of sophistication by Shoshana Zuboff, *In the Age of the Smart Machine: The Future of Work and Power* (New York: Basic Books, 1988).

52. For price/performance of hardware, see James W. Cortada, *Historical Dictionary of Data Processing: Technology* (Westport, Conn.: Greenwood Press, 1987): 110–117.

53. ''Deconstructing the Computer Industry,'' *Business Week* (November 23, 1992): 90–100.

54. For a sampling of this bibliography, see Cortada, *Second Bibliographic Guide*, passim.

55. The issues concerning productivity are well summarized in Landauer, *The Trouble with Computers: Usefulness, Usability, and Productivity.*

56. Paul A. Strassmann, *Information Payoff: The Transformation of Work in the Electronic Age* (New York: Free Press, 1985): 97.

57. Paul A. Strassmann, *The Business Value of Computers: An Executive's Guide* (New Canaan, Conn.: The Information Economics Press, 1990): xvii.

58. Kevin Maney, ''Digital Age: PCs Power '90s Renaissance,'' *USA Today* (July 27, 1995), 1B–2B.

59. To get a sense of what was changing, see Charles H. Ferguson and Charles R. Morris, *Computer Wars: How the West Can Win in a Post-IBM World* (New York: Times Book, 1993) and the earlier extremely well-informed volume by Regis McKenna, *Who's Afraid of Big Blue? How Companies Are Challenging IBM—And Winning* (Reading, Mass.: Addison-Wesley, 1989).

60. For a sampling see articles in Thomas J. Allen and Michael S. Scott Morton (eds.), *Information Technology and the Corporation of the 1990s: Research Studies* (New York: Oxford University Press, 1994); Thomas H. Davenport, *Process Innovation: Reengi-*

neering Work Through Information Technology (Boston: Harvard Business School Press, 1993); James W. Cortada, *TQM for Information Systems Management: Quality Practices for Continuous Improvement* (New York: McGraw-Hill, 1995).

61. For trends, see Weizer, *The Arthur D. Little Forecast*, and John C. Dvorak, *Dvorak Predicts* (Berkeley: Osborne McGraw-Hill, 1994).

62. Phil McDade, "Computer Force Energizes Campus," *Wisconsin State Journal* (September 3, 1995): 1A, 10A.

3

Patterns in Office Equipment Technology and Business Practices

The development of office machines, such as typewriters, adding and calculating devices, bookkeeping equipment, punch card devices like tabulators and key-punches, cash registers, even coin changers, and finally the computer in all its variants from large mainframes to the humble palm top, followed some common patterns over the past century. These patterns involve (1) how t chnology was channeled into marketable forms you and I know as products and (2) the business practices and strategies implemented to make sure customers had the opportunity to acquire and use these products. While many devices were invented outside the context of any industry (for example, the first typewriter, the first microcomputer), ultimately they became historically important once a company manufactured and sold them. There were many people who invented machines who never sold any, or at best a few. Charles Babbage worked on his engines for decades during the 1800s but none of them became operational, let alone products. On the other hand, there were individuals in the United States who were trying to solve business problems using machines of their creation. That is how, for example, companies like (NCR), Burroughs, and the ancestors of (IBM) came into existence. Technology unapplied did not make an inventor rich, and many wanted to make money of their creations. So the pull of economic opportunity, and later of market demand, ensured that almost from the beginning technological creativity and business issues would be intertwined.

The examples are everywhere. J. Prespert Eckert and John Mauchly had an argument over patent rights with the University of Pennsylvania where they built the ENIAC. They left, formed their own company, sold a few machines and then their firm to Remington Rand, which then, with their help and leadership, built and introduced the UNIVAC I—the first widely available digital computer. That was in the early 1950s. Barely two decades later, college students were assembling small, portable machines that in time we came to know as micro-computers. One of these individuals, working primarily on operating systems for such devices, was Bill Gates, founder of Microsoft. In the mid-1990s, well over 80 percent of all IBM and IBM-compatible microcomputers around the world used his Windows products, and his personal worth hovered around $10 billion. Pick another decade, any decade since the end of the American Civil War, and you see examples of people who built machines and then found a way to get them to market. The modern typewriter was invented by a printer in Milwaukee at the end of the 1860s and within several years was being sold by Remington. In the 1880s the inventor of the modern cash register was hawking products through the National Cash Register Company, with Burroughs right behind him with adding machines in the 1890s. Herman Hollerith designed his machines and set up his Tabulating Machine Company to market services and supplies based on his machines. His company would become the centerpiece of IBM. Both NCR and IBM scoured the countryside for technicians who were inventing machines, making them employees of NCR and C-T-R (later IBM) from the earliest days of their corporate history. Cryptographers in the 1920s and 1930s developed and sold code machines to military agencies all over the world.

New startups after World War II in what would become the computer business continued the process: Engineering Research Associates (ERA) and CDC are obvious examples. Pick any of the thousands of small software and component companies of the 1960s, 1970s, 1980s, and 1990s and you understand what was happening along Route 128 outside Boston and what we have all come to know as Silicon Valley in California. The phenomenon is so well recognized today that no self-respecting state economic planning commission would leave out the opportunity to encourage some sort of high-tech corridor where hackers and tinkerers could invent, find venture capital, and bring their products to market. By the 1980s, such mainstream publications as *Time* would even discuss trends in venture capital investments in computing product opportunities, bewailing the momentary lack of creativity in product development.[1] It was not uncommon in that decade to see professional venture capitalists invest annually between $700 million and $1.2 billion in such projects, and even then only account for between 23 and 42 percent of total investments in such ventures![2]

VALUE OF UNDERSTANDING HISTORICAL PATTERNS

So what? If we could understand the process better—and we do not really appreciate long-term patterns of behavior—investors could identify opportuni-ties earlier, and startup businesses would learn sooner some best practices, avoiding some of the common sins committed by most young companies. We could hope, from the point of view of the historian, for a deeper understanding of a company's corporate culture and, for that matter, an industry's historic culture. We are quick to characterize an industry, but very slow to understand its historical characteristics. Some of those in time become an inhibitor to change and progress, but in other cases were critical to the industry's success. Taking an historical perspective, therefore, is a useful method for reaching a clearer understanding of how companies and industries work, and how best to find ways to change them. Business leaders are very weak in the application of historical perspectives; business historians forget that there are good reasons a great deal happens. Both could learn from each other.

Using history as a tool for improving the management of businesses is slowly coming into its own. Where it is applied, business managers want to understand *patterns of behavior*, not simply how an individual historic event occurred, no matter how interesting. Thus, for example, there is extraordinary value in having senior executives of the largest companies in the information processing industry understand the historic role played by the Antitrust Division of the U.S. Department of Justice which caused the breakup of AT&T and the near breakup of IBM, and which today still views the industry's practices with suspicion as witnessed by its sparring with Microsoft in 1994 and 1995.

There is extraordinary value in manufacturing executives learning how IBM could package products such that it moved from the industry practice of making one-at-a-time computers in the 1940s and early 1950s to mass production by the middle of the decade, giving it runaway capacity to lower costs, build products, and outsell many rivals.[3] There is extraordinary value to historians, economists, and business leaders in understanding technology transfer; it occurred in every decade. Don't you find it just a little curious that the keyboard of a 1990s microcomputer looks very similar to a Remington Typewriter Model 1 keyboard of the 1870s and 1880s? Or that the calculating pad on a Burroughs machine of the 1920s and 1930s looked very similar to that on an NCR cash register of the 1890s or to Texas Instruments calculator of the 1980s? It is no accident, it is technology transfer at work. While a great deal of research has been done by engineers and economists on technology transfer, we should understand that it is not a new phenomenon. Our challenge is to link the knowledge we have of how this occurs in modern times with more long-standing patterns of behavior that date back at least to the 1840s.

While throughout this book I will keep asking for more research to be done on specific historical issues, we must at some point elevate our findings to "rules of the road" or become marginalized by business managers who are becoming more aware of the value of history. Already, we see history being applied, to the horror of some historians who believe history should not be applied. Yet if there is a lesson from the computer industry, it is that all lessons are applied, particularly if there is a dollar to be made at it. Nobody can accuse the inventors of this industry of not being entrepreneurial.

History began in business as an ego trip, to celebrate anniversaries of foundings, and birthdays of Chief Executive Officers (CEOs) and products.[4] Corporate lawyers told executives to create archives to support defense attorneys in the myriad of lawsuits that have always plagued this industry. This industry was very good about that. NCR's is still housed within the legal department. IBM's is more widely used by company lawyers than by anybody else. Archives are also destroyed when they could embarrass a company; enter in the concept of communications policies and strategies following World War II. Some manufacturing and product development operations relied quietly on historical perspective to guide their work. Two obvious candidates for this approach were IBM's Watson Laboratory and AT&T's Bell Laboratories.[5]

The information processing industry has only just begun to apply history. IBM, AT&T, and NCR have supported or published histories. A few other, younger companies have done the same. Another group, including companies such as Apple and Microsoft, has allowed writers and journalists access to papers or to interview executives. But little else has been done. On the other hand, if you look outside this industry, there appears to have been a far more active exploitation of history—for example, in U.S. government decision making.[6] For-profit organizations have also studied their past, preserved records, used anniversaries to reinforce corporate cultures and improve employee morale, displayed products in high-customer-traffic locations such as education centers, and conducted research for lawyers preparing defenses in lawsuits.[7] A lawsuit story: The Remington typewriter people bought a copy of every competitor's machine they could find beginning in the 1880s and continuing to World War II so that their lawyers could demonstrate that other companies were poaching on their patents—they had most of the basic technology patents in the industry in the beginning. In the process, their engineers would occasionally "borrow" a good idea from another machine and apply it to subsequent models. What an application of history and technology transfer!

Some industries are more inclined to exploit history than others.[8] Information processing thinks of itself as a young industry even though it often exhibits the habits of a mature one. Industries that pay more attention to history, and from whom the information processing community could learn, include financial services, insurance, manufacturing, energy and utilities, consumer goods, and non-profit organizations. Many are household names: Marriott Corporation, Campbell Soup, General Mills, Sara Lee, Shell Oil, Texaco, The *Washington Post*, Mellon Bank, CIGNA, and Boeing.

Executives in the information processing industry are closet historians anyway. Leaving aside those who have written history or memoirs (e.g., Emerson Pugh and even Thomas J. Watson, Jr.), anybody who looks at trends (even economic and financial) is practicing history. Barbara Tuchman pointed this out about executives in general:

Policy is formed by preconceptions and by long implanted bias. When information is relayed to policy makers, they respond in terms of what is already inside their heads and consequently make policy less to fit the facts than to fit the baggage that has accumulated since childhood.[9]

The growing body of business literature on how decisions are made and how corporate cultures operate simply confirms Tuchman's blunt statement of the obvious.[10]

OFFICE MACHINES AND COMPUTERS: PATTERNS OF THE INVENTION PROCESS

But more to our case in point—the data processing world—there are some universal questions for students of computing's history to worry about. To what extent does a tool such as the computer build on the experience of earlier machines used for similar tasks? What was the process by which humans began gathering and controlling data outside the brain, and how did that create the kind of chain reaction which, thousands of years later, makes it possible for me to write this book on a 486-chip-based personal computer with enough memory to hold a small library of books or the data from a large pile of Syrian or Roman tablets? Data entry has a rich history; I still marvel over the humble pencil; now picture image scanning and voice recognition as data entry!

Historians of technology generally agree that tools are not developed in the abstract, especially sophisticated implements, which means just about everything you and I use today. Indeed, if there is any consensus, it is that tools evolve in variety (usually called novel ways) and purpose one upon the other.[11] Anybody who has walked through the Computer Museum in Boston and has seen the many different types of data-entry devices and terminals understands. A quick look through an IBM product catalog of the 1930s would astonish anyone with the variety of punch card equipment, tabulators, and peripheral equipment. A Burroughs catalog from the same period displays an even larger range of products for billing, adding, and calculating. Yet one must, for example, enjoy the benefits of black and white television before wanting TV manufacturers to invent color, as in the movies, or to provide stereo sound. It also takes the vendor a level of understanding before he or she can come to the same conclusion. In fact, the most innovative products have grown out of an appreciation of the possible by vendors, not customers. The list of examples is noble: the light bulb, movies, television, radio, instant photography, xeroxing, personal computers, and camcorders. With business machines, the power of a word processor becomes more evident if the user is already familiar with the benefits and limitations of a typewriter. It is a lesson drawn from even low-tech realities. Could you enjoy, really enjoy, a meal at a five-star French restaurant if you knew little or nothing about French food? Or would such an experience just be the cat's meow if you had lived in France, gone to many fine two- and three-star restaurants, and had a solid working knowledge of French wine, regions, and history? Now who enjoys the French five-star restaurant the most? Now how much would you enjoy a personal computer that did not have an occasional software bug in its footnote functions, or the ability to move a mouse without the arrow disappearing momentarily?

In an earlier book I argued that long before the advent of the computer, technologies were manipulating data and an industry existed to supply appropriate machines for this task.[12] The office appliance industry supplied such devices as typewriters, adding and calculating machines, cash registers, and punch card equipment. The suppliers of such office equipment saw the computer ultimately as an extension of these earlier devices and adopted it, taking it away from laboratories, universities, specialized computer vendors, and electronics firms and successfully bringing it to market. In other words, they were right: the largest group of customers for these new machines were those who had used their products before. Like the individual who really appreciates good French food, the right customers were willing to drive to our mythical five-star restaurant, even plunking down way too much for a good meal. The data presented in Chapter 2 suggest what an outrageously successful decision it was for the office industry to adopt the computer as its own. Because of that link with the past, comparing patterns of evolution and adoption between the computer and earlier office machines suggests tangible and direct patterns more universal than those evident with one machine (e.g., the computer), while acknowledging that more than technological considerations were at work (e.g., vendors and public perceptions). This is an "ethno-office" view, one that discounts the effects of scientific and engineering sectors of the new business on purpose, even though these were still very important, particularly in the very early 1950s and possibly the late 1940s.

The interaction among engineers, tinkerers, and scientists has increasingly been studied in recent years, and common patterns of discovery and invention have been uncovered.[13] As much tied to the way these people think and work, however, are some institutional observations from the perspective of the office appliance industry. These observations confirm and complement this growing body of knowledge about the act of invention, creation, and improvement.

Developers of machines ranging from the typewriter to the computer evolved increasingly from single individuals to teams of engineers, from work done literally on a kitchen table (the macaroni box that became a simple calculator)[14] to projects carried out in world-class laboratories (e.g., MIT, AT&T, and IBM). The more complex or more expensive the equipment became, the less one saw a lone inventor at work. Hollerith had a small team working with him on product development by the end of the 1890s; George R. Stibitz at Bell Labs quickly went from working on his kitchen table to a team that eventually built five generations of specialized computers in the 1940s and 1950s. But always there were the exceptions: Thomas Edison with his laboratory in the nineteenth century, but even then only in the beginning. His laboratory eventually became a veritable invention factory. Stibitz was an exception to the rule, but only in 1939–1940. Historians of the microcomputer talk about college students working in dorms and in garages inventing what would become the Apple, DOS operating system, and a host of application software, including word processors and spreadsheets. We won't even get into the issue of computer-based games: that constitutes a virtual industry composed of individuals making up what must eventually be recognized as the ultimate in a high-tech cottage industry.[15] So the exceptions existed from the 1870s to the 1990s but the pattern generally held; as office appliance technology became more complex, larger numbers of people had to be involved in its development. Thus we find at all the major office equipment companies a staff of engineers and inventors who were responsible for product development. The demand for new devices was constantly high. There are no exceptions to this rule; all such companies put together teams from almost the first decade of a company's life to create new machines.

The establishment of teams is such an obvious feature that as a subject it is worth more historical attention. There developed in the 1980s and 1990s a vast body of literature about the value of teams, largely an outgrowth of quality management practices, which need not detain us here.[16] However, the long and the short of the research on teams, which I might add began decades ago, is that teams of people tend to make more correct decisions than individuals and that teams of people are more effective in designing, building, and delivering products and services. It is a central tenant of management practices in most industries in the 1990s.[17] Team-based research and development (R&D) and product development are the norm for many reasons, including the fact that as products become more complex, they require more skills and manpower than one can house in a single person. Think of all the skills required to design and manufacture a car or a personal computer and you understand the magnitude of the problems involved. Then we must consider everything we are learning from students of human behavior. They tell us that group activity can spur individuals on to greater levels of confidence, boldness, and results. But we lack good historical analysis of how this process worked in the office appliance industry or in the age of computers. To be sure, Emerson Pugh and some of his colleagues (yes, team) have done yeoman work, using IBM as the example, in explaining how computers were developed and built in one company, but that is not enough. I believe IBM's practices were evident elsewhere since this company always paid attention to what everyone else was doing and did not hesitate to adopt and adapt from others. Archivists also work in teams, suggesting another case of what is effective. Robert Seidel at CBI and William Aspry at the IEEE are emerging as role models in the 1990s of how to work with staffs who demonstrate the behavior patterns of teams with clear missions, rather than as heads of functional departments. But let us drop back in time for examples of the process at work.

Christopher Lathan Sholes (1819–1890) was a printer with knowledge of how to construct movable type. Looking for a way to create printed-like text in Milwaukee, he tinkered with different devices, and blended various mechanical processes together until he was able to build the first wooden typewriter. O.K., so it needed a little work. But by the end of the 1860s he had reached the point where he had a working typewriter that had potential market attractiveness. He next sought a way to get the thing manufactured. In short, he negotiated a deal with Remington, which had the fine machining skills required to build type-writers. Over time new models were developed and built. William Burroughs (1855–1898) followed a similar path. He spent the 1880s and 1890s developing adding machines. Sensitized to the need for such a device, and not unfamiliar with some of the aspects of machine building, he designed and built various devices. Some worked, others didn't, and he lived many frustrating years before crafting a design that could be manufactured and sold. In fact, he died before the company selling his machine experienced its great period of initial growth.

Herman Hollerith (1860–1929) began his process in the 1880s, again address-ing a known need—the ability to analyze rapidly large bodies of census data—tinkering with various designs and devices. Since complexity will quickly influence whether one does the work alone or in teams, it is interesting to see what happened here. His machines were big and complicated, and therefore it is no surprise that he would move to a machine shop approach to the devel-opment of tabulators faster than Sholes or Burroughs had. Thus by the 1890s we see Hollerith in Washington, D.C., with a machine shop in which both development and manufacture occurred in the same room by the same people. The historical record of Sholes and Burroughs does not clearly indicate whether the same people worked in the same rooms. However, we do know that by the end of the century, engineers in the typewriter company facilities were designing machines with manufacturability considerations in mind. In all three cases, we see design departments in operation by World War I, all three attached to man-ufacturing facilities.

By World War I we also see equipment designers in the office appliance industry enhancing existing base designs. At C-T-R (later IBM, and an out-growth of Hollerith's tabulating machine company, the T in C-T-R) James A. Bryce (1880–1949) and Frederick L. Fuller (1861–1943) were full-time design engineers inventing and expanding the product line, then moving their creations to manufacturing, usually in the same building. Fuller had designed cash reg-isters for NCR using existing patents that he enhanced in the late 1800s and early 1900s, and doing essentially the same thing for tabulating equipment at C-T-R.[18] Bryce was responsible for almost all of the innovations in punch card equipment at IBM from the mid-1920s to the end of World War II. He moved beyond Fuller, from a small shop operation to a fully staffed development lab that included engineers, machinists, and administrative support functions. By World War II he was recognized as one of the most prolific patent holders in the United States, in the same league as Thomas Edison.

By the 1920s a shift occurred across the office appliance industry to more complex development work as major corporations began establishing facilities stocked with hundreds of engineers and scientists before World War II. In this pattern we see the office appliance industry performing R&D much as in other industries in the United States. Bell Labs opened its doors in 1925 as an amal-gam of craft shops and development departments from various divisions and departments in AT&T. That explains why AT&T could instantly have a sophisticated operation in Bell Labs and why it could build technical momentum almost from day one. At the same time Bell Labs came into being, smaller yet similar development labs were cropping up around the United States. Burroughs, NCR, and IBM began placing these labs on manufacturing campuses. Burroughs had theirs in Detroit, home and major manufacturing location, NCR in similar facilities in Dayton, Ohio, and IBM at Endicott, N.Y. In fact, the strategy of putting development labs in manufacturing locations is still widely deployed in most computer and manufacturing industries. Similar patterns have been evident in industries besides office appliances since the 1920s: GE, RCA, and DuPont are the obvious examples, all similar in that they relied on science and technology for new products, often deploying product development teams closely linked to manufacturing. A dialogue between manufacturing and development became crucial as one moved from a new design to the realities of cost-effective manufacturability. The office appliance industry was a model of that kind of effectiveness. By World War II, when the U.S. government needed delicate instrumentation to be invented, refined, or mass produced it turned to the office appliance industry, often finding that all the skills needed were on one site (Dayton, Detroit, Endicott, and so on).

Universities also began to invest in engineering capabilities housed in specialized laboratories in the 1920s and 1930s, although small one-, two-, or three-person operations had existed since the 1880s at some of the more mature universities. Up-and-coming young engineering schools, like MIT, moved quickly to this model by World War I. Links to technical communities in business were formed almost immediately. For example, the Astronomical Laboratory at Columbia University was strongly supported by IBM with funds and equipment in exchange for development work on tabulators and new scientific applications of such devices. MIT had established similar relations with the military and utility companies.[19] Hollerith had taught at MIT for a short while, too. The University of Pennsylvania at Philadelphia, the city that in the early twentieth century was the radio capital of the United States, had many engineers, some of whom worked on computers for the army and with the cooperation and support of IBM, NCR, and GE. This same university had close research ties to almost all the major electronics firms in the United States.[20] Similarly, land grant universities in the Midwest, such as the University of Wisconsin and Iowa State University, had similar relations. Also, by the 1940s one could see R&D work for computers at RCA linked to the Institute for Advanced Studies, while other projects were underway at Stanford. In the 1930s Iowa State College (later Iowa State University) did extraordinarily important research on the architecture and design of what eventually would become the modern digital computer.[21] Thus, the pattern of commercial laboratories and teams developed on the one hand, while on the other closer bonds grew between university facilities and the U.S. government after the turn of the century, with examples existing even in the 1880s and 1890s.[22]

Looking at the performance of individuals suggests another pattern evident over the past century. The earlier inventors and developers were best able to bring their products to market, probably because they had no choice. But on a more universal basis, no single inventor saw his product arrive successfully to market without extensive and successful marketing by him personally. The earlier ones (late 1800s) had the most difficult situation since they had no logical industry to plug into as would a computer components inventor or software author today. That may explain why the earlier ones had a more difficult task. If they were successful, however, it was because they demonstrated extraordinary marketing and organizational initiative. These earlier ones had to find manufacturing and capital wherever they could, and to develop methods of distribution, even creating whole channels from scratch. By the early decades of the century, the last requirement became easier to implement since existing office supply channels existed (e.g., existing vendors or retail outlets). They were better at developing equipment than at marketing it, however, just like their counterparts in the second half of the twentieth century. Like their counterparts, they soon turned distribution over to others more capable of selling their creations. This was true in every case early in the nineteenth century and almost every case in the late 1800s (Hollerith was an exception), and by World War I channels existed to accept a wide variety of products and get them into the market quickly.

By 1910–1914 the major lines of information-handling equipment—typewriters, cash registers, adding and calculating equipment, and punch card devices—were housed in companies that could develop, refine, manufacture, distribute, and service these machines. By then, with minor exceptions, engineers developing machines specialized—first, by concentrating on refining existing technologies, and second by focusing on specific subsets of machines. For example, by the end of the 1920s some engineers at IBM's Endicott (N.Y.) laboratory were experts on printing mechanisms, others on tabulators, and still others on cards and papermaking.[23] Similar patterns of specialization were evident at Burroughs, NCR, Felt & Tarrant, and, by 1910, at the key American typewriter manufacturing companies. In the absence of more definitive evidence, we must assume that the European vendors had a similar experience, just as they did in other industries that we are aware of.

The one modern exception to the patterns about personal behavior, and even then only for a short while, was the team of Eckert and Mauchly, who left the Moore School of Engineering at the University of Pennsylvania (home of ENIAC, the first functioning digital computer in the United States), started their own firm, built a number of machines, and finally sold their business to Remington Rand. They then completed work on the UNIVAC I for that company. Enhancements to that machine and development of the UNIVAC II in the 1950s came about in the same context as for many other computers—with teams and corporate structures.

The experience of the microcomputer generation of inventors was not too dissimilar. Since capital requirements were low for the invention phase of their work, there were no financial barriers to tinkering. Once configured, however, manufacturing (and its attendant appetite for capital) drove them into the arms of existing manufacturers or subcontractors to get product built and into distribution channels. No major vendor by definition became major without access to manufacturing facilities, some of which they only owned after becoming successful providers of products. Software's experience is a little different since the degree of capital requirements to produce software is not as extensive as with hardware. But even here, systematizing the production and distribution of software through company-owned or retail channels became critical for the success of a product over and above its reliability, function, or marketing.[24]

The manner in which invention, creation, or development of machines came about was thus remarkably uniform. In the initial development of machines— the first typewriter, cash register, or calculator, for example—the inventor had a good idea of what the machine should be used for, and therefore designed it to satisfy that application. Once these machines were built, however, other applications emerged from the minds of developers or users; in turn, these new ideas served as design points for enhancements or other changes in the equipment. The result was that the form and configuration of both office and computer equipment evolved over time as users and vendors saw needs for changes. No radically new technologies ever emerged overnight. Applications served as the map to new functions. Thus, for instance, punch card users insisted that computers also use cards,[25] and even when computer builders added magnetic tape storage, they kept punch card equipment as part of the system for more than 30 years.[26]

OFFICE MACHINES AND COMPUTERS: THE ROLE OF TECHNOLOGY

Other examples for each decade are everywhere. A few illustrate the process. Just after World War I accounting auditors made it very clear to C-T-R that its card printers would no longer be attractive to them unless they could print text on the cards that reflected what the holes said. So printing-punch functions were added. Lashing equipment together for data entry, processing, and output electronically done appeared in products from Burroughs, NCR, and IBM throughout the period from World War I to the Korean War. The extent was dramatic. It was not uncommon, for instance, in the inter-war years to see base products from these companies available in two, three, even ten models (variation of capacity, speed, and function). We saw the exact same thing with microcomputers in the 1980s and 1990s. Go to an I/T industry show like Comdex today and you get lost and bewildered by the array of computer-related products. At next year's show there will be as many new ones as you saw this year! When IBM announced its S/360 in 1964, it introduced a total of 150 products, including five different processors, and by 1970 had announced many dozens more devices, additional models of its computers, and many, many releases of all its

various operating systems, utilities, compilers, and application packages.[27] By
the early 1970s, the average IBM salesperson ran the risk of having to describe
over 3,000 products to customers! In short, the office appliance/information
processing community demonstrated the behavior pattern of innovation so
widely accepted today by historians of technology.

A second observable pattern was the inclination of engineers to use existing
components to build on previous applications. Many examples exist from the
typewriter to the computer. Sholes relied on the work of others dating back to
the early 1700s, to printers, and even to bicycle and sewing manufacturing and
engineering techniques. Both Burroughs, with his adding machine made in a
humble machine shop in the 1880s, and Stibitz, with miscellaneous components
taken from Bell Labs to work with on his kitchen table in the late 1930s, built
their initial devices in this fashion. The story of how early computers were
constructed is often a tale of lashing existing parts together, particularly in the
early phases. Even in relatively well-stocked laboratories, like Vannevar Bush's
at MIT, photographs of the devices of the 1920s and 1930s clearly demonstrate
a strategy of lashing together existing components.[28] Familiar components available long before the computer included vacuum tubes, telephone relays, electricity, and cathode ray tubes. Even the transistor was available for nearly one
decade before it was incorporated into computers; the same was true for integrated circuits. RISC technology, developed in the 1970s, finally was adopted
by high-function workstation manufacturers in the 1980s. Reduced instruction
set computers (RISC) made it possible to build a powerful processor out of very
high-speed, simple components, bringing tremendous power to desktop computers. In the 1970s, early "inventors" of microcomputers built them entirely
from existing electrical components. Their genius was in packaging these into
a useful new device for which a prior need already existed.[29]

We could just as easily draw examples from the nineteenth century. Key-
boards on adding machines, typewriters, and (to a certain extent) cash registers
looked the same. Indeed, the components and mechanics of physically pushing
keys down and causing imprints to be made on paper were essentially the same
across thousands of products for a half dozen decades. Electrical circuits, even
wiring, was fairly standardized. Components from bicycles and sewing machines
are perhaps the best known examples of component transfer from one device to
another.

As an aside, one could also build a case arguing that marketing and distribution strategies that worked for an earlier product were applied to subsequent
machines. For example, how typewriters were distributed and sold, and under
what terms and conditions, essentially detailed for vendors of adding, calculating, and other office machines how they would sell products. Thus, distribution
techniques used with typewriters in the 1870s and 1880s profoundly influenced
the hundreds of vendors of office machines who came into the market after the
arrival of the typewriter. Many of the same companies that sold one type of
machine sold another, using the exact same marketing strategies, same retail

outlets or direct sales forces, and very similar terms and conditions. By World War II, Burroughs, NCR, and IBM were all selling calculators, typewriters, and billing machines! To be sure, each had its specialized products, too (e.g., NCR its cash registers, IBM its tabulators), but the observation holds.

The key to rapid availability of new products often lay with the existence of components that could be put together—a fact often overlooked by both historians and business executives in this industry. Crucial in many cases was speed to market, which could be optimized only by using components that already existed, whose price, performance, and manufacturability were all known variables. This was especially the case as competition heated up (e.g., typewriters between about 1885 and 1910, adding machines from about 1900 to 1925, computers in the 1950s and 1960s, and microcomputers from 1985–88 to the present). Application was always rapid. For example, once available components were applied (by the late 1940s) to the computer, additional demand for new technologies was created, approaching urgency. This need encouraged the development of magnetic storage media, the transistor as a practical component, and a variety of integrated circuits. These developments were driven specifically by the invention of high-performance electronic parts designed for use in computers.[30]

What the experience with the computer suggests, however, is that as information-handling products became more complex, the rush to market with products built on existing components needed to be viewed at two levels. First, there is the macro perspective—"I need a new computer of x size and function"—which both customers and vendors spoke of as replacement products for earlier devices. Second, there is the micro perspective—"I the inventor need new components so that I can design and build x computer"—which manufacturers, engineers, and computer scientists spoke of. The speed and breadth of new introductions varied at each level, a process we do not yet understand. For example, base technologies seemed to evolve more slowly—e.g., vacuum tube to transistor, transistor to integrated circuit, integrated circuit to whatever will be next—yet computers based on them changed constantly. Tubes were around for a half century, transistors were used in computers for over a decade, integrated circuits for similar times (usually about one decade, today several years) per generation of integrated circuits. Yet IBM and all the other vendors introduced new computer models every year, and almost every year new models of key peripherals (e.g., printers and tape, and disk drives).

The base technologies of pre-computer information-handling equipment remained fairly constant for many decades (e.g., manual typewriters from the 1890s to their demise in the 1970s, electric typewriters from the 1930s to their end in the 1980s, and manual and electric cash registers from the 1800s to the 1980s, after which computer chips began to appear in these products). The same could be demonstrated for every class of machine in the office appliance industry. Yet, as I stated earlier in this chapter, all the key vendors introduced thousands of new products between the 1870s and the arrival of the computer.

Thinking in terms of a hierarchy, we could therefore envision market demand (customer and vendor defined) as changing the fastest, products transforming a little slower but still quickly (vendor engineers and manufacturing personnel dictating the realities here despite marketing's wishes), and base technologies the slowest of all (defined and determined by engineers and scientists, and the proclivities of the laws of nature, chaos, and luck). My three-phase model of transformation suggests that both the office appliance and computer industries were not as revolutionary in their technologies as many journalists, marketing experts, and industry pundits would suggest. The revolution, as I will demonstrate in Chapter 5 on applications, was more of an evolution.

The revolution—which one usually defines as radical and rapid change—was more in the acceptance and deployment of these tools. Even there we have to move into third generation computers (second half of the 1960s) and to the microcomputer (early to mid-1980s) before we have the right to use the word revolution. Why do we care? We care because as we look at either this industry or another "high-tech" industry (e.g., telecommunications, aviation, and space-related technologies.) we want to understand how change comes about, the interplay among technology, vendor activities, and customer applications, and the speed with which these things have happened or could be expected to in the future. The venture capitalist does not want to be the last person to invest in yesterday's technology (e.g., tape on the eve of disk drives in computers, phonograph records on the eve of tape or compact disks (CDs) in stereo systems). The customer does not want to buy a 386-chip-based personal computer when 486 is about to become the required standard for use with his or her favorite Lotus application. The vendor does not want to get stuck with a warehouse full of products that nobody will buy because it has been superseded (leapfrogged) by a competitor, much like IBM did in 1964 with its S/360 to RCA, GE, Burroughs, and so many others. The concern is greater today than it was in the age of office appliances because the cost of obsolescence or innovation is so much greater, and the speed with which innovation occurs appears to have increased somewhat despite my previous comments.

Another observation about the role of technology involves complexity. The more complicated a device became, the more frequently one saw special modifications either to existing components, to manufacturing, or to new parts and processes for manufacture. In other words, complexity in itself influenced the behavior of those who had to change and apply technology and existing components. We do not yet fully understand the effects of this process on the rate of change in office equipment, but it is there nonetheless. Factories that made typewriters and adding machines looked very different from those that manufactured computers. The latter often had craft rooms that developed uniquely shaped repair tools, screws, and bolts of unique sizes and shapes, while the adding machines of the 1800s, for example, used standard size screws and bolts. As a product line or technology matured, standardization of components increased, which in turn drove down costs and complexity and made change and variety easier. The process has remained relentless. Thus computers with unique bolts and nuts in the 1950s would wind up using standard nuts and bolts later. Is this a contradiction to the earlier comment about the use of off-the-shelf components? Not really, because while off-the-shelf components were the norm, unique items were often low tech and could be simply and easily developed in order to facilitate the creation of a new product using high-tech-based components. Today as we introduce new machines all the time— look under the covers of a computer, you will see Honeywell thermostats such as are used in aircraft and process equipment, the same kind of fiber optics as deployed by telephone companies, and the same nuts and bolts, panels, and metal sheeting, and carbon casing as used in thousands of products that are not computers.

Cross-pollination of technologies was a common feature in the progress from typewriter to computer. The keyboard first introduced on typewriters soon appeared on cash registers, adding machines, later tabulating equipment, and finally on the consoles on computers. Some computers not made by IBM in the 1950s and 1960s even used IBM Selectric typewriters as their consoles! A typewriter and an adding machine had many of the same components, albeit shaped differently, and manufacturing was essentially the same. The lessons learned from creating, machining, and manufacturing sewing machines were applied to typewriters and adding machines.[31] By 1900 some companies made both types of office equipment in the same plant. Ideas developed by electrical firms, telephone companies, and office appliance vendors were constantly copied and borrowed all through the twentieth century. Firms applied components differently, and new uses therefore emerged. By the 1950s a pattern had developed of formalizing the process through cross-licensing. Remington Rand and IBM cross-licensed their computer technologies in the 1950s, as had Powers and IBM in the 1930s and Remington Rand and some typewriter firms in the late 1800s.[32] A variation of this form of access to new capabilities was the licensing of technologies. AT&T may have invented the transistor, and even figured out how to manufacture it effectively by the early 1950s, but it was the computer vendor community that introduced this component into computers and electrical appliance companies that brought this technology over to radios. This was done by licensing out rights to manufacture and use of the transistor in specific products.

Cross-pollination also was applied as a competitive strategy, sometimes in direct violation of patent law, sometimes in notorious ways in the early decades. Vendors used ''retro-engineering,'' or ''reverse engineering''; that is, they acquired a competitor's product, took it apart to see how it was built, and then often offered the almost duplicate product with either a few enhancements or at a lower price, thereby taking advantage of the other's R&D investment. This was a notorious practice with cash registers in the 1890s; as early as the 1880s Remington Rand faced the same problem from dozens of typewriter firms.[33] Although this was not as severe a problem with the most sophisticated office equipment of the middle decades of the twentieth century, by the 1970s it appeared again with disk and tape drives, and in the 1980s with microcomputer "clones."[34] By the 1990s the problem had actually gotten worse, having spread to software that sold not as clones, but as exact duplicates of the original. The conflict over patent and copyright infringements concerning software, video, and CDs, for example, strained relations between the United States and China, since the late 1980s.[35]

This has always been a very emotional issue and, on occasion, has resulted in significant losses of business (e.g., with tape and disk drives for IBM in the 1970s and 1980s), and to a raft of lawsuits (e.g., NCR and Remington from the 1880s through the early 1920s). But a more basic question is to what extent does the complexity of machines build on experiences gained from older ones. Is there a direct line of evolution from typewriters to computers? Could the computer have developed if the adding machine had not been created first? These are important questions for historians of technology as well as for vendors interested in determing whether or not a market is ready for some new product. The issue is one of sophistication, much like the question, Can an individual appreciate the subtleties of a fine French meal without first learning a great deal about French food? Research on the history of technology strongly suggests that one must know about French food before being able to appreciate fully the quality offered by a five-star French restaurant.[36]

Historans of computing have not always done a good job in exploring the technological lineages of computers; we are still learning how to do this. Two examples illustrate blind alleys. In the 1970s and 1980s there was considerable debate about what role Charles Babbage played in the invention of the computer, and about who invented the digital computer. The Babbage issue involved the extent to which builders of computers in the 1930s knew about his work in Britain in the nineteenth century and borrowed from it. To the chagrin of many Babbage fans, most of the young engineers and mathematicians working on these machines barely knew who he was and never had access to his drawings. But it took a while to quell the issue and it has not gone away completely; the bibliography of articles and books that continue to link him somehow to the history of computers is a virtual sub-industry![37]

The second debate was more serious and involved the extent to which work done by John Atanasoff at Iowa State College in the late 1930s influenced the thinking of the design team working at the Moore School on the ENIAC in the 1940s. The fact that the ENIAC was the first operating digital computer, while Atanasoff's was simply a combination of concepts and some working parts, did nothing to stop the heated debate among historians.[38] The issue has not been extensively debated in the 1990s, probably because many of the protagonists and their defenders are dead or long in the tooth. Whether some of Atanasoff's ideas influenced development of the ENIAC or not, given what he actually designed and built makes the debate strictly an off-Broadway drama because there were many other, more important, even obvious influences at work that should have occupied the attention of historians. That they did not is less a criticism of Atanasoff, Mauchly and others, than evidence of the immaturity of the process by which historians study the lineage of a technology.

What is a more effective lineage to chase? For starters, those computer engineers of the 1930s and 1940s who have published their memoirs are fairly open about what influenced them. The most common technological influence was the radio; the majority loved them and built them as children, some were ham operators, and many were intimately familiar with their components. Second, a few studied electrical engineering while working on computational projects at such schools as MIT and the University of Wisconsin in the 1930s, and at Harvard University in the 1940s. So what went on at those institutions are good leads.[39] Third, many developers of computers in the late 1940s and throughout the 1950s served in various military units that depended on the use of state-of-the-art electronics components for weaponry, cryptoanalysis, and aviation. Those are all good leads for understanding the technical heritage of computers. The issues involved are not as glamorous as trying to annotate someone as the FIRST builder of the computer, or linking the modern machine back to a handsome if eccentric English gentleman. It makes for good reading but not necessarily good history.

While this indictment may appear harsh, the point to keep in mind is that when historical research is being done in a field that has so much to be unearthed, as is the case with computers and office equipment, the temptation to become sidetracked is enormous, as is the risk of running up some blind alley. It is part of the discovery process itself. Historians of computing need to understand the history of other technologies as much as, for example, historians of clocks and manufacturing devices should appreciate office equipment to understand applicable patterns of behavior.

For the modern manager involved in technology, an understanding of patterns of technology transfer, sources of component options, and so forth, can mean success or failure, so we need to understand how best to perform this kind of research. In short, the issue is too serious not to handle effectively.[40]

It is also a complicated one. The answer to my question about the French restaurant may seem easy enough: Yes you must know something about French food before going to a five-star restaurant. But the experience does not have to be the same for every guest at the metaphorical French restaurant. Does that mean we are back at the Atanasoff/Moore School problem of firsts? Not at all. However, historians of technology are coming to learn that those who go to our French restaurant must share a common body of knowledge and sense of expectations. For our guests that could mean some learned about French food during trips to France, another through a cooking school, a third at home from a French mother, and a fourth from books. But they all must know about French food! In the case of the office appliance it was necessary to have developed and used tabulating equipment for various applications to appreciate the potential commercial use of computers. Someone had to use computers with very small memories to recognize passionately the need for larger memories. Someone had to use tabulating equipment that did not print results on paper to require both IBM and Powers to develop printing tabulators that would conform to conventional accounting practices.[41] Someone had to use a typewriter designed to print words out of sight at the back of the machine to see the need for a typewriter that displayed what was typed on a sheet of paper in front of the user. Adding machines called for calculators, which, in turn, pointed to the need for huge increases in capacities, and, hence, to the electromechanical monsters built by Bush (1890–1974) and Howard Aiken (1900–1973).

So how do we come to understand the technical relationship of machines from one period to another? Essentially, there are three approaches. First, as just described, pursue backwards the source of application requirements or forward, chasing the use of machines from one decade or century to another to see where the string of applications leads. Second, ask the inventors. Those who write memoirs usually make statements about why that they invented their device. Furthermore, people who write biographies of these developers are sure to ask that question. Research on computing in the 1930s–50s has clearly demonstrated the connection between radios, mathematics, and the military. If you look at the extant literature to date on the developers of microcomputers and their software, you also find a wealth of information about applications and who influenced whom. In the case of the machine and software developers of the 1970s and 1980s (e.g., Steve Jobs, Mitch Kapor, Adam Osborne, Bill Gates), you see a group of people familiar with the rudiments of computing and the hardware components of computers of their day, and who, like their predecessors of the 1930s–50s, had the technical skills and interest to play with available components.[42] The third approach is to conduct classical archaeology. That is to say, pull the covers off machines and see what parts they have in them, then find out where those were made and by whom, and trace back their trip from factory to your computer.

The first approach—chasing applications—is a variation of the great French historian Fernand Braudel's strategy of understanding European history by chasing the money to see where the key events and motivations were from the Age of Philip II to the present.[43] In our more humble case, it is chasing benefits which come only from applications. The second approach—what the inventors knew and said—is the fine literature approach that says for most activities someone has taken the time to document and explain why they did it. The third approach—looking at components—is the most technical and, in some ways, the easiest of the three to begin with because it is the one which most appeals to historians of technology.

However, at the level of what parts to put into a machine, the lineage can quickly become less clear. It was common, for example, for engineers to reach outside their spheres of knowledge for components. For instance, just like many radio operators happened to get into the computer invention business in the 1930s, so, too, many of them did not fully understand all the available radio components. Yet they found their way to these, co-opting many into computers of the 1930s, 1940s, and 1950s. Typewriters of the 1870s were designed and manufactured much like sewing machines, whereas punch-card concepts owed greatly to early-nineteenth century looms. How do we identify those links and verify their influences? Now the problem is more like social, economic, and political history than the history of technology. The key to use of components in new devices was the ability of the developer to remain aware of their existence in other business or science applications. That is why looking at scientific meetings, the availability of technical journals, and the role of competition and wartime activities is so crucial to any understanding of how a technology moved from laboratory to market. Obviously, the easier it was to be aware of applicable components and their uses, the faster one could expect them to be applied in novel ways. That ability to build novel devices spurred demand for even more specialized components, and then equipment.

Thus, what you have probably concluded is that all three strategies must be applied if we are to understand either how technology evolved or, if you are a manager in the information processing industry today, how you might appreciate what new product to develop or upon what technical platform to place your company's next major applications. Now the history of technology becomes useful and a part of the process of innovation itself.

Related to the requirement to understand component history in much broader terms is the need to appreciate that, in fact, the ability to specialize (in order to satisfy an application need or reflect what a specific engineer knows about inventing) is a significant characteristic of all the information processing technologies available from the typewriter to the computer. Once a machine has been in existence for one decade or more, variations multiplied, sometimes into dozens with hundreds of possible configurations. We have already made that point about adding machines, calculators, tabulators, computers, and microcomputers. But as early as 1950 computer builders also spoke of machines intended for scientific or commercial use, of analog compared with digital designs.[44] By the end of the 1970s computing capability was being built and software written and embedded in other industrial and military devices (e.g., papermaking machinery, rockets, space ships, and smart bombs). At what point did a typewriter stop being a typewriter and become a billing machine? In old photographs it is obvious that they were close relatives. Or to call out a more contemporaneous example, at what point does a photocopy machine stop being a normal Xerox-like device and become either a printer or a telecommunications instrument (a FAX machine)? To illustrate the cross currents at work, at the time Xerox machines were becoming more than copiers, Xerox Corporation was beginning to call itself the Document Company. Which was driving what: strategy or technological innovation, customer requests or creative Japanese competition? What we do know is that the evidence demonstrates for each decade that machines and components build one on the other, that applications expand and become more sophisticated, dependent on more specialized, higher function machines, and that inventors and users get used to going to five-star restaurants.[45]

OFFICE MACHINES AND COMPUTERS: BUSINESS ISSUES

People, machines, and components operate most frequently within some business context, as suggested in Chapters 1 and 2. There are some patterns evident that are similar from one period to another which are useful to keep in mind as we look at the history of computing. Office machine vendors in the 1950s worried about how big the market was for computers, whereas computer startup firms worried about being too small. For small firms the risk of building unprofitable products was enormous. To one degree or another that concern existed for all types of office equipment. All also experienced slow acceptance, which injected uncertainty into business plans. In each instance the new technology had to be introduced, its application explained along with anticipated benefits of use, and then training provided. When typewriters were first marketed, nobody knew how to type! Because people knew how to add, they accepted adding machines more easily, but firms such as Burroughs and Felt & Tarrant had to either develop training manuals or run hundreds of training schools. As computers came into use, the same issue came up again: Who knew what they were, how to use them, and why? In each instance from typewriter to PCs, the degree of acceptance of a new product was tied to how well customers understood the benefits and use of machines.[46]

The two keys to this issue are ability to use a device (e.g., technical competence, computer literacy, typing skills) and the applications to which they are put. The first is fairly straightforward, we do not need to add to this issue. The second is a more difficult issue. While I will have a great deal to say about applications in Chapter 5, let me add that applications as an historical issue go back to the dawn of information handling. When applications were obvious, machines sold, when they were not, sales slowed. An example or two from our own personal experiences illustrates the point. In the 1970s and 1980s we all heard a great deal about home banking using personal computers; it failed to take off because nobody saw the benefits of typing checks into a computer rather than writing them out, and then getting a balance online which the bank was giving us anyway.[47] Industry pundits said at the end of the 1970s that one-third of all Americans would have PCs in their homes within several years. The public asked: What for? The answer that emerged was, buy a $2,500 machine and use it for Christmas card labels, playing games, some word processing, and for recipes. Wisely, the American public looked at those applications and said "not for $2,500." It took an additional decade of product improvement, price reductions, easier-to-use software applications, and the delivery of network-based applications (e.g., from Prodigy, Internet, etc.) before home sales took off.

However, from the first day that microcomputers were available, some people bought them, ten of thousands in the early 1980s, not very many, but some nonetheless. It appears that Mark Twain was the kind of individual who would have been first to get a PC; he was one of the first American writers to compose on a typewriter. With every generation of technology there were always a few people who wanted to try it out. In sales circles in the information processing world, they are usually called "heat seakers," folks who wear digital watches with many additional functions more appropriate for underwater divers than for office use. But they existed in each decade of this industry and provided the early testimonials that caused others to want to try machines. Marketing strategies often will build around first satisfying these people, followed by using them as references. Every generation has them. Go through the eighteenth century home of Thomas Jefferson (Monticello) and you will understand. While the office appliance industry was not maintained just by this group, this sector was important enough to teach the industry many lessons. We know very little about them. What little we do understand is often presented in a negative way (e.g., we call some PC users "hackers").[48] But we should learn more about their role because some even became builders of machines.

Another constant over the past century is that all successful marketing efforts had several common elements. First, vendors explained (sold) what the machines were and how they could be used. Second, a great deal of initial support was required until users had the skills needed to use the equipment (e.g., typewriter schools in the 1890s, Microsoft help desks to install Windows '95 in 1995). Third, formal training programs were frequently required. The one exception was the typewriter; by World War II training was best obtained from schools and colleges, not vendors. We may be approaching a similar situation with the personal computer at a much faster pace than with typewriters, with community colleges and K–12 schools beginning to take on from PC dealers the responsibility for teaching computer literacy. Fourth, service organizations were necessarily close to the customer. That meant repair people had to be available in every state, store fronts in every major urban center, and, with the early computers, maintenance engineers in the same rooms as the machines.

That requirement profoundly influenced the economics of marketing options. If you were a vendor and needed to have repair people situated in a state, with a building and offices and parts, did it make sense to also open a store front or have a sales team headquartered there? Typically the answer was yes. As the installed number of machines in a region increased, finally reaching the point where local repair people were needed, one could reasonably expect soon after to see sales personnel with geographic coverage responsibilities. In analyzing the historic records of IBM sales offices in Tennessee, New Jersey, and Wisconsin, it became very clear that between the 1920s and the late 1950s (when most previously uncovered U.S. geographies were blanketed with IBM local presence) sales followed repairs.[49] Yet sales had earlier been done by sales personnel who made the rounds but not resident in rural or small urban areas, mostly housed out of major cities. As geographic coverage extended and became more comprehensive, geographic coverage strategies with retail arms added became the norm. As equipment became more complex, customers also wanted industry or application expertise, which put pressure on vendors to provide some industry and application coverage—a direct confrontation with the geographic approach, complete with decades of debate about which salesman should get credit for a sale, the local rep or the person who sold the business. This debate never was resolved and continues today. Historians can document this by looking at sales organization charts and titles of individuals, or at compensation plans (what salespeople were paid for). But as a rule of thumb, the bigger the product line the more likely an application and geographic coverage strategy would be deployed. The smaller the machine the less support would be available, and the more the preferred channels of distribution were retail outlets (e.g., dealers in cities) and business partners (usually with specific application skills). This observation applies to the 1920s as much as to the 1980s. We sell PCs today the way we sold typewriters in 1896.

Fifth, a public relations effort was crucial. NCR mailed millions of advertisements from the Dayton (Ohio) post office in the 1890s, approximately 25 percent of all third-class mail in that city. All widely distributed magazines in the United States have carried advertisements for office appliances from World War II to the present. Efforts had to be made to ensure that thousands of articles appeared in trade publications on the beneficial uses of typewriters, calculators, adding machines, tabulating equipment, cash registers, and computers in each decade of their existence. In fact, the volume of publications is still rising. On approximately the fifteenth anniversary of the microcomputer (1990), for example, more than 150 magazines devoted to this device existed worldwide.[50] As of this writing (1996), the number of magazines devoted to the Internet is increasing by several each month. But they were always extensive. Systems magazines were very popular in the period 1905–1935, while technical magazines on computing became a rapidly expanding subset of the magazine business in the United States in the 1960s and 1970s. This has always been an industry that publishes a great deal and is published about a great deal, too.[51]

Office machines became very profitable when sold in volume. In each instance, vendors sought to standardize manufacturing and distribution and for each class of device were generally successful. Although individual companies either were more successful or failed, as a whole these devices returned consistent profits from one decade to another once significant volumes had been achieved: The smaller and less complicated the device, the more copies that had to be sold, and the more sophisticated a machine, the more the opposite held true. This meant, for example, that by 1900 the business of a typewriter vendor could be very profitable, selling tens of thousands of machines yearly. The same held true for adding and calculating equipment. For tabulating machines thousands or even just hundreds satisfied the need for profitability. In the 1950s it was difficult to make a profit on dozens of machines but easy on hundreds. As competition within a particular device's market intensified, the volume required to make a profit rose because, in part, a vendor's response to competitors was through price reductions, which required great manufacturing efficiencies. This clearly was the case with each device type and has continued to the present with microcomputers.

Hand-held calculators illustrated the extent to which this could happen. In the early 1970s Hewlett-Packard sold a device for $700. The same function became available on Texas Instruments' products by 1976 for approximately $90, and, by the end of the 1980s, programmable calculators sold for $50. Simpler devices that performed just the four basic mathematical functions, calculated interests, and had memory could be purchased in the 1990s for as little as $3.00 and had shrunk from a large handful to a device the size of a credit card.[52]

EFFECTS OF NEW TECHNOLOGY ON AN EXISTING INDUSTRY

Increasingly, technologies have come into a wide variety of industries in the twentieth century at a rate that has far surpassed even that of the previous century. The examples are obvious and blunt: aviation, telecommunications, medicine, and transportation (trucks and cars), just to mention a few. Less obvious but probably just as dramatic are the smaller array of technologies that have influenced industry structures and tasks (e.g., electricity and electrical motors, telephones, light bulbs, and so on). While historians and technologists tend to look at the effects of a technology from the perspective of the technology at hand—for example the impact of the telephone or the car—less often do they look at the impact of a technology from the view of a particular industry. The two obvious paths would be to ask how has a specific technology affected a particular industry, or how has a particular industry been affected by one or more technologies. These are areas that require vast amounts of research by future historians. However, the connections between the computer and old office appliance technologies and the computer's position as the latest technology incorporated into the industry offer an opportunity to explore the general question of what effect a new technology has on an existing industry. The discussion below is not definitive, merely suggestive, based on my research on this industry's century-old history. The caveat is important because it is not yet clear that what happened here transports over to other industries as common patterns, hence my interest in seeing industry-by-industry research. Nonetheless, the world of information processing is important enough on its own to warrant some observations, even if it turns out that its patterns were not similar to those in other industries.

Perhaps the most obvious observation we can make is that as with most sets of new products in the information processing industry, and in many others where a high level of technology content existed, the computer business started small but changed later. In 1950 few companies other than the Electronic Computer Company (Elecom) and Computer Research Corporation (CRC) were attempting to sell computers commercially; by 1955 some fifteen U.S. and one British firm had installed computers for nonmilitary purposes. These early enterprises were often tied to U.S. defense work, frequently located in the same community as a major university, and had strong skills in electronics and no ties to the office equipment world. But between the late 1940s and the mid-1950s the office equipment industry came to dominate the manufacture and sale of commercial computers. Office equipment vendors, not small computer firms staffed with engineers and few or no marketing personnel, created commercial markets for computers.

The process of taking over the market was, in hindsight, relatively straightforward. Firms like IBM and Remington Rand acquired technical skills—such as in advanced electronics and radar—as part of doing business with the U.S. military during both World War II and the Korean War. The U.S. government asked them, in turn, to take on computer-related projects, which it funded. Finally, armed with potential products, a sales force, manufacturing capability, and a customer base most suited to use computers, it was possible to add such machines to the product line when the timing was right. In turn, that process heated up demand, which reinforced initial forays into the market and led dominant companies such as IBM and Sperry to invest more and introduce additional computer products. Their knowledge of the office world and ability to bridge old technologies with newer ones was a workable symbiotic relationship that resulted in the acceptance of computers by long-standing customers of the industry.[53] In short, the largest office equipment vendors had the capital and knowledge of the information-handling business to sell computers profitably.

The key finding is the link between vendors and customers, not the availability of a new technology. The critical path to consider is the influence of customer needs and wants, and access to these people. Electronics, small computer manufacturers, and aviation companies were the first enterprises to display a strong interest in commercial computers. Their attraction grew out of experiences like those of office equipment vendors; they, too, had developed expertise and worked for the U.S. military. In fact, one could easily build a strong case that these firms had better and more technical expertise than the office appliance companies. They had built more machines, had individuals who had, in effect, invented the devices (e.g., Eckert, Mauchly), and would have appeared to many as the most competent group to turn to.

But they all shared one major weakness: They lacked the customer base to sell to, or the appreciation needed to translate computer technology into practical commercial products for wide use in offices and factories. Even in the 1940s and early 1950s, it was very clear to office appliance executives that high-tech machines required many high-tech customers. Their definition of many customers was not a dozen or so, but many hundreds or thousands, an order of magnitude difference minimally between their view and that of the computer experts of the day, who saw only dozens of opportunities. That is why, for example, you could have the president of IBM and other executives in the industry quoted in the late 1940s as saying the market for computers was of little interest to them because they could only see a few dozen customers. Observers of the industry like to point out these kinds of quotes almost in mocking fashion, little realizing what was behind these statements. The engineering communities in small computer companies, like EMC and ERA, did not understand. So they went after the dozen companies and while they hardly made a dent in the market, were perceived later by historians as visionary. All these visionary companies ran out of customers and capital and had to be sold off to companies who had customers. It is quite possible that in, say, 1948, there were only a dozen possible customers for the kind of computers available at the time.[54] From an office appliance vendor's point of view, the same investment of required dollars made in calculating gear instead of computers presented less risk and higher profits (e.g., at net after taxes above 25 percent).

The marketing assessments that have survived in the IBM Archives and in the Burroughs Papers, not to mention the testimony given in the IBM antitrust suit of the 1970s, clearly prove the difference in perspectives between the new computer companies and the old-line office appliance firms. The latter recognized that the real market for any new information-handling equipment consisted of hundreds of thousands of commercial enterprises around the world employing millions of workers, not just the military or a few universities. The leading vendors constantly tracked industries, number of enterprises, and distribution of work forces, looked at education levels, and demographics; and, of course, knew who had what kinds of equipment installed. Given the mindset of the industry that it was always easiest to sell to an existing customer, and they knew what their existing customers already had installed, it was not difficult for this industry to appreciate in fairly precise terms who were real customers for computers at about any time from the 1940s to the present. Almost from the beginning of the industry in the nineteenth century, market intelligence operations were extensive, sophisticated, and effective. In short, to borrow Alfred D. Chandler's basic thesis from *Scale and Scope*, this is an industry that had made the major investments required to do the job.[55] Yet this was not necessarily fully appreciated outside the old-line office appliance world. In the early days of the computer large electronic firms appeared better positioned to compete (e.g., GE, Sylvania, and RCA) if one only looked at marketing capability through the eyes of technical prowess, which is the way that both computer and electronics firms viewed the market. The office appliance community looked at opportunity through marketing and customer lenses and, when they felt the technology had reached a marketable level of sophistication, simply went out and bought the technical talent they needed.

That process was easy. Remington Rand bought all the talent they needed quickly; IBM chose to hire an army of engineers; NCR and Burroughs combined the two strategies. Over time, balancing of resources and market access was also done through acquisition and deacquisition (e.g., think of GE, Honeywell, and the French firm, Bull, and their activities in the 1960s–1980s). Thus, well-run office equipment vendors moved effectively, and by the late 1950s came to dominate the fledgling business worldwide, serving as an ideal example of Chandler's own observation. This industry moved from competing on price and technology to battling its own on function, service, and technical reliability. It took less than a decade to pounce on the new market. Electronic firms came in and out of the computer business over the next four decades but with little success. In fact, the churn continues as of this writing. European and Asian firms were also entering and exiting the market, but leaving it to such companies as IBM, Sperry, and Burroughs to dominate throughout the 1960s and into the 1970s.

Yet the reader might ask, "What about the Japanese electronics firms that did well with computers?" "Does that contradict the model described?" The answer is, not really. For one thing, the traditional office appliance companies were major providers of computers in Asia all during the period in question (1950s–1990s). Electronic firms in Japan were successful because (a) they had large commercial customer bases and (b) either had also sold office equipment or had marketing links to such firms. While the structure of Asian firms has only just recently become a topic of serious research in the West, we do not understand in detail the relationships among computer providers, office appliance vendors, and commercial customers in that period of transition (1930s–1960s) to either challenge my model or fully endorse it as valid globally. It would also be interesting to understand more fully the evolution of the microcomputer business in Asia as an extension of the small office appliance industry, since until, for all intents and purposes, the early 1990s, most microcomputers were sold to commercial and public sector establishments. Since access to customers is the key to understanding generational links in the acceptance of technologies, we may find a similar pattern at work as existed in the United States.[56]

Apart from the fact that the computer business started out small and grew, another feature of the computer's effect was the compulsion evident on the part of many American office equipment vendors to enter the market by the mid-1950s. As sales of UNIVACs and IBM 701s and 650s accelerated in the mid-1950s, it became obvious to other vendors that if they, too, did not sell computers, their installed base of large accounting machines would be displaced by the likes of IBM and Sperry. These two companies had already realized this fact to such an extent that it would be correct to argue that they, too, reacted out of fear in entering the computer business. As a self-protective and reactive act, therefore, most office appliance vendors saw the need to participate in the new market by the late 1950s; many had entered by the early 1960s. That many of them did so ineffectively is another issue, but their recognition of the need to participate simply strengthened the process by which computers were fully integrated into the office equipment industry.[57]

But let us deal briefly with the issue of ineffectiveness. I have described elsewhere in more detail some of the problems involved. However, it is important to put into perspective what happened. Typically, both computer-centric companies and office appliance-centric vendors brought to the issue of computer markets their own set of experiences and opinions which prevented them from understanding as well as historians do today what it would take to be successful in the world of computers. Computer-centric companies failed to understand the importance of having a pre-existing customer base and underestimated the amount of capital it would require to build, market, and support a profitable computer product line. Into this camp we must add electronic firms that shared, in common with Remington Rand, the chronic problem of having too many product lines fracturing the attention and capital of senior management. The majority of the office appliance companies, while they understood and had customers ripe for computers, usually underestimated the capital and technical requirements to design, manufacture, service, and then replace products with new ones. Once they found out what the price of admission would be to this new market, commitments were often insufficient, or of a too brief duration (e.g., Burroughs), often almost unaffordable (probably NCR), and management attention distracted by too many other activities (especially Remington Rand and RCA).[58]

The one obvious exception was IBM which, in hindsight, we know really had no choice but to throw everything it had at the process of developing the market if it were to survive, since its bread-and-butter business—tabulating equipment—was about to be taken over by computers. Besides the talent of its employees, the real key here was commitment backed up by the fortuitous availability of a great deal of capital, right-skilled employees, and an appropriate manufacturing capability. Senior management was also prepared to change more than we thought in the 1970s or 1980s. For example, today we know that the legendary sales force at IBM, which has been given credit by just about every historian, economist, business leader, professor, and consultant for selling computers better than Remington or anybody else in the 1950s and 1960s, had to be replaced in order to do the job. In the late 1950s, this legendary sales force was superb at selling punch card equipment, but knew little to almost nothing about how to sell computer systems. Some salesmen managed to learn—the company invested mightily in training its employees about these new machines—but in the end were quietly replaced with college graduates, people with technical education and experience using such machines, beginning in the late 1950s. The last of the old tabulating machine peddlers were gone in the early 1960s when IBM sold its punch card equipment business.[59] After that, its salesmen looked and acted much more like the engineers who had invented computers a decade or more before. The exception was that this renovated sales force was led by experienced sales and marketing managers who understood and had contacts with potential customers.

Ironically, history also seemed to repeat itself. IBM, for instance, had been able to seize a large share of the punch card market in the 1920s because of good marketing, its corporate structure stabilized earlier than that of its rivals,[60] and, by the end of the 1930s, sufficient capital and critical mass were available to support the product line against all competitors. In the 1950s it again was armed with capital, reasonably good marketing resources, and technical expertise, and effectively challenged rivals sooner rather than later. Although companies such as Underwood, Monroe, Olivetti, and Machines Bull introduced computers in the 1950s, they were either weak financially or less effective in marketing them than IBM.

History repeated itself even in the sales force's operations. When Thomas J. Watson, Sr., decided to focus his attention on the punch card business during World War I, he discovered that the sales force had to split its time across multiple products ranging from the complicated tabulating business all the way to hawking scales. He fixed that problem by collecting his best sales people into a group to concentrate on selling punch card equipment, constantly added more salesmen suited to this kind of selling, and trained them extensively. IBM's "Sales School" had originated at NCR in the nineteenth century and had been personally copied by Watson at IBM. But it was not enough; he found that as the product line to be sold increased in sophistication, so too did the sales force have to change. Just like in the early 1960s a "tab" salesman might have difficulty selling computers, so, too, a scale or clock salesman might find it difficult to sell tabulating services. In both situations other support functions had to be in place: training, market intelligence gathering, strong sales and marketing management leadership, and the right kind of rewards and incentives. In both cases, they were. In the 1950s, the marketing and sales structures required for selling computers often were weak or nonexistent in IBM's competitors.

That is not to say they were absent. Larger firms also quickly acquired the expertise they needed, although these acquisitions were more frequently of a technical nature, not in selling or marketing. Remington Rand, Burroughs, NCR, and others bought talent to move rapidly into the computer business. Those not able to do so found the new market too expensive to enter. Underwood, for example, risked financial disaster as it attempted to develop its own computer product line. Small rivals, in time, were also neutralized by mergers when not defeated outright by failure. So the market landscape became less cluttered. Monroe and Marchant, respectively, folded into Litton and Smith-Corona; Underwood's computer business went to Olivetti; Remington Rand became part of Sperry. The same happened with electronic firms. Of the eleven companies working on commercial computers in the United States before 1955, four were acquired by office equipment vendors by 1955, five simply stopped developing computer products, while two lingered (J. B. Rea and Teleregister) for years before disappearing.[61]

The capital requirements of the new technology thus did cause industry restructuring. The same had happened several generations earlier in the office appliance industry. For example, more than 150 typewriter manufacturing companies shrunk to less than a dozen in the United States by World War I. A less dramatic but nonetheless significant consolidation occurred among vendors of cash registers, and adding and calculating devices. In many cases, critical mass was achieved for both market coverage and product development and manufacture, by combining product lines. Thus, for example, by World War II one could buy from Burroughs typewriters, adding machines, calculators, cash registers, billing machines, coin changers, and so forth. NCR—the dominant provider of cash registers— had acquired some of its competitors or their patents, and over the years had added products that competed toe-to-toe with Burroughs' machines.

It is so much clearer to historians today that it is logical that in time the office equipment industry would assume control over the development and marketing of computer equipment. That result appears reasonable because, as with all technologies, in the final analysis it is the use to which something is put that determines its destiny. Initially, computers were the next round of technologies introduced to handle information and were perceived as such by users. That perception placed computers historically in a continuum of machines under development since the mid-nineteenth century aimed specifically at improving the efficiency and speed with which information is gathered and used by both scientific/engineering and commercial users. Viewed that way, who initially developed the computer is less important than who ultimately came to sell or buy it.

The computer came into an industry with long-established roots in the economies of the United States, Canada, East Asia, and Western Europe. Before the computer, data processing had an important history and its practices became those of the early computer market, giving it many of the characteristics evident in the late twentieth century. The computer's journey from laboratory to market also mirrored the path taken by many complex technologies in the twentieth century, from airlines to telephones, from trucks and cars to radios and television.

CONCLUSION

The story presented in this and other chapters of this book might lead one to conclude that the journey from kitchen table or laboratory to market and twentieth-century icon was part of a well-connected paradigm. Historians, and particularly journalists, are quite effective in creating such illusions. In reality, however, events often occurred in complete isolation from others; the opposite was equally true. Chaos and an uncertain future were the daily realities. The memoirs of this industry are full of testimonials about how the protagonists had no clue where this business was going or how much they would make. PC inventors and software writers in the 1980s and 1990s made the same comment. Did Bill Gates have any idea two decades ago that he would be a multibillionaire or that PCs would be sold by the tens of millions each year? Cause-and-effect relationships were not necessarily obvious at the time. They are more neatly the product of industry observers after the fact—a useful exercise that could influence future behavior, however. Historians and economists like to build elegant models or theses to explain what happened, it is their job to do that. Links, however, were always messy at best and rarely if ever clear. What was always obvious at any time, however, and clearer today, is that nobody had a master plan, any well-defined road map. All felt their way along as best they could, usually building on the activities of others who had come before them.[62]

Tradition and experience have a long history in this industry, despite the image of 24-year-old executives running around in Silicon Valley. Many of the senior executives in this industry have, from the 1880s to the present, worked all of their adult lives in this industry, spending 30, even 40 or more years in it. The most senior executives of all the major office appliance firms of the 1920s–1940s in the United States had served their companies for 30 or more years. Even the major generational changes in corporate leadership that took place in the 1920s, 1940s, 1950s/60s, and again in the 1980s did not change that fact. While turnover in leadership was a constant—as in any industry—it was quite remarkable how many people worked 30 to over 40 years in one company and in one industry. That fact helps explain why on the one hand there was always a vast amount of experience to help guide companies, and why, on the other hand, companies were sometimes reluctant to move to new products and markets quickly enough. Burroughs had to flush out a whole generation of intransigent executives at the end of World War II in order to revitalize itself, IBM did the same thing in the 1990s. But the examples are everywhere: NCR in the 1910s, IBM in the 1950s, Remington Rand in the 1950s, Remington Typewriter in the 1880s, and so forth.

I began this chapter by calling out the need to search for universal "rules of the road" useful in the management of any "high-tech" industry. Let me conclude by suggesting five points of similarity with other industries and challenge the reader to refine this list.

1. Base technologies in an industry usually, if not always, build substantially on nineteenth-century scientific studies.

2. As science was moved to technological applications, many people working in teams at universities and within companies were required in order to produce useful products.

3. Scarcely any significant technology of the twentieth century came into existence without an extraordinary investment by national governments. This was particularly pronounced in the United States in the period 1930–1980.[63] After 1960, the dynamics began to change as, for example, the Japanese, and, to a lesser extent, the Europeans invested in strategic technologies and their associated industries.

4. The transfer of technology to widespread use required adoption of this technology by pre-existing corporations, although startup enterprises provided initial commercial leadership.

5. Public awareness of a particular technology occurred at approximately the same time that the technology moved from being highly specialized (e.g., only for military or scientific uses) to commercially applicable. Related to this is the strong role played by print media in getting the word out both to the public at large and to buyers through widely distributed publications and narrowly focused trade and industry journals touting the wonders of the new technologies.

There are other observations that can be made which may be directly observable in other industries but which would have to be validated. My suspicion is that they are observable elsewhere but not as universally as the five listed above. The list, while not exhaustive, includes the following:

1. Nineteenth-century variants of high-tech products were frequently introduced by their inventors, who usually experienced only moderate success in marketing these products. Twentieth-century counterparts were more effective.

2. High-Tech devices (including, for example, farm machinery of the 1800s) quickly required a complex of investments and skills to sell effectively and that required small companies being formed which grew in size rapidly.

3. In both centuries, basic and innovative configurations of components to create new products came most frequently from outside the industry or profession. Corollary Number One: Companies were better at then taking these configurations and continuously enhancing them (e.g., PCs invented by young engineers, but companies turning them into product lines). Corollary Number Two: As one moves deeper into the twentieth century, science becomes a greater contributor to technology. We have only to think about the research done on the transistor and integrated circuit to recognize the pattern.

4. The biggest barriers to entry for companies were insufficient capital and lack of the right kind of customers.

5. The easiest skills to acquire in both centuries were technical (e.g., machinists in the 1800s, programmers and engineers in the 1900s).

In addition to these multi-generational observations, we can say with some certainty that the computer had particular characteristics that distinguished it from other technologies. For one thing, it ultimately joined the mainstream of office applications, hence the value of linking office appliances to computers to a far greater degree than has been done by historians. This link was no accident. In addition, this technology became widely applied to other technologies that one would be tempted to use for comparison, such as airplanes and military equipment. People simply did not use as many rockets and spaceships on a daily basis. No perfect paradigm exists, however, to describe technology transfer: Each device has some unique characteristics over and above general observation, including the computer or, for that matter, adding and calculating machines, typewriters and cash registers. But this is also true for other classes of machines: telephones, television, trucks and cars, airplanes, and a host of other devices.

Less understood are questions about the influence of various technologies. Some generalities on the issue of computer impact on society as an indicator of patterns of behavior of any twentieth-century technology would be welcome because they could enhance our appreciation of how technologies go from laboratory to market. But historians are too close to many of these technologies, and it is, perhaps, still too early in the life cycles of these classes of devices to see patterns correctly. They have enough to do just tracking the emergence of specific technologies. But social historians want answers; they will have to provide them in time.[64] For example, I doubt historians will ignore the impact of microcomputers on American life during the historic period 1975–2025, an era when one might conclude this technology made as much of a penetration in the fabric of the nation as it was possible to do. If true, in 1996—when I wrote these words—we were not even halfway through the cycle for microcomputers, merely one of many waves of information technology we have to study!

There are many issues at work that complicate the story beyond what was just covered. For example, while the thrust of this chapter has been to suggest that more, rather than less, computers folded into a longer continuum of office appliances, there are some departures from the pre-computer era, too. The two obvious ones are the extensive role played by governments around the world in funding and influencing the course of R&D related to computers. The second concerns the reliance and influence of scientific research on the base technologies of these machines. From a corporation's point of view it did not matter if machinists, engineers, or scientists were inventing or discovering the bases of products, it was all R&D. But, nonetheless, the picture becomes more complicated, particularly by the end of the 1940s. Government roles are hardly understood. We best appreciate what has happened with the U.S. government, thanks to Kenneth Flamm. But what about the British, French, Poles, Russians, Japanese, and Chinese? All had extensive government investment programs in computing. We know almost nothing about these, snipets at best about the Japanese and the British (in London's case most about its role during World War II). But those are the two grand differences with the past—government and science—that we now need to put into context. The exceptions, however, do not fundamentally alter the main thesis of this chapter, that computers were yet another information processing technology bought and sold the same way as earlier office appliance companies and more often than not, by the same vendors.

Economists have come closer to identifying common patterns of technology behavior than historians of either technology or society. They recognize the profound need for capital, for example, to make it possible for a technology to move out of the laboratory to market in this century.[65] In fact, if we play out their logic, economists would lead you to conclude that capital requirements for high-tech products may actually go up, yet other new technology-based industries may provide counter arguments to this (e.g., in biotech products). What may be clearer for the longer term is that new technologies cost more proportionately to do research on than in the nineteenth or first half of the twentieth century. But this is not the place to discuss R&D productivity, merely to point out what complex technologies like those of the computer do to economies of scale.

Economists have started the important work of identifying national patterns of investment in technologies as a critical cause of specific devices coming to the fore in one nation rather than another.[66] The work done, for example, in comparing and contrasting Japanese, U.S., and European investments in technological development crosses many devices, and is not limited to computers. Patterns exist, suggesting that government investment strategies have a direct correlation to technological developments, especially in military-related spheres; that does represent a major departure from the old office appliance industry which did not receive any government support to speak of. Nothing did the computer as much good as the 40-year Cold War. Of course, with that behind us, economists will have new issues to worry about. But in the case of the computer, it does not matter because the impetus for new product development will come, as it has now for almost two decades, from the demands of the market place because the computer now lives in a well-established, some even say mature, industry that has everything the machine needs: capital, R&D, manufacturing, sales, distribution, and customers.

Economists, however, do tend to take a far too narrow view of reality. Just because the cost of calculating a number on a computer dropped from $1.50 to a fraction of a penny in and of itself did not make customers use these machines. The historical evidence is clear on this point. In fact, most living executives who have had information systems departments reporting to them complain that I/S budgets never went down, only up. Recall Paul A. Strassmann's analysis.[67] Thus, simple economic cause and effect explanations or the hunt for the tyranny of economic imperatives is an incomplete view of reality. Closer to the truth is the analysis of a technology and of its industry alignments across many decades involving an appreciation of the interrelationships among its developers, supporters, vendors, and the public/customers at large. This is how we can arrive at a different, more specific, and accurate view of the history of any technology.

NOTES

1. "Just Squeaking Along," *Time*, October 30, 1989: 70, 73.

2. Ibid.

3. It is this issue of manufacturability that makes IBM's technical history of the period so crucial. Fortunately there is the excellent study to consult by Charles J. Bashe et al., *IBM's Early Computers* (Cambridge, Mass.: MIT Press, 1986), massive and comprehensive.

4. Some of these histories add significantly to our understanding, however, on the history of the company. See, for example, NCR, *NCR: Celebrating the Future, 1884–1984* (Dayton, Ohio: NCR, 1984).

5. For bibliography on these two, see James W. Cortada, *A Bibliographic Guide to the History of Computing, Computers, and the Information Processing Industry* (Westport, Conn.: Greenwood Press, 1990): 494–495, 548–555.

6. The best summary of this process is by Richard E. Neustadt and Ernest R. May, *Thinking in Time: The Uses of History for Decision Makers* (New York: Free Press, 1986).

7. For a sampling of the issues involved in applying history to business decisions, see Les Garner, "History for the Corporate Executive: Cultivating the Historical Imagination in MBA Students," *The History Teacher* 18, no. 2 (February 1985): 199–226.

8. A practical "hands on" approach is explained by Robert Heilbroner, *The Future as History* (New York: Harper and Brothers, 1960).

9. Barbara Tuchman, *Practicing History: Selected Essays* (New York: A. A. Knopf, 1981): 289.

10. Corporate culture treated as historical issues is well demonstrated in Terrence E. Deal and Allan A. Kennedy, *Corporate Cultures: The Rites and Rituals of Corporate Life* (Reading, Mass.: Addison-Wesley Publishing Co., 1982); a well-reasoned argument for the use of history, humanities, and social sciences in business is now available in Patricia Pitcher, *Artists, Craftsmen and Technocrats: The Dreams, Realities and Illusions of Leadership* (Toronto: Stoddart, 1995): 171–182.

11. George Basalla, *The Evolution of Technology* (Cambridge, Mass.: Cambridge University Press, 1988): 64–134.

12. James W. Cortada, *Before the Computer: IBM, NCR, Burroughs, and Remington Rand and the Industry They Created, 1865–1956* (Princeton, N.J.: Princeton University Press, 1993).

13. To cite an information processing industry example, see Susan Lammers, *Programmers at Work Interviews* (Redmont, Wash.: Microsoft Press, 1986); for an excellent bibliography of the literature, see Pierce, J. Howard, *The Owner's Manual for the Brain* (Austin, Tex.: Leornian Press, 1994).

14. Cortada, *Before the Computer*, 39–41.

15. For an introduction to this world, see Steven Levy, *Hackers: Heroes of the Computer Revolution* (New York: Anchor Press, 1984).

16. Peter R. Scholtes, *The Team Handbook: How to Use Teams to Improve Quality* (Madison: Joiner Associates, 1988); Jack D. Orsburn et al., *Self-Directed Work Teams* (Burr Rodge, Ill.: Irwin Professional Publishing, 1990).

17. David A. Garvin, *Managing Quality* (New York: Free Press, 1988): 3–92.

18. Frederick L. Fuller, *My Half Century as an Inventor* (n.p.: privately printed, 1938).

19. Karl L. Wildes and Nilo A. Lindgren, *A Century of Electrical Engineering and Computer Science at MIT, 1882–1982* (Cambridge, Mass.: MIT Press, 1985): 32–178.

20. Nancy Stern, *From ENIAC to UNIVAC: An Appraisal of the Eckert-Mauchly Computers* (Bedford, Mass.: Digital Press, 1981).

21. Alice R. Burks and Arthur W. Burks, *The First Electronic Computer: The Atanasoff Story* (Ann Arbor: University of Michigan Press, 1988).

22. For bibliography on this theme, see David A. Hounshell and John Kenly Smith, Jr., *Science and Corporate Strategy: DuPont R&D, 1902–1980* (Cambridge: Cambridge University Press, 1988): 731.

23. Frederick L. W. Richardson and Charles R. Walker, *Human Relations in an Expanding Company: A Study of the Manufacturing Departments in the Endicott Plant of the International Business Machines Corporation* (New Haven: Labor and Management Center, Yale University, 1948).

24. For an analysis of the microcomputer business in its early days, see Paul Freiberger and Michael Swaine, *Fire in the Valley: The Making of the Personal Computer* (Berkeley: Osborne/McGraw-Hill, 1984); software is well covered in Robert T. Fertig, *The Software Revolution: Trends, Players, Market Dynamics in Personal Computer Software* (New York: North-Holland, 1985) and in Stephen E. Siwek and Harold W. Furchtgott-Roth, *International Trade in Computer Software* (Westport, Conn.: Quorum Books, 1993). Two case studies of companies in this era are Jerry Kaplan, *Startup: A Silicon*

Valley Adventure (Boston: Houghton Mifflin, 1995) and Michael S. Malone, *Going Public: MIPS Computer and the Entrepreneurial Dream* (New York: HarperCollins, 1991).

25. Most U.S. data processing centers continued to use punch cards into the early 1980s.

26. This pattern also conforms to the research done on product life cycles by Richard N. Foster, *Innovation: The Attacker's Advantage* (New York: Simon and Schuster, 1986): 29–43.

27. This product line and its evolution through the S/370 is well described by Emerson W. Pugh, Lyle R. Johnson, and John H. Palmer, *IBM's 360 and Early 370 Systems* (Cambridge, Mass.: MIT Press, 1991) and in Emerson W. Pugh, *Building IBM: Shaping an Industry and Its Technology* (Cambridge, Mass.: MIT Press, 1995): 263–307.

28. See, for example, the photographs in Wildes and Lindgren, *A Century of Electrical Engineering and Computer Science at MIT*, 82–95.

29. James Chposky and Ted Leonsis, *Blue Magic: The People, Power and Politics Behind the IBM Personal Computer* (New York: Facts on File Publications, 1988); Freiberger and Swaine, *Fire in the Valley*; Harold A. Layer, "Microcomputer History and Prehistory—An Archaeological Beginning," *Annals of the History of Computing* 11, no. 2 (1989): 127–130.

30. This process has been studied extensively. Typically, one of the first references historians use is the study by Ernest Braun and Stuart Macdonald, *Revolution in Miniature: The History and Impact of Semiconductor Electronics* (Cambridge: Cambridge University Press, 1982), but do not overlook the pre-chip era, see Paul E. Ceruzzi, *Reckoners: The Prehistory of the Digital Computer, from Relays to the Stored Program Concept, 1935–1945* (Westport, Conn.: Greenwood Press, 1983). For a large collection of essays dealing with the present and future states of chip technology, see Tom Forester (ed.), *The Microelectronics Revolution: The Complete Guide to the New Technology and Its Impact on Society* (Oxford: Basil Blackwell, 1982).

31. Alfred D. Chandler, Jr., *The Visible Hand: The Managerial Revolution in American Business* (Cambridge, Mass.: Harvard University Press, 1977), describes the process with many examples.

32. See Bashe, *IBM's Early Computers*, 167, for how sensitive the issue had become at IBM in the 1950s.

33. Isaac F. Marcosson, *Wherever Men Trade: The Romance of the Cash Register* (New York: Dodd, Mead, 1945): 92–108.

34. Franklin M. Fisher, James W. McKie, and Richard B. Mancke, *IBM and the U.S. Data Processing Industry: An Economic History* (New York: Praeger, 1983): 289–291, 399–401.

35. The legal wranglings over technologies and software are extensive and serious. The best study of the problem is by an IBM corporate lawyer and expert on copyrights and patents, Anthony Lawrence Clapes, *Softwars: The Legal Battles for Control of the Global Software Industry* (Westport, Conn.: Quorum, 1993) and his earlier book, *Software, Copyright and Competition: The "Look and Feel" of the Law* (Westport, Conn.: Quorum, 1989).

36. Cortada, *Before the Computer*.

37. You can see the issue at work just in the title of an excellent biography by Anthony Hyman, *Charles Babbage: Pioneer of the Computer* (Princeton, N.J.: Princeton University Press, 1982). Howard Aiken supposedly was influenced by Babbage's ideas, see Michael R. Williams, *A History of Computing Technology* (Englewood Cliffs, N.J.: Pren-

tice-Hall, 1985): 241. For a large yet incomplete listing of materials on Babbage, see Cortada, *A Bibliographic Guide*, 74–93, which cites over 140 references.

38. The definitive pro-Mauchly discussion is by Stern, *From ENIAC to UNIVAC*, and the definitive pro-Atanasoff accounts are by Burks and Burks, *The First Electronic Computer*, and by Clark R. Mollenhoff, *Atanasoff: Forgotten Father of the Computer* (Ames: Iowa State University Press, 1988). The most balanced judgment on the matter is probably by Ceruzzi, *Reckoners*, "The ENIAC worked, Atanasoff's computer was never reliable enough to put into routine use solving practical problems," p. 110.

39. For a brief account of their views, see James W. Cortada, *The Computer in the United States: From Laboratory to Market, 1930 to 1960* (Armonk, N.Y.: M. E. Sharpe, 1993): 54–63.

40. Periodically historians need a call to arms. Most recently this was done through a large conference held at the University of Wisconsin in Madison in 1991 by historians of both science and technology. The proceedings are a wealth of information on research issues, *Conference on Critical Problems and Research Frontiers in History of Science and History of Technology, October 30–November 3, 1991* (Madison, Wis.: n.p., 1991). A conference devoted to similar issues but focused on information processing was held in France in 1993 and its proceedings are equally rich, *3ème Colloque Histoire de L'informatique 13–15 Octobre 1993* (Sophia Antipolis: Institut National de Recherche en Informatique et en Automatique, n.d. [1993]).

41. These were some of the most sophisticated products: tabulators in the 1920s, computers in the 1950s. These could be used only by large organizations conducting large volumes of transactions that justified their cost and staffing support.

42. For a wealth of information on this generation of inventors, see Robert Levering, Michael Katz, and Milton Moskowitz, *The Computer Entrepreneurs: Who's Making It Big and How in America's Upstart Industry* (New York: New American Library, 1984).

43. While he commented on this issue frequently in many books, the two key studies are, Fernand Braudel, *The Wheels of Commerce: Civilization and Capitalism 15th–18th Century*, English trans. (New York: Harper & Row, 1982), and his earlier *The Mediterranean and the Mediterranean World in the Age of Philip II* (New York: Harper & Row, 1973), both multi-volume studies that are today considered major works in twentieth-century historiography.

44. The obvious example from the period is B. V. Bowden (ed.), *Faster than Thought* (London: Sir Isaac Pitman & Sons, 1953). But the literature is vast; see Cortada, *A Bibliographic Guide*, and its sequel, *A Second Bibliographic Guide to the History of Computing, Computers, and the Information Processing Industry* (Westport, Conn.: Greenwood Press, 1996) for hundreds of citations.

45. Experts sometimes, however, still stick to specific cases rather than looking at evolutions over time, see for example, Newton Copp and Andrew Zanella, *Discovery, Innovation, and Risk: Case Studies in Science and Technology* (Cambridge, Mass.: MIT Press, 1993), while policy makers are quick to understand the value of core competencies, see, for example, Lewis M. Branscomb (ed.), *Empowering Technology: Implementing a U.S. Strategy* (Cambridge, Mass.: MIT Press, 1993), especially 135–166.

46. An IBM salesman of the 1940s and 1950s described the problem of little training. William W. Simmons noted that in the early 1950s "There was a lack of capability at the branch offices responsible for servicing the installations, and customer training and technical literature were also inadequate," *Inside IBM: The Watson Years* (Bryn Mawr, Pa.: Dorrance & Co., 1988): 82.

47. Tom Forester, *High-Tech Society* (Cambridge, Mass.: MIT Press, 197): 128, 129, 239. Banking in general posed a variety of problems for consumers, regardless if done at home or through computers at banks. For insight see Nancy Stern and Robert A Stern, *Computers in Society* (Englewood Cliffs, N.J.: Prentice-Hall, 1983): 363–377.

48. For "true confessions" on how hackers think and act, see Eric S. Raymond (ed.), *The New Hacker's Dictionary* (Cambridge, Mass.: MIT Press, 1991): ix-xx.

49. I have documented the Tennessee case in Cortada, *Before the Computer*, 119–120.

50. For hundreds of examples, see Cortada, *A Bibliographic Guide.*

51. Many advertise in *ComputerWorld, Datamation,* and *PC World,* three leading publications in the information processing industry.

52. The little electronic calculators of the 1970s–1990s have yet to be fully studied by historians and are only casually mentioned by commentators on the computer industry.

53. Cortada, *The Computer in the United States,* 64–124.

54. Insider views of marketing opportunities by people steeped in sales and strategic planning are very limited for the period 1940s-early 1950s. However, an important first-hand source is Simmons, *Inside IBM.* He sold machines for IBM in the 1940s and early 1950s and then went on in the decade to do market analysis for the company.

55. Alfred D. Chandler, Jr., *Scale and Scope: The Dynamics of Industrial Capitalism* (Cambridge, Mass.: Harvard University Press, 1990): 8, 14–45.

56. We are not completely without some data, particularly for the post-1960 period. See Marie Anchordoguy, *Computers Inc.: Japan's Challenge to IBM* (Cambridge, Mass.: Harvard Council on East Asian Studies, 1989) and Michael A. Cusumano, *Japan's Software Factories: A Challenge to U.S. Management* (New York: Oxford University Press, 1991). For contrasting models on how to look at national information processing industries, see Ian Mackintosh, *Sunrise Europe: The Dynamics of Information Technology* (Oxford: Basil Blackwell, 1986) and Paulo Bastos Tigre, *Technology and Competition in the Brazilian Computer Industry* (New York: St. Martin's Press, 1983).

57. The memoirs of IBM's president at the time, Thomas J. Watson, Jr., on the matter offer powerful evidence: "demand for those products was accelerating, and it seemed clear the market wasn't going to wait. If IBM didn't grab the business, somebody else would, and we would never have this kind of opportunity again," *Father, Son & Co.: My Life at IBM and Beyond* (New York: Bantam, 1990): 253.

58. We know too little about RCA's operations despite the fact that a business historian has looked at the company, only to devote less time to technology than to more traditional business and corporate political issues, Robert Sobel, *RCA* (New York: Stein and Day, 1986): 170–183.

59. Comments all through Simmons, *Inside IBM,* and sporadically in Watson, *Father, Son & Co.,* passim, provided the major source for this insight.

60. This is a crucial point because at the time IBM's arch rival, Remington Rand, was attempting to deploy its sales force in a focused manner, proving to be too late. For details, see Cortada, *Before the Computer,* 149–157.

61. Fisher, *IBM and the U.S. Data Processing Industry,* 3–100.

62. This view of the interaction between industry and technology developments parallels in a remarkable fashion how scientific knowledge evolved per Thomas S. Kuhn, *The Structure of Scientific Revolutions, Second Edition, Enlarged* (New York: New American Library, 1970).

63. This has been very well demonstrated with the computer industry in the United

States with the role of the American government, by Kenneth Flamm, *Targeting the Computer: Government Support and International Competition* (Washington, D.C.: Brookings Institution, 1987) and his *Creating the Computer: Government, Industry, and High Technology* (Washington, D.C.: Brookings Institution, 1988).

64. Already the process has started across many technologies, industries, and issues. Two anthologies are representative of the broad array of studies underway: Wiebe E. Bijker, Thomas P. Hughes, and Trevor Pinch (eds.), *The Social Construction of Technological Systems: New Directions in the Sociology and History of Technology* (Cambridge, Mass.: MIT Press, 1987) and Wiebe E. Bijker and John Law, *Shaping Technology/Building a Society: Studies in Sociotechnical Change* (Cambridge, Mass.: MIT Press, 1992).

65. Dale W. Jorgenson, "Capital as a Factor of Production," in Dale W. Jorgenson and Ralph Landua (eds.), *Technology and Capital Formation* (Cambridge, Mass.: MIT Press, 1989): 1–35.

66. For a recent summary of what economists are thinking about computers, see Thomas K. Landauer, *The Trouble with Computers: Usefulness, Usability, and Productivity* (Cambridge, Mass.: MIT Press, 1995): 13–46, 73–136; but also see Charles Jonscher, "An Economic Study of the Information Technology Revolution," in Thomas J. Allen and Michael S. Scott Morton (eds.), *Information Technology and the Corporation of the 1990s: Research Studies* (New York: Oxford University Press, 1994): 5–42, which also includes a healthy bibliography on economic literature and computing.

67. See Chapter 2 but also Paul A. Strassmann, *The Business Value of Computers: An Executive's Guide* (New Canaan, Conn.: The Information Economics Press, 1990).

II _____

The Applications for Computers

Part II consists of two views on the value and nature of looking at how computers were used. Both historians and the public at large tend to focus attention on computers—the machines—and very little on their uses. About the one great exception is that everyone seems to want to discuss how difficult they are to use. But without uses, there is no need for computers. Yet historians primarily, economists and technologists, too, often fail to study adequately to what uses these machines have been put. It is the purpose of the next two chapters to look at that theme.

Chapter 4 presents the argument for why and how we should look at the history of applications, what they teach historians, technologists, and business management. While the case may seem obvious, it obviously is not, because it lacks defenders. So I will lay the case out, obvious or not, for looking at the history of applications. The timing is good because historians needed first to forcus on the history of the machines and their technologies if for no other reason than simply to catalog what they were and how many existed. But now we need to move on to how they were used. This represents the next major step forward in understanding the value and influence of the computer.

Chapter 5 demonstrates what that history looks like. As will become obvious to the reader, it is a high-level overview of the history of commercial applications. It suggests an approach—looking at applications primarily through an industry-by-industry focus—and demonstrates what such an exercise would yield. It is not the only way to look at the topic, but it is a useful first step in understanding better how these machines have been applied to the operations of corporations, governments, and educational and medical institutions. It focuses on the commercial side because ultimately businesses came to use these machines more than other sectors of the economy. It also illustrates the kinds of materials available to the historian, suggesting that there is a vast wealth of research that can be done on the topic that is both rewarding and very important.

Bottom line: Part II is a call to arms, a move from just the study of machines to an understanding of what they were used for, from a narrow focus on chips and how cheap they were to their effect on the operations of organizations.

4

The Case for Studying the History of How Computers Were Used

The evolution of the computer's historiography has reached the point where historians can no longer ignore the broad and complicated issue of what people have used computers for. Like the history of clocks, we have studied the history of specific computers and how their base technologies emerged. Hardly any major computer system built before the PC has been ignored. The personal computer has even attracted the attention of the historian. But in time, historians of clocks moved on to study how clocks were used and their effects on society.[1] In fact, until this next step was taken, the study of clocks remained almost an antiquarian activity. But once the hunt got underway for knowledge about their use, historians came to realize the profound importance of this device in regulating and influencing the patterns of work and life in the Western world, ultimately the whole world.[2] What the experience of the clock historians teaches us is that the most important work that can be done on the history of computing is not the study of the machines but of their use and effects. The evolution of the work of the clock historians suggests the analysis of the computer can and must pass on to an appreciation of more than its mechanics.

What the experience of the clock historians also instructs us is that a great deal of the future research on the uses and effects of the computer will be done by individuals who have little experience studying the history of specific machines. As we move from studying any specific technology toward an analysis of its use, we will see historians from many fields coming to the task. Historians of politics, society, economics, business, and even philosophy will take up the work. The effect will be to take what always starts out as a marginalized activity (the study of machine history) and will bring it into the mainstream of intellectual activity. The sociologists, economists, and business professors and consultants have long kept the computer at the center of many discussions about the role of technology on society. The literature on this topic is vast. But now the historian will take the concerns of these other scholars and practitioners and document their historical evolution, giving us insight into how this technology came to influence the way life is lived in the late twentieth century. Thus we move from a highly specialized sub-field of history to a broader one. Think of the process as a journey on a train. The historian of a machine sets foot onto the train and the first few stops are at stations devoted to specific machines and classes of devices. As we get closer to the urban center of history, the stops are at stations devoted to the history of science and technology. Finally, at the downtown station, our historian steps down from the train entering one for economic, social, and business history. Our historian has arrived at his or her place of work.

In this metaphor the history of applications is the train itself. As will be demonstrated below and in the next chapter, from the very beginning of the computer's journey someone was always concerned about applications—that is to say, to what uses such machines should be put. As the historian rides the train toward downtown, the topic becomes more compelling as the study of these machines becomes intertwined in the affairs of other intellectual communities—the study of the history of science, technology, society, economics, politics, and so forth. By the time our historian reaches downtown, applications—the work people do—must absorb his or her attention, just like work does for commuters who finally arrive at their offices. The activities and thoughts of the weekend or of home (e.g., the history of these machines) must be put aside while the activities of work (i.e., applications) are taken up and come to dominate the rest of the working day.

ISSUES AT HAND

The study of applications of computers is a relatively new field; as such, it would be normal, indeed necessary, to ask the simple question: What is this? What do we need to study? Why? How do we go about performing this research? What are the issues that we must deal with? Do they change over time as we learn more about the topic, and if so, how? These are all good concerns typically present at new bends in the road of historical research. Basically, we need to understand three issues:

- What are applications?
- What are their roles in computer technology?
- What affect do they have on human activity?

We could add many more questions to the list but, given where we are in the study of the history of applications, these three should keep historians busy for a long time.

The first question—what are applications—appears to be simple enough: An application is the use to which a computer is put. However, immediately after we set down this definition comes the problem of defining the application's functions, the role of individuals and organizations, and then the dependencies associated with these applications. For example, is a billing application simply the act of entering data into a computer and then having that data spit out a bill? Or is it the process by which information is gathered on billable activities, decisions made concerning practices, and actions taken after a bill is created to ensure its delivery to customers, and, finally, collection? A technology historian's more narrow view of the question would probably suggest understanding the applications only in terms of what its steps or activities were within a computer (e.g., data entry and data processing) and later the actions taken by people with the output from these applications. An example of output might be the bill that is printed out and what the mailroom staff does with it and what customers do (e.g., pay it). A business manager would argue for a broader view; namely, from when the need for a bill surfaced to when it was collected and the receipts tucked into the bank. Historians of different mindsets would have other perspectives. For instance, a social historian might be interested in the effects of receiving monthly bills on the lives of customers, the economic historian might want to understand the time and rate of flow of money through the economy since it would be influenced by how often bills were sent and paid, while the political historian might be curious about how customers react to politicians and their influence on jobs and the health of the economy if customers view their own well being by the degree to which they can pay their bills.

Historians need to consider the definition of an application's scope because of how information comes to them. An application from the information processing manager's point of view is usually seen as a piece of software—in our case a billing "package"—and possibly even the actions taken by the information processing community to "run" that software in the computer. Since most technical history begins with the study of a specific technology from that technology's perspective,[3] one might expect data processing's view of an application to dominate initial historical research. Indeed, application briefs and the vast majority of the bibliographic citations on the subject take this narrow perspective.[4] However, if the historian chooses to look at the application from the perspective of the organization that has it—in our case either the billing department or the corporation—then the role of billing software is only part of the story.

Historians need to be aware of a development in the management community of the 1980s and 1990s that will influence their view of applications. Across the industrialized world businesses and government agencies began to look at the activities of their organizations in new ways, primarily as collections of processes rather than as applications. A process in this context is defined as all the activities required to carry it out.[5] Buried in any examination of a process is the use of information technology. What can be confusing is the fact that many processes have the same name as many applications, e.g., billing application, billing process. Process views sublimate the emphasis on computer-based applications. Application views do the reverse; emphasis is on the software or actions of the computer and the activities surrounding them are de-emphasized or ignored. The documentation that has been emerging since the late 1980s on what activities are being performed in business and government has increasingly been of the process type. As a result, the historian of applications will be encouraged to broaden his or her perspective on what makes up an application, particularly for the period since the 1980s.[6] But that model—of processes—will be very useful in looking at how computing was applied in the 1950s through the mid-1980s because it is more comprehensive and realistic.

The process view requires the historian to understand two points. First, applications of computers undergirds processes and thus may involve multiple software packages, uses of hardware, and application design principles. In short, a historian may have to look at what earlier might have been several applications in order to understand the role technology was playing in one process. Second, there is a large body of business practice in the design, re-engineering, and management of processes that calls for their design and operation to be computer-centric.[7] In other words, many processes have, at their heart, an application package. Confused yet? Exactly my point. The redesign of many critical business processes that occurred in the 1980s and 1990s called for the application of computers to processes, leading to a variety of new results. These included such things as:

- elimination of process steps
- increased accuracy of operations
- faster performance
- detailed performance measurements

Thus the centrality of application software in our thinking about applications could become a trap, narrowing the focus of the historian too much, much the same way the study of specific hardware has done that. There obviously is a delicate balance between the examination of specific application packages and software products on the one hand, and, on the other, the total operations (i.e., processes) into which these packages were dropped as part of the fabric of an organization's operations.

Software's importance thus varies depending on which period is studied. In fact, the further back in the history of computers one goes, the less important software is and the closer one arrives at a period when process views dominate the thinking of users. One dynamic operating in the background is that as time progresses and more functions are automated, the greater the role played by an application package. A simple example illustrates the evolution of software's role. If you had a billing problem in the mid-1970s, you would call the company, get connected directly to a customer service representative, and immediately have a conversation. Changes to your bill (if any) would be entered into the system by the clerk, and a new bill or credit issued. Today, the billing inquiry process might include a link between automated telephone services and the billing process. You call to question a bill and are greeted by a recording asking you to dial 1 if your problem is of a certain type, 2 if it is another type, and 3 if a third type before you are connected to a service representative. As a part of the billing application, a piece of software in a telephone switch (a computer in itself) gathers data on the types of billing problems being reported; it is not simply increasing the productivity of the call takers. Then you are passed over to a clerk who uses more traditional billing software to gather information about your issues. In the mid-1970s you would have paid your bill only by check or cash. Today the same application might well accept a credit card payment if you dial your credit card number and amount to be charged, or you might authorize your bank to deduct automatically a set amount to be credited to the billing company. Now where does the billing application begin or end?

Take a process view and the questions become more complicated. Clearly the addition of telephone options at the start of the process and the ability to tie-in bank services suggest that the application, or process, has evolved over time. In other words, billing is not a static activity so obvious and pervasive that once in place it stays the same. Far from it. Even a mundane activity such as billing has a life of its own, evolving over time in response to a variety of influences: availability of telephonic application software, databases on customers and bills, customer demands for services, changing needs of an organization, and process simplification or enhancement. The point is, applications and processes evolve over time, a point historians cannot ignore.

In addition to defining an application, the relationship of the application to the technology must be questioned. It is more than just the chicken and the egg dilemma. Does technology drive the demand and function of applications, or do applications drive the nature of technology's evolution and role? I have argued elsewhere that both are at work here.[8] On the one hand, increased processing, faster cycle time, greater reliability, and lower operating costs historically encouraged greater use of computers. The evolution of the underlying technologies made computers a more attractive alternative to processing than earlier methods. New functions, such as on-line processing instead of batch processing, changed the way applications ran. The development of microcomputers made it possible to transfer applications from mainframes to personal computers.[9]

On the other hand, reliance on applications gave users insights into possible new requirements of technology, and they never hesitated to go back to their inventors and to ask for more. For example, Northrop Aviation in the late 1940s used International Business Machines (IBM) tabulating equipment and went back to the company to ask that a variety of "standalone" products be connected together to form a more continuous processing systems.[10] User demands for more memory, lower costs, greater reliability, and additional application function has led to a flood of continuous changes in technology throughout the history of the company. Those who have been using PCs for years have experienced this phenomenon, particularly as they moved from one release of a word processor to another, from one generation of PCs to a newer one.

Thus for the historian interested in applications, one of the central issues becomes the investigation of the dynamics among applications, technologies, users, and suppliers. This is not a simple task. For one thing, we do not know what is most influential: hardware, software, users, suppliers. Does influence vary by application, user, or technology? If so, how and why? Studies of other technologies suggest that the answers are diverse and complex, but also, yes.

These are important issues because they lead to the third concern—effects of technology and applications on human activity—which is probably the real issue we ultimately want to address. The history of a billing application or process in and of itself is probably not terribly interesting, but the effect of that application on a company's ability to collect receipts, or to maintain relationships with customers, or to use computers is very important. While most commentators on computers have been quick to announce profound impacts of the computer, we do not even know the extent of deployment of these machines and their applications across the economies of the industrialized world. At best we can discuss only how many machines have been built and sold, not the extent to which they have been used industry by industry. Today we have only vague notions of the extent of deployment and even there, our best data are only for one country—the United States—yet computer usage extends around the world. Until we better understand the extent and nature of deployment, we will not be in a position to move past the rhetoric to a more realistic understanding of the nature of our dependence on computers.

However, we are not without some appreciation of the role of computers. We know, for instance, that initial users were government agencies in the United States and in Europe because they were the only organizations financially willing and capable of funding research and development in this technology during its early stages. We also understand that commercial uses became viable by the mid-1950s and that commercial enterprises became the greatest users of computers, and hence of applications. So a good early step would be to study the role of computers in business. That quickly gets you to an examination of what computers, normally applications, were used for. It was the use of applications which in turn made advances in technology sufficient to support what became known as the information processing industry.

PHASES IN THE HISTORY OF APPLICATIONS

Historians may quickly find that commercial applications primarily (and scientific applications incidentally in the 1950s and 1960s and increasingly more so beginning in the 1970s) fall conveniently into four general phases of evolution:

- era when computers were first introduced to business, 1945–1952
- initial implementation phase, 1952–1965
- time of wide and rapid adoption, 1965–1981
- time of massive use by most business, 1981–1995

The first period was characterized by heavy reliance on pre-computer machines, such as adding machines, billing machines, and tabulators. Businesses simply became aware of the existence of computers, but did not find many applications for them. Companies with close ties to government funding agencies were the first to begin studying these devices (e.g., aircraft manufacturers). However, commercial applications did not appear in these years, only a few scientific and engineering uses. We will have more to say about scientific applications below.

During the initial implementation phase (1952–1965) circumstances changed rapidly. Machines were installed, and large numbers of accounting and inventory control applications were moved from earlier technologies to computers. Additional function was added to these applications, and the demand for more computing power became evident. During this period, most of the major issues associated with cost justification, management, installation, and use of computers as we know them today were identified. The underlying technologies evolved rapidly into large-capacity, cheaper to use, and more reliable products culminating in the introduction of fully integrated systems of computers, peripherals, operating systems, and applications, such as the IBM System 360 in the mid-1960s. In the United States alone, the number of installed systems went from hundreds to thousands, with sales from tens of millions of dollars to billions of dollars. And importantly, it was in this period that applications, while very expensive, began to pay for themselves.

Historians of applications will quickly find that the issue of cost justification and the reasons for initial installations are hotly contested subjects in the business and economic literature for both the period in question and subsequently. It permeates each phase in the development of the computer.[11] This is an area in which historians can do everyone an enormous service by answering for each period to what extent computers added value to the enterprises and societies in which they ran? Business managers and economists have difficulty documenting whether increases in productivity resulted from the use of computers. Theoretically, computers were either to save money on the cost of doing something because you automated a function, or to enable people to do a great deal more. We have many examples of both. However, most users of computers never went back and documented the benefits of computing, they simply either assumed it helped or realized that they could no longer go back to a pre-computerized situation.[12] So what the historian can do to add value to the debate is to document how decisions were made to acquire applications in all periods, why these decisions were made, and then study how computers increased or decreased costs and productivity, case by case.

The effort is complicated by the fact that the issues shifted over time. For example, in this early phase (to the mid-1960s), most commercial applications (we think) were installed to displace expensive labor. Thus, if you could use automation you would need fewer people and thus one could measure exactly the displaced cost of these people versus the expense of computers. Anecdotal data suggest that the bulk of the benefits anticipated from computers in the 1950s and early 1960s were of this type, expense displacement.[13] Indeed, if you had well-defined tasks one could document very accurately the expense of that task as done by people versus by computers. But in the mid-1960s we began to see implementation of new applications that supported more ill-defined decision making processes. These have been almost impossible to quantify with the same precision as earlier applications.[14] Therefore, they posed new and different challenges for the historian attempting to answer questions concerning the value of computers. Yet the anecdotal evidence suggests that a large number of users found value in having computers assist in new functions even though one could not document fully their benefits.

These kinds of questions—cost avoidance versus decision-making applications—rest concurrently in all periods. That is to say, in any given year, one can find examples of new installations of applications that fall into either category, particularly after 1965. Therefore, even the process of attaching periodization to types of decisions and benefits is very complicated. So generalizations become more hazardous to make. But we march on anyway looking for patterns because they help subsequent historians working on the same themes.

The expansion of computers simply added to the work facing historians. In the third period, 1965–1981, the computer became ubiquitous. Just about every major corporation had computers to do accounting, inventory control, and financial, manufacturing, and distribution applications. Work became a combination of batch and online applications. Applications resided on large mainframes and on more specialized minicomputers. Certain industries became more reliant on computers than others, typically those whose primary inventory was information: insurance, banking, and airlines, for example. Manufacturing companies, long users of information-handling equipment, quickly adopted this new technology and applied it to the control of manufacturing and distribution processes. By the end of this period, hardly any industry existed that did not extensively rely on this technology.

One concern that surfaces as a result of looking at what was happening in this period is the extent to which applications penetrated through individual industries. To what extent were they implemented? In fact, what were the implemented applications? Related to these concerns is another: we do not know how the experiences of one industry influenced adoption patterns in others. Historians, business managers, and economists assume that industries tend to look within themselves for role models, not across industries.[15] Does the experience of the computer support or contradict that assumption? We do not know yet. However, the answer is important because it sheds light on a bigger issue facing historians of technology and science—the patterns of dissemination of technology within a society. What contemporary literature of the period does suggest, however, is why new applications were installed:

- reduced labor content in existing work
- lowered operating overhead expenses
- resulted in more effective performance of work[16]

Most dramatic from the point of view of applications was the development of new ways to use computers. The biggest collection of new uses were decision-making or decision-support systems. In the early years of applications, people used computers to capture large quantities of data, perform simple mathematical calculations on them, and generate reports and bills. By the mid-1960s, functional departments were successfully using computers to perform rudimentary "what if" types of analysis of data, suggesting alternative decisions for humans to make.

Because computing spread across so many industries in this period, the whole issue of deployment must be addressed, as suggested above. What might historians look at? It would be helpful to understand what was written about applications in industry publications and in others that transcend a particular industry, read by many (e.g., *Time*, *Newsweek*, *Harvard Business Review*). Documenting where people came from as they moved from job to job would be important, too. We know, for example, that there are some definable migration patterns, but no serious historical research on job migrations has been done, for example, of managers. We know, for instance, that in the 1990s the U.S. utility industry is undergoing deregulation and, in an attempt to respond to that new environment, utilities have hired many executives from banking, insurance, and telecommunications. These people bring with them skills, attitudes, and experiences with computing that they are introducing into the utility industry. That happened in every decade. The deregulated telephone companies in the 1980s raided computer companies for executives and management, who in turn did what is happening in the utility industry in the 1990s.[17] In the 1970s the paper industry hired manufacturing executives and managers. In each period, there are evident patterns of career migrations that suggest how applications traveled. These need to be documented.

A second approach is to look at how vendors of software and business consultants moved across industries. For example, at IBM application software was developed that could be sold across multiple industries because that was the way to improve profitability. Other vendors sold industry-specific packages, making handsome profits without having the pressure to sell across multiple industries because they did not have IBM's overhead to contend with. Consultants in business always operated in multiple industries. In fact, for most industries the attraction to a specific consultant or his or her firm was precisely the fact that they had experience in other industries that could be applied to theirs. That process of cross-fertilization of ideas has not been studied. Yet in each decade, the use of consultants to figure out what applications to implement and then to actually install the programs was extensive. Studies could begin with examination of accounting and manufacturing applications, where the greatest amount of consulting and hiring cross-fertilization occurred, and extend to other application areas. So studies could be of application migrations, or the movement of that vast herd of employees we call managers, with their metaphorical wagons filled with applications, management practices, industry-specific experiences, and attitudes. As will be demonstrated in Chapter 8, when we look at information processing personnel, these migrations did build common views about key application issues that crossed industry boundaries.

For many living business people the history of modern computing could easily be divided into two periods: that before the personal computer and the time after. For many, the arrival of the microcomputer was the great watershed event in modern information processing. In fact, a century from now historians may agree with them. But for us mortals looking at the problem of periodization at the end of the twentieth century, we are rather more prepared simply to state that the current period in application history is that of post-1981. This forms an era in which personal computers came into their own. In fact, it is very difficult today to think of a time when PCs were not everywhere. Today tens of millions are sold each year, but it is hard to imagine that as recently as 1981 and 1982, less than a million were sold per year. Yet very quickly PCs made it possible to place computing physically anywhere in the economy: data centers, large buildings, offices, factory floors, and in our homes. Large, medium, and small computers in thousands of models made it possible to distribute computing to the point where almost every business depended on them in one fashion or another in the 1990s.

In this period, we find, for the first time in the history of computing, that application software is sold almost as commodity products through a vast network of retail outlets. Products became popular and began to display the same marketing patterns evident with other consumer goods. Best-seller lists of software appeared, reviews of their quality and functions were published, and rankings readily available. Traditional retail marketing practices were evident. For example, when Microsoft began shipping its new operating system, Windows 95, vendors of hardware quickly either gave away this software (often with some application packages) or sold it at a reduced price from that recommended by the vendor in exchange for customers buying hardware or other software packages. In short, the world of applications changes profoundly. We barely can even guess how. But the historian will ultimately have to understand and explain the process; it simply is too big a part of the gross national product of any developed nation to ignore.

To a large extent the discussion above, and that in Chapter 5, looks at applications through the lens of industry—my preference for the historian at this juncture. However, there is a class of applications that does not lend itself to this approach: scientific applications. This class of applications is massive, visible, and transcends any particular industry. There never was or is an industry called science. It is a field of study, a set of disciplines and, more to the point, a class of activities that existed in most if not all industries throughout the period of the computer. Thus scientific applications need to be treated differently.[18] Yet even here we can speak of periodization. Let me suggest three.

First, the age of discovery of the computer, 1930s–1940s. While engineers and scientists were the first to apply computers, the amount of work they did was little in comparison to subsequent periods. However, what scientists quickly came to realize is that computers could help with calculations.[19]

Second, the age of data gathering and numerical calculations, 1950s-mid-1980s. Science, thanks largely to the computer, adopted highly mathematical, numeric-intensive practices. If you studied physics in high school in the 1930s you ran into far less mathematics in that class than you did in the 1980s. Quantitative approaches became widespread, made possible by the ability of computers to crunch many numbers quickly and cost effectively. Looking at numerical calculations can lead historians down the path to many applications.[20]

Third, the age of visualization, mid-1980s to the present. As the power of computers reached the point where graphical representation of data became a reality, whole new ways of studying, teaching, and applying computers became possible. For example, by the late 1980s, students of weather systems could metaphorically fly through a tornado or severe storm by sitting down at a terminal that demonstrated what that storm would look like on a screen. By using graphical representations on terminal screens, students could see what the molecular structure was, understand what DNA—deoxyribonucleic acid—was and does, and conceptualize the activities of atoms and diseases because they could visualize, that is to say, see, a model of these created real-time by computers.

STRATEGIES FOR THE STUDY OF APPLICATIONS

What is the most effective strategy for studying the history of applications? Or, should we ask, what is the most effective strategy for studying processes that extensively used application software and computers? Should applications be studied as cases of individual company implementations, or as products of vendors? Should studies be of adoptions and experiences by industry? Or should histories emerge out of the study of the adoption experiences by computer or technology type (e.g., as might have to be the case with scientific applications)? The answers are not categorical; however, if one starts with the evidence available at the moment, there are four convenient starting points.

One way to go after the problem is by the case study method, looking at the experience of specific companies one by one. This is made possible by the availability of archival records in some companies (e.g., Dupont, Ford, IBM), with which historians can document specific experiences through traditional ar-

chival-based research. A second source at the company level is the large body
of articles and books published over the years in which actual users and information processing personnel describe their experiences with specific machines
and applications. Role model applications, such as ERMA in banking or SABRE
in the airline industry, are relatively well documented and therefore provide
another source of information. Because the computer is still a relatively new
technology, it is also possible to interview individuals who developed and used
applications in any period. While this is not the place to debate the pros and
cons of oral history, the fact remains it is a source of information. Various
organizations, such as the Charles Babbage Institute and the Smithsonian Institution, to mention only two, have an extensive collection of oral histories that
they continue to expand.[21] There exist in the United States alone over one thousand oral histories of key players in the information processing world. That
number will continue to grow. While many of the early pioneers are now reaching the end of their lives (particularly those most active in the 1930s and 1940s),
there are many people to interview from the 1950s to the present.

A second strategy for studying applications is to look at the adoption of
applications by specific industries. Thus, for example, one might look at the
adoption of automatic teller machines in the banking industry and from that
effort expand to other applications within the banking world. Many government
studies of computer adoptions are by industry and comment on rates of use of
specific applications.[22] Much of this kind of government research was done by
interviewing and surveying thousands of companies. That is why we know, for
example, that in the United States in the 1970s extensive users of computers
included banks, utilities, insurance companies, large manufacturers, processing
industries, and the telephone service providers.[23] U.S. government studies tried
to quantify the percent of companies in specific industries that had computers
or that used computers for named applications. Such surveys also suggest the
reasons why applications were adopted, an important issue since the logic varied
by industry.

The industry approach is also facilitated by the fact that specific configurations
of technology were almost exclusively the domain of one industry or another.
Examples are everywhere: teller machines in banking, film automation in movies
and entertainment, and scanning initially in medicine, now elsewhere. If an
historian wants to move from the study of technology outward to applications,
this is the logical path, and a useful way to demonstrate how technologies respond to end user needs and evolve, providing a convenient link to patterns
evident, for instance, with tabulating equipment which initially were the preserve
of people who handled large volumes of numbers (e.g., accountants and census
takers) and later of data (e.g., insurance firms, those doing inventory control,
and manufacturing personnel).

A third approach is to look at specific applications or groups of applications.
Obvious candidates include accounting, manufacturing, and financial modeling.
All three can be studied by going through journals devoted to those disciplines

and applications, through records of the discipline's own national associations (e.g., auditors, bankers, and so on), and the body of published literature on the disciplines to track the integration of computers into them (e.g., through text-books over time and industry publications). I used a combination of this approach and the second suggested strategy to write the next chapter.

There is a fourth strategy; namely, to look at applications not so much from the perspective of information processing being deployed in an organization but instead by studying how various activities were carried out that happened to have a high level of information technology content. In other words, this approach would call for the historian to look at a specific process and comment on computing whenever it appeared within the process. This approach has the benefit of helping the historian avoid the trap of becoming computer-centric in his or her view of an organization's activities. After all, from this vantage point, it would be easier for the historian to appreciate that a process could be developed that had little or no computer content. That has happened frequently. A case in point: When Harley-Davidson, the manufacturer of the famed motor-cycle, was attempting to recover from bankruptcy in the 1980s, it stopped automating activities and instead began re-engineering processes. Some resulted in new uses of computers while others did not.[24] Now which is the historically more important story: how the company used process re-engineering as a strategy of recovery or what were its applications portfolio? Clearly the former teaches us a great deal more about technology's role and about business.

Historians normally are not experts on process mapping or process re-engineering. These techniques are not taught them, and higher education represents the last industry to hold out against this kind of fundamental redesign of its operations.[25] Thus the opportunities to learn these kinds of approaches have not existed for the historian, leaving those individuals very much handicapped in their study of industry circa post 1970. While this is an import deficiency in their training, it is not one difficult to overcome. Process management and design techniques are relatively simple to understand and identify.[26] Applying them is another matter, also a topic that business historians will someday have to deal with. However, for purposes of understanding applications, the role of technology, and the consequences of the use of computers, process approaches represent a wonderful technique.

The quality management practices of the 1980s, which are closely linked to process management techniques, adds the promise of additional documentation for the historian to study. A core principle of process management is that decisions to fix problems and to improve operations must be based on data and that calls for information covering the performance of a process over an extended period of time.[27] Process teams, therefore, have to collect and preserve data and other forms of documentation (e.g., analyses of problems) for many years. In fact, certain types of business certification (e.g., ISO 9000) and candidacy for national quality awards (e.g., Malcolm Baldrige National Quality Award in the United States) require thorough and meaningful record keeping.

These records must demonstrate clear understanding of existing issues, what was done in response to them, and the consequences of these actions.[28] In short, for the historian this approach represents research nirvana!

Finally, what about the natural impulse of historians to want to perform comparative analysis across industries and countries? While this is a noble quest and a sound principle of modern scholarship, it is premature, given the poor state of our understanding of the purposes to which computers have been put. As it is, we are just barely getting our arms around the history of specific machines and technologies, have a superficial understanding of the vendors who supplied hardware and software, and even less of an appreciation in historical terms of such bread-and-butter applications as accounts receivable, accounts payable, payroll, and inventory control. Until these lower order themes are flushed out in more detail, comparative studies will be difficult to conduct. They simply require mountains of pre-analyzed information that can come only from the more specialized studies. The problem posed by the lack of information is international, cutting across all of North America, Western Europe, and East Asia, not to mention other parts of the world that have also used computers.

The history of computing in general has been written about by many people; historians actually represent a minority in this collection of commentators. Journalists, memoirists, economists, and others have not hesitated to generalize about patterns of behavior concerning computing with insufficient basis in fact. Thus we have a literature that has made errors yet to be corrected.[29] The same situation could occur with applications, representing a more serious breach of intellectual discipline since such errors would, because they cover much broader topics than specific machines and software, misguide those studying such issues as the history of companies and government operations, the role of technology on management practices, and even the nature of what future software tools are needed.

As we move away from academic studies of computing to business practices, the impulse to apply what someone thinks they have learned grows. Therefore, the opportunity to cause real damage actually exists. Historians of applications have to be very careful about what they generalize about, and the actual conclusions they reach. Business managers do read about technology's contemporary history. Thomas Watson, Jr.'s autobiography was not purchased by 300,000 historians and graduate students; yet his publisher sold that many volumes.[30] Alfred D. Chandler's books on the history of business have sometimes become best sellers and one was awarded the Pulitzer Prize.[31] A variety of books on computing have done well over the years. The successful ones have usually provided some historical perspective that later turns out to have influenced the thinking of some executive attempting to figure out how best to deploy a computer.[32]

CONCLUSION

It is a compliment to a whole generation of historians that so much work has been done to bring the history of computers into the mainstream of the history of technology. We have gone from just understanding what the big questions are in the history of technology,[33] past debates that justified the study of computer history,[34] to dealing with the kinds of issues Michael S. Mahoney called on historians to address.[35] A next logical evolution of this historiography is the study of applications. It moves us from issues of a highly technical nature to broader ones concerning business and economic history. This next step links the work of computer scientists and engineers to the daily lives of millions in societies that have come to depend on a vast array of technologies with which to carry out their functions. It is the study of applications that ultimately places the history of computing square in the middle of modern historiography and in the inner circle of critical issues of concern to historians of late twentieth century human life.

NOTES

1. Martin Campbell-Kelley and William Aspray, *Computers: A History of the Information Machine* (New York: Basic Books, 1996).

2. David S. Landes, *Revolution in Time: Clocks and the Making of the Modern World* (Cambridge, Mass.: Harvard University Press, 1983).

3. For a well-written perspective on the history of technology useful to the historian of information processing, see George Basalla, *The Evolution of Technology* (Cambridge: Cambridge University Press, 1988).

4. For over a thousand examples, see James W. Cortada, *A Bibliographic Guide to the History of Computer Applications, 1950–1990* (Westport, Conn.: Greenwood Press, 1996).

5. For an introduction to this perspective, see Don Tapscott and Art Caston, *Paradigm Shift: The New Promise of Information Technology* (New York: McGraw-Hill, 1993): 207–230; James W. Cortada, *TQM for Information Systems Management: Quality Practices for Continuous Improvement* (New York: McGraw-Hill, 1995).

6. The best explanation of the interrelationships among processes, applications, and information technology is by Thomas H. Davenport, *Process Innovation: Reengineering Work through Information Technology* (Boston, Mass.: Harvard Business School Press, 1993).

7. The primary source of bibliography and assessments of trends in this area is by James W. Cortada and John A. Woods, *The Quality Yearbook* (New York: McGraw-Hill, 1994–present), published annually. These yearbooks contain hundreds of citations each year, assessments of key publications, and over 60 are reprinted.

8. James W. Cortada, *Before the Computer* (Princeton, N.J.: Princeton University Press, 1993) and his *The Computer in the United States: From Laboratory to Market, 1930–1960* (Armonk, N.Y.: M. E. Sharpe, 1993).

9. On the application perspective of the microcomputer, see Tom Forester, *High-Tech Society* (Cambridge, Mass.: MIT Press, 1987): 131–169.

10. Known as "Betsy," Northrop wanted to combine its IBM 405 and IBM 603 to make, in effect, a "poor man's ENIAC." For details, see Charles J. Bashe et al., *IBM's Early Computers* (Cambridge, Mass.: MIT Press, 1986): 68–72.

11. The issues involved in this debate have been recently updated by Thomas K. Landauer, *The Trouble with Computers: Usefulness, Usability, and Productivity* (Cambridge, Mass.: MIT Press, 1995): 9–136.

12. On the problem of evidence see Paul A. Strassmann, *The Business Value of Computers: An Executive's Guide* (New Canaan, Conn.: The Information Economics Press, 1990): 97–160, 246–252, 259–261.

13. Cortada, *The Computer in the United States*, 112–116.

14. Strassmann, *The Business Value of Computers*, passim.

15. Most instructive on industry perspectives is Michael E. Porter, *Competitive Strategy: Techniques for Analyzing Industries and Competitors* (New York: Free Press, 1980) and for comparisons of industries across nations, his *The Competitive Advantage of Nations* (New York: Free Press, 1990). Benchmarking of a strategic nature is well covered by Gregory H. Watson, *Strategic Benchmarking: How to Rate Your Company's Performance Against the World's Best* (New York: John Wiley & Sons, 1993). The best example of a business executive's perspective is by Thomas J. Watson, Jr., *Father, Son & Co.: My Life at IBM and Beyond* (New York: Bantam, 1990).

16. The literature is vast; however, for a sense of the logic see John Diebold, *The World of the Computer* (New York: Random House, 1973): 86–94.

17. In the 1970s and 1980s I worked in the IBM sales office closest to AT&T in New Jersey. Every manager and sales person in that office was interviewed by AT&T; 12 people went to the phone company. In 1981 over 50 IBM managers in the New York area were recruited into AT&T.

18. The subject has hardly been touched by historians. One of the few studies—and not a comprehensive one—on the topic is Stephen G. Nash (ed.), *A History of Scientific Computing* (New York: ACM Press, 1990).

19. For insight on early scientific uses of computing see Herman H. Goldstine, *The Computer from Pascal to von Neumann* (Princeton, N.J.: Princeton University Press, 1972).

20. Ibid.; but also, as an example, Bruce I. Blum and Karen Duncan (eds.), *A History of Medical Informatics* (New York: ACM Press, 1990).

21. Lists of such interviews are beginning to make their way into the Internet. For example, the Charles Babbage Institute has its own page in the Internet with finding aids to these research materials.

22. For various listings of these studies, see Cortada, *Second Bibliographic Guide*, passim. Also see notes in Chapter 8.

23. See Chapter 8 for details.

24. Gregory M. Bounds, Gregory H. Dobbins, and Oscar S. Fowler, *Management: A Total Quality Perspective* (Cincinnati: South-Western, 1995): 60, 115, 116, 437, 517.

25. Higher education in the United States has increasingly come under attack for not adopting modern management methods. For a recent, well-informed study of the problem, see Stan Davis and Jim Botkin, *The Monster Under the Bed* (New York: Simon and Schuster, 1994), which also includes many comments on the role of information processing in this industry.

26. A good introduction is by Raymond L. Manganelli and Mark M. Klein, *The Reengineering Handbook: A Step-by-Step Guide to Business Transformation* (New York: AMACOM, 1994).

27. The clearest explanation of this is by Brian L. Joiner, *Fourth Generation Management* (New York: McGraw-Hill, 1994).

28. For a comparison of the Baldrige and ISO 9000, see the essay written by Curt W. Reimann, head administrator of the Baldrige Award, and his colleague, Harry S. Hertz, "The Malcolm Baldrige National Quality Award and ISO 9000 Registration: Understand-

ing Their Many Important Differences,'' in Cortada and Woods, *The Quality Yearbook, 1994 Edition* (New York: McGraw-Hill, 1994): 611–627; includes bibliography.

29. To single out one example of many that has many errors of fact and judgment, and written by a member of the information processing industry, is R. Moreau, *The Computer Comes of Age: The People, the Hardware, and the Software* (Cambrige, Mass.: MIT Press, 1984).

30. Watson, Jr., *Father, Son & Co.*

31. Chandler's prize-winning book is *The Visible Hand: The Managerial Revolution in American Business* (Cambridge, Mass.: Harvard University Press, 1977).

32. Examples include Paul A. Strassmann, *Information Payoff: The Transformation of Work in the Electronic Age* (New York: Free Press, 1985); Katharine Davis Fishman, *The Computer Establishment* (New York: Harper & Row, 1981); Paul Carroll, *Big Blues: The Unmaking of IBM* (New York: Crown, 1993); and Charles H. Ferguson and Charles R. Morris, *Computer Wars: How the West Can Win in a Post-IBM World* (New York: Times Books, 1993).

33. G. Daniels, ''The Big Questions in The History of American Technology,'' *Technology and Culture* 11 (1970): 1–21.

34. Arthur L. Norberg, ''Another Impact of the Computer: The History of Computing,'' *IEEE Transactions on Education* E-27, no. 4 (1984): 197–203.

35. Michael S. Mahoney, ''The History of Computing in the History of Technology,'' *Annals of the History of Computing* 10, no. 2 (1988): 113–125.

5

Commercial Applications of the Digital Computer in American Corporations, 1945–1995

On the occasion of the fiftieth anniversary of the arrival of the digital computer, it is difficult to imagine a time when such computers did not exist, when paychecks were produced on other types of office machines or were handwritten, when invoices were often typed, and accounting records were historical records produced often six to twelve weeks after the events they documented. Yet we have gone from no commercial uses of computers in the mid-1940s to a situation where, in the mid-1990s, companies spend over $600 billion each year on computers and software,[1] functioning within an economy in which between 70 and 85 percent of all workers rely on such technology directly or indirectly to get their work done.[2] We went from a handful of experimental machines in the 1940s to the annual sale of tens of millions of digital computers (mostly PCs) in the mid-1990s. By any measure, the story of the digital computer is profoundly important not only for the history of technology, but even more so for the history of late twentieth-century national economies and businesses.

The biggest users of digital computers became commercial enterprises. While the earliest were universities and government agencies, by the end of the 1950s businesses also installed machines in quantity. By the end of the next decade, the largest segment of the user community was comprised of businesses, and it has remained so to the present.[3] Internal IBM marketing studies throughout the period documented the rate of penetration, suggesting that by the end of the 1980s, well over 70 percent of all commercial enterprises with 50 or more employees in the United States relied on digital computing *in-house* while in Western Europe the figure surpassed 40 percent.[4]

There are three lines of historical development which account for the acceptance of digital computing. First, there was the invention of and continuous improvement in the reliability, function, and economics of digital computing—the topic which has most interested historians of computing.[5] Second, there were the activities of companies which either existed or came into being capable of manufacturing, selling, and supporting the use of digital computers—the subject which has most recently begun to draw the attention of historians.[6] Third was the adoption of computers by commercial enterprises for performing their daily chores—the subject least studied by historians but which may ultimately be the most important of the three to explore over the next decade.[7]

Without the use of digital computers in business processes, computers would simply not have become as pervasive as they did. Commercial applications provided computer vendors with the economic wherewithal to build and sell more machines. Customers provided economic incentives and demands for additional function that motivated computer designers to provide newer, different, faster, cheaper, and more reliable devices and software.

The story of the computer is the history of the continuous interaction among the three lines of historical development, with no one element operating in isolation from the others. Historians have usually found it more convenient to describe one line of development to the virtual exclusion of the others. Histories of how computers were developed, and descriptions of their functions, are numerous. Other historians have looked at the companies that manufactured and sold such devices. Commercial uses of the computer remain a virtual desert of historiography and yet without an appreciation of what these machines were used for and why, the full story of the digital computer cannot be understood.[8]

The purpose of this chapter is to identify in the briefest of terms some of the major trends in the commercial use of digital computers over the past half-century, suggesting lines for future investigation. My focus will be primarily on the experience of businesses in the United States, where use of digital computing in a commercial setting occurred first and most extensively. Europe's pattern of adoption, while similar to that observed in the United States, lagged by five to seven years. Thus a quick look at how computers were used suggests that the history of the digital computer is at least every bit as much a business story as it is a tale of technological evolution. I will not look at engineering or scientific applications per se, even though they also existed in businesses, because over time they represented a smaller portion of the computing pie than did commercial applications (e.g., accounting and customer service).

The history of commercial uses of digital computers can conveniently be subdivided into four historical periods which are remarkably distinct, even though patterns of use from an earlier period survived in subsequent years. The introduction of new machines and software makes it possible to divide commercial applications into precise historical periods because the installation of new devices encouraged either further dependence on these machines or the implementation of new uses. The four historical periods proposed for the history of commercial applications are:

- introduction of computers, 1945–1952
- initial implementation of computers, 1952–1965
- era of major adoption in business, 1965–1981
- extensive implementation to all corners of business, 1981–1995

BUSINESSES MEET THE COMPUTER, 1945–1952

In this period, neither corporations in the United States or Europe, nor government and university computer users, applied digital computing to traditional business applications, such as accounting or inventory control. Rather, they became aware of the existence of the digital computer, began to study its potential, and used them (under government contracts) to perform very narrow-based engineering and scientific applications. Commercial uses were nonexistent, the exception being engineering applications within defense-related firms. Accounting functions were still performed using bookkeeping machines and punched card tabulating systems.[9]

The ENIAC began the process of awareness, particularly in the United States, as articles on the device began to appear in the second half of the 1940s.[10] Scientific and engineering journals began discussing the new technology in the same period, making it possible for large corporations to begin the process of disseminating within their enterprises knowledge about the new machines and their potential.[11] Aircraft manufacturing firms and electronic component manufacturers first, and later large banks and insurance companies, learned of this technology mainly through publications, later from vendors. In the period 1945 through 1952, between 180 and 225 magazine and journal articles on digital computers were published in the United States, a number which doubled in the subsequent three years.[12] Influential business journals did not begin to publish on the digital computer until the end of this first phase. For instance, the *Harvard Business Review* published its first article about computers in the September-October 1952 issue; its first article on the application of digital computers in commercial settings did not appear until the November-December 1953 issue.[13] Mainly published were articles concerning scientific or engineering uses of digital computers in this period.[14]

The story of how various large corporations came to learn about the digital computer through government-sponsored projects is well known. Suffice it to point out three trends that historians have identified in this period as significant. First, electronics and office supply companies did development work on such devices at the behest of the American and British governments.[15] Major participants included GE, RCA, IBM, NCR, Burroughs, and Boeing, to mention a few. That experience injected into these companies and their sub-contractors some awareness of how to use the machines.

However, businesses did not see the economic advantage of applying digital computers in commercial applications in this period. An internal report at General Electric, written in 1952, illustrates the widely held view in business concerning this new technology. In essence it reported that computers had a long way to go despite their enormous potential. The irony of this report is that it was written at the exact moment that GE was installing its first digital computer intended for commercial applications. While it cataloged a large list of technical problems associated with the lack of functionality, reliability, and capacity, it did note that "The computer is so much faster at routine computational work" and that "the inherent speed also makes it possible to test a variety of assumptions."[16] This same report began to inventory, however, the obvious possible commercial applications for the new technology: when direct labor in handling information could be reduced, when indirect labor could be eliminated, when "what if" analysis could be performed.[17] Already at this point a common theme evident throughout the next four decades had appeared—using the computer to reduce the labor content of commercial work.

In short, commercial application of these machines did not exist. Scientific and engineering applications, funded by government contracts, occurred in over twenty instances in this period in the United States. Machines were highly experimental, one-of-a-kind. Digital machines first appeared as a commercial application in the second period.

COMPUTERS COME TO COMMERCE, 1952–1965

The year 1952 is as good a date as any for declaring that commercial applications began to appear on digital computers, although, as already noted, business interest in this technology dated back to the end of World War II. In 1952 GE installed a digital computer in its Lexington, Ky., appliance manufacturing facility and, over the next half dozen years, loaded it up with a variety of applications associated with inventory control, shop floor scheduling, and related manufacturing processes.[18]

By the early to mid-1950s, digital computing technology had reached a point where businesses were willing to adopt it. Three fundamental conditions had been met by the new technology:

- It performed reliably enough so that it was more attractive than such predecessor equipment as punch card devices.

- While very expensive, the economic benefits usually appeared to managers of the day to outweigh the costs, even though the expenses of installation were normally underestimated while the prestige of having a computer was overrated.

- Computer systems now had enough capacity to perform commercial applications: central processing unit (CPU) power, memory, channel speeds, and input/output compatibility with previous technologies (e.g., punch card machines and printers).

Improvements in performance, reliability, capacity, and costs continued unabated throughout the 1950s and 1960s despite enormous problems to overcome in how software worked, programming occurred, and systems balanced to improve throughput. The degree of improvements proved substantial. Using the cost of computer horsepower as an example, the expense of CPU power declined between 22 and 26 percent each year, depending upon whose calculations you use.[19] Because of these improvements, it became increasingly possible to apply this technology to commercial applications. That is why digital computers became very attractive as the decade of the 1950s progressed.

Evidence is rapidly mounting that the breath of commercial applications installed in the 1950s and early 1960s was greater than previously supposed. Furthermore, the same evidence suggests that the number of these far exceeded what historians might have believed a decade ago.[20] To a large extent in this period, companies that already were extensive users of punch card equipment were the first to apply digital computers.

So what were the earliest applications?

Accounting

An early candidate was a variety of accounting applications, a natural outgrowth of such applications on earlier information processing technologies. These included calculation of financial statements, purchase control, payroll accounting, accounts payable, billing, accounts receivable, sales analysis, and inventory costs.[21] So much was moved to digital computers that, by the late 1950s, the accounting profession, and more specifically auditors, had to develop a new set of auditing practices to monitor computer-based accounting applications.[22]

A casual reading of the major accounting journals of the period 1954–1965 suggests that accountants were changing profoundly how they performed their work in corporations, due largely to the digital computer. Historians of accounting have confirmed that accountants did adopt the computer, attracted by its calculating capacity, and over the next two decades began to modify basic accounting practices to take advantage of the speed and capacity of computers. In fact, by the end of the 1970s, traditional accounting practices came under attack precisely because the computer was providing more current information. Therefore, monthly and quarterly accounting reports increasingly became a hindrance to businesses now used to having information hourly, daily, or weekly in other operational functions (e.g., unit counts of things made).[23]

Banking

A second area of activity concerned a wide range of banking applications. All through the 1950s, the industry did historically significant work on standardizing check formats using magnetic ink character recognition. While that was the most important computer-related project underway in this industry during the 1950s, and a story well documented, we need not be detained here.[24] Suffice it to say that what made it important is that this industry sought to standardize check formats while using computers to read data on them and was able to get this accomplished. To this day, the decisions and actions taken have governed how checks look and are processed. However, banks aggressively went after other applications as well. They worked on deposit slip applications, credit card processing, online savings and loan functions, and checking and saving account management.[25] Large commercial banks were the first to move in this direction while smaller ones held back, waiting for smaller machines and less expense, even as late as 1964.[26]

Insurance

This was an American industry with a long history of using advanced information-handling technologies. It was an industry that had many large companies and very labor-intensive data handling. Therefore, it should be expected that insurance companies would not be absent from the wave of automation taking place in the 1950s and 1960s. This industry's burden of very large data-entry and data-handling problems gave it solid economic incentive to explore better ways of doing important daily information processing. It constantly sought less expensive and faster ways to get data into machine-readable form and, by the mid-1950s, that meant into computers so that companies could handle this information more effectively. That hunt for productive ways of manipulating information has continued to the present. A variety of applications began to appear, such as optical character sensing for reading data and case and account management systems; also popular was the broad range of billing and accounting applications, along with actuarial calculations.[27] Of particular interest to this industry was reducing the labor content of data handling, a subject that drew much attention in these early years.[28]

Manufacturing

It should be no surprise that the largest sector in the U.S. economy, and the one with the greatest number of employees and size of firms, would have become early users of digital computers. While more will be said below concerning the degree of adoption of computer technology in many industries, suffice it to say here that they adopted the technology rapidly and extensively. One almost gets the feeling, while reading the literature of the day, that every data processing manager in manufacturing rushed to print with their account of initial installation, in the process giving historians a substantial body of material to work with. Applications involved remote transmittal of production data, shop floor data collection, production forecasting, automation of shop floor activities,

Table 5.1
Early Users of Computers in the Manufacturing Sector, 1950s–Early 1960s

Aircraft
Automobiles
Computer and Office Machine Products
Electrical and Electronic Equipment
Steel
Telephone Communications Equipment
Trucks and Busses

Source: BLS studies.

numerical control and CAD/CAM for design and manufacturing, work simplification, and production control.[29] As in insurance and banking, reducing labor content of work became a major incentive for using digital computers.[30]

Applications spread across a wide variety of manufacturing industries: automotive, aeronautics, steel, appliances, and defense being some of the more obvious. However, in a multi-decade study of the adoption of all kinds of technology conducted by the U.S. government, evidence turned up of all major segments of manufacturing adopting computers in the 1950s and early 1960s.[31] Table 5.1 lists manufacturing industries that reported extensive use of digital computers in the United States in the period 1955–1965.

Process industries, which had many applications similar to those found in discrete manufacturing, also turned to the digital computer. In addition, process industries had requirements for computing in continuous flow operations and thus were extensive users of analog devices as well. Paper manufacturing companies in both the United States and Western Europe, for instance, were early users. An industry publication, *Pulp & Paper*, reported many cases over the years.[32] Petroleum and chemical industries also turned to digital computers to help with normal accounting and industry-specific applications in the 1950s and early 1960s. Modeling flows and scheduling work in these capital-intensive industries were imperative.[33] As with manufacturing, the evidence demonstrates that installation of digital computer-based applications began in earnest after 1957 and was in full swing by the end of 1962.

Inventory Control

I began discussing applications in commercial settings with accounting and finance because they cut across over 40 industries that, at least in the United States, adopted digital computers by the early 1960s. Inventory control is another of those cross-industry applications, but it first appeared in manufacturing and process industries, then, by the end of the 1960s, existed in all sectors of both the U.S. and Western European economies. It used to be said by computer salesmen in the 1950s and 1960s that more computers were cost justified by reductions in the costs of inventory than by any other means! And there is some truth to that quip because the challenge was, and continues to be, how to keep the least amount of raw and finished goods in inventory and yet have what is needed in order to run a profitable business. For decades large companies used huge punch card tub files to track what they had and used. The digital computer represented a major improvement over tabulators and thus was applied to inventory control between the 1950s and the end of the 1970s, after which most companies had sophisticated applications in place. Extant evidence suggests that this was one of the most widespread and satisfactory of all the early uses of digital computers, something worth more study by historians.[34] This is also a computer application that developed into a discipline at the same time as accounting processes. Many managers and professors have even viewed inventory control as a branch of accounting.[35]

Retail

Other than for normal accounting applications, this industry started late in the adoption of computers, largely because most companies in this sector were—as they are today—smaller than, for example, insurance or manufacturing firms, and thus did not have the economic or application critical mass to justify installing digital computers in the 1950s and 1960s. However, many did use such devices. For example, Lake End Sales used an IBM 1440 to do order processing, as did food distributors.[36] Yet the potential for applying this technology in industry-specific applications had already been explored in the early 1950s, yet had to wait for a time when the economics of the computer were right for this industry; this occurred at the start of the 1970s.[37]

Other service industries did not show up in my surveys of applications as significant. Absent in the 1950s, and just starting to use digital computers by the mid-1960s, were trucking firms, although airlines and railroads were aggressive users; private hospitals (most were public institutions) used them for some accounting; and they were used a little in movie making and distribution. They were used extensively, however, by major radio and television broadcasters in the United States.

Why Used

Large companies normally commissioned studies on the potentials of the new technology, visited other users, and worked with vendors to configure, cost justify, and implement applications. Three reasons typically justified use of digital computers:

- They reduced significantly labor content of some activity (e.g., data entry).
- They made possible lower operating overhead (e.g., cost of inventory).
- They led to more effective performance of work (e.g., modeling production schedules in manufacturing). Other reasons included the prestige of being seen as "modern" because of the company's use of this technology, or the ability to handle much larger volumes of work than was possible before. In some cases, new applications became practical (e.g., in engineering and design).[38] These reasons applied across the entire U.S. economy. We still have little data on what applications were used on digital computers in Western Europe. One important study done on four Dutch companies covering many decades suggests convincingly that the pattern of adoption was very similar in Europe. The one major difference uncovered by this study is that such application began several years later than in the United States.[39] Sales of computers in Europe confirm the later start.[40]

DIGITAL COMPUTERS BECOME PART OF THE CORPORATE SCENE, 1965–1981

It is in the period roughly from the mid-1960s to the late 1970s-early 1980s that the digital computer becomes almost the premier icon of late twentieth-century society. During these years, for example, all the Fortune 1000 companies became users of digital computing; a paycheck in almost any company in the United States having 50 or more employees was prepared by a computer; and the forms of computing that we are familiar with today were initially released.

What caused this huge and rapid explosion in the use of digital computing? The economists have argued that the cost of computing continued to decline, making the technology attractive. Indeed, costs dropped at a rate of between 22 and 28 percent a year, citing both the actual cost of technology and the similar expansion of the sales volumes of information products vendors (also in the range of 22 to 28 percent in the 1960s, but much lower in the 1970s).[41] There was also, to be sure, an economic "turnpiking effect" at work. This is the effect of lowering costs for a function, making it more attractive to a broader range of potential users or to existing ones who now felt inclined to use more computers and related I/O equipment.

A second explanation was provided by those who spoke of technological imperatives—that is to say, they argued that computers became more reliable, bigger, faster, and easier to use, describing what amounted to another variant of the "turnpiking effect."[42] Their case is more compelling than that of the economists for two reasons. First, in April 1964, IBM introduced over 150 new products with its announcement of the S/360 family of computers, soon followed by similar introductions by its competitors. What made the S/360 attractive from the perspective of business applications was the fact that certain technological components of the system could handle larger amounts of data (the new disk drives for example), and permit the potential of more multi-processing (e.g., the new operating systems OS and DOS).

Second, and also very important, was the possibility of migrating to larger computers (when capacity requirements called for this) without the horribly expensive, hair-pulling experiences that data processing managers underwent in the late 1950s and early 1960s when they migrated to different computers. In fact, this point—the availability of a migration path—has been almost totally ignored by historians of computers as a critical point of attraction of third-generation computing to that community most involved in the decision to acquire new machines—the data processing manager. Yet the extant published literature of the period written by these decision makers, and as also reflected in the marketing documentation of the day, clearly shows without a doubt that the avoidance of conversions made third-generation computing an attractive platform.[43] The fact that this new generation of equipment was not without its problems (e.g., initial quality of operating systems) did not matter enough to slow installations of the new machines. In the case of IBM, for example, the S/360 caused a doubling of the company's revenues in less than eight years! In fact, the whole computer industry boomed.[44]

Therefore, for the history of commercial applications, while the economists are correct, their arguments were not as compelling to buyers of computers as were technical considerations. But other environmental circumstances also affected events in these years. For one thing, early users of the new computers had been successful users of second-generation systems. The huge expansion in the use of such systems as IBM's 650s, 1401s, and 1440s in the late 1950s and early 1960s, for instance, created an install base (to use a marketing term) of successful customers who needed more capacity as their applications grew in size. By the mid-1960s, when S/360s and machines from other companies were being shipped, either dependence on computing had grown—there was no turning back—or the experience had been positive enough to encourage development of additional applications.[45]

For another, the technology had undergone several significant changes that made conversion of old applications to new forms possible, along with additional applications not practical before. The two biggest technological changes involved the widespread acceptance of disk drives in which to store direct access information and the implementation of online systems. Disk drives made direct access of information possible which, in turn, made online systems practical (something virtually impossible with tape-based systems). Thus, while batch processing continued to expand all through the 1960s and 1970s, online processing grew from nearly zero in commercial environments to the preferred choice by the end of the 1970s. In other words, as the 1960s and 1970s progressed, more applications were being developed that were online rather than batch; both became possible since all computers now could handle multiprocessing with batch applications operating in background.[46] While inventories of applications that were batch versus online have yet to be made, leaving us with only impressionistic accounts from the period, the evidence suggests strongly that demand for the machines required for batch and online systems was strong.

Further, it appeared that the changeover to online systems was massive and quick because of the large numbers of terminals and disk drives installed.

Terminals—the most obvious device required for online systems—were installed in large numbers. Using U.S. dollar values to measure quantities, we see that from a negligible few millions of dollars in sales prior to 1963, there is a steady climb all through the 1960s and 1970s, with the billion-dollar mark reached in 1968, the two-billion-dollar mark achieved in 1972 (a recessionary year in the data processing industry), and sales at three billion dollars in the mid-1980s.[47]

Disk drives were also installed in large numbers as they became less expensive and more reliable. Using disk packs deployed with IBM 3330 DASD—the industry standard—as our indicator of growth in the use of this technology, we see that costs went from $1,000 each at the start of the 1970s to under $500 by the end of the decade, costs driven more by economies of scale than by competitive pressures. Disk pack sales increased through the second half of the 1960s, dipped slightly during the recessionary years of the early 1970s, and then continued to grow until the late 1970s when fixed disk technology began to make the portable disk pack obsolete.[48] Magnetic tape sales essentially remained flat from 1960 through the 1970s; their cost went down only slightly in the period, suggesting that the huge growth in machine-readable data was put on disk drives—the base technology required for online systems.[49]

What applications were implemented in the 1960s and 1970s? Did these change in type from the late 1950s/early 1960s? Several lines of evolution occurred. First, accounting and manufacturing applications, which had been the majority of application groups in the 1950s and early 1960s, continued to be implemented in more companies and across more organizations within firms. Batch systems were enhanced with online applications, while the introduction of minicomputers, particularly in manufacturing and engineering environments, contributed mightily to the expanded use of distributed processing, particularly in the second half of the 1970s for data collection, shop floor scheduling, accounting, and a variety of engineering functions.[50]

Second, something relatively new in the 1960s, and much more common in the 1970s, was a myriad of online applications that could be performed in offices. Office applications ranged from online access to accounting and financial information (developed originally in batch or online) to such inter-office functions as word processing, E-mail, and calendar management. Office applications crossed all industries in this period as one of the highest growth areas for new commercial applications.[51]

Third, a body of new applications came into being called decision-making or decision-support systems. These were both batch and online, going beyond operational research applications of the 1950s in that they were reports and online access to a wide variety of information. Unlike operations research applications of the 1950s and 1960s, which required the use of technical experts in mathematics and programming, these new decision-support systems were far simpler to execute and thus made it possible for growing numbers of people to make business decisions who had little or no understanding of OR. Some executives in the 1970s, for example, began accessing information about the financial performance of their companies on a daily basis from a terminal at their desk (often these were called executive support systems). These applications became more popular in the 1980s when the use of databases on mainframes became widespread.[52] Modeling occurred in finance, strategic planning, sales and marketing, and human resource management, to mention only a few.[53]

The one major sector of the American economy that finally waded into the world of digital computing in a very aggressive manner was retail. Declining investments in mainframe computing (as a proportion of total hardware/software expenditures) and availability of minicomputers made adoption of this technology cost-effective in this period. In addition, beginning in the mid-1960s, point-of-sale (POS) technology became available. This technology proved important to retail companies because it allowed them to capture information on sales and inventory at the store level in real-time, making possible a whole myriad of new applications (such as just-in-time buying by the late 1970s), better cash flow management (in the 1960s), and improved inventory management in all years. Other applications included optical character recognition (OCR), first in supermarkets in the 1970s and then across large sectors of American retail operations by the early 1980s, electronic data interchange (EDI) to suppliers, and of course, adoption of the Universal Product Code (UPC). Of all the industries in the American economy, perhaps no other was so delighted by the application of computers as retail because its executives had access to technologies that were specifically bent to their needs (OCR, POS) despite the fact that they had been slow to embrace digital computing in the beginning.[54]

EXTENT OF ADOPTION OF COMMERCIAL APPLICATIONS IN THE UNITED STATES

Before surveying the evolution of commercial applications in the period following the introduction of microcomputers, we have a very basic question to address: to what extent and in which industries was the digital computer adopted in the period from the mid-1950s to the end of the 1970s? While the question is very important, it also is very difficult to answer with any precision. Yet at least having a sense of the degree of deployment helps us begin defining correctly the historical significance of digital computers to American society. Fortunately, the U.S. Bureau of Labor Statistics (BLS) has conducted a number of important research projects to understand the general role of technology in the economy since the 1960s, in its attempt to understand the effects of all manner of machines (not just computers) on employment and productivity. Using this material suggests the extent of digital computing in the United States. The data leads to the unequivocal conclusion that American businesses have been aggressive adopters of all manner of technologies, not just computers. Second, the

Table 5.2
Extensive Users of Digital Computers, Mid-1970s–Early 1980s

Banking
Electric and Gas Utilities
Electrical and Electronic Equipment
Insurance
Motor Vehicles
Petroleum Refining
Petroleum Pipeline Transportation
Printing and Publishing
Pulp, Paper, Paperboard
Railroads
Steel
Telephone Communications
Tires and Inner Tubes

Source: BLS studies.

information BLS gathered makes it clear that the rate of adoption and the degree of acceptance varied widely by industry.

Table 5.2 lists those industries that the Bureau of Labor Statistics identified as extensive users of computers by the late 1970s. Surveys conducted in these industries concluded that all major companies in these industries used computers not only for normal accounting applications but also for specific manufacturing and logistical operations. In some service industries, such as banking and insurance, 100 percent of the firms were using computers in one fashion or another by the late 1970s.

Table 5.3 lists industries that the BLS concluded were moderate users of computers by the late 1970s and early 1980s. By moderate I mean most used computer services for normal accounting applications, but less than roughly 50 percent of the firms were using computers for industry-specific applications. Note that the retail industry, which in the 1990s is characterized by most observers as an extensive user of computer technology, was only just beginning to apply industry-specific applications on an aggressive basis.

Table 5.4 lists industries the BLS observed were very limited in their use of computers. Again, most used computers to perform accounting functions, particularly the larger firms within these industries, and often used other technologies extensively, but when it came to industry-specific applications, were less deployed than industries listed in the previous two tables. Again, circumstances changed over time. In this case, wholesale trade is listed as a limited user due to its cumulative action through the 1970s and early 1980s, but by the end of the 1980s, had become a very extensive user of information technology.

Table 5.3
Moderate Users of Digital Computers, Mid-1970s–Early 1980s

Aerospace
Air Transportation
Apparel
Folding Paperboard Box
Hosiery
Intercity Trucking
Metal Working Machinery
Oil and Gas Extraction
Textiles

Source: BLS studies.

Table 5.5 gives a more detailed breakdown of some moderate and all extensive users of computers by the early 1980s, showing what the major application
areas were by industry along with some comments about extent of use. In some
instances quantitative data were available, most in only narrative impressions.
Yet several observations can be drawn from these data.

First, where industry-specific uses of computers had been developed, they
generally were used first by large companies and then by smaller ones as costs
for these devices declined. Second, most of the users cataloged in Table 5.5 are
in manufacturing industries because that is where the largest percent of employees were in the economy; recall that a primary reason for using automation
tools was to reduce labor content in work to improve productivity. Third, the
table assumes that most if not all companies of moderate to large size used
computers for some or all of their basic accounting functions (e.g., payroll,
accounts receivable and payables, general ledger, and financial reporting).

Fourth, adoption of digital computers varied in rate of installation and extent
of deployment by industry. In other words, some were quicker to use computers
than others. A related observation, variously made by BLS researchers over a
period of a decade, is that larger firms within an industry used computers sooner
and more extensively than other companies. The breadth of implementations
simply calls out the need for additional scholarly attention to the history of
applications *by industry*.

Service sector companies required less industry-specific configurations of digital computing to perform many core applications (e.g., case load management
in insurance, checking account management in banking) yet also had specific
industry-related devices (e.g., POS in retail, ATMs in banking) just like manufacturing had some unique devices (e.g., numerical control (N/C) and CAD/
CAM). All of these industry-specific technologies and applications were initially
developed in the 1960s and were in relatively wide use by the end of the 1970s.

Table 5.4
Limited Users of Digital Computers, Mid-1970s–Early 1980s

Aluminum
Bakery Products
Coal Mining
Concrete Manufacturing
Copper Ore Mining
Fabricated Structural Metal
Foot Wear
Hydraulic Cement
Laundry and Cleaning
Lumber and Wood
Meat Products
Water Transportation
Wholesale Trade

Source: BLS studies.

What is remarkable in reading the industry literature and in analyzing the nearly two-dozen BLS reports covering almost 40 industries is the speed with which digital computers were adopted for such a broad array of applications—going from a few industries leading the pack in the late 1950s (aerospace, computer manufacturers, banking, and insurance) to more than fifteen major industries falling into that category by the end of the 1970s (and probably by the very early 1970s).

The industries examined covered all the largest segments of the manufacturing and service sectors within the economy; they continue to be studied by the BLS. The data presented in this agency's reports, and very briefly summarized in the tables above, also reflect the cumulative introduction of computers throughout the period of the 1950s through the early 1980s. For example, if tire and inner tube manufacturers used computer-based testing and inspection in 80 percent of their plants, these were installed plant-by-plant over a long period of time, not in the year of the survey. So what we see is a steady, fairly massive diffusion of digital technology across a wide spectrum of American industry, penetrating all corners of the economy within one generation of employees. Thus a 21-year-old worker entering the labor force in 1955 would, by the age of 45, while ostensibly only midway through his or her working career, find computers everywhere. And that was before the broad adoption of microcomputers in the mainstream of the American economy!

The BLS material also suggests why this technology was embraced, suggesting part of the answer for why some industries were quicker or slower, or more thorough and broader, in their use of digital computers. Already suggested was one answer: the availability of industry-specific computing equipment, such as

Table 5.5
Applications and Diffusion by Industry, Mid-1970s–Early 1980s

Industry	Applications	Diffusion
Aerospace	manufacturing processes, N/C, DNC, CAD/CAM	9% of machine tools used N/C in 1983; 8% in missile industry; in large plants only; CAD/CAM extensive
Apparel	laser cutting, N/C, inventory	moderate (297 CPUs installed late 1970s)
Banking	all major functions, EFT, check processing, ATM	97% of all banks used CPUs in 1984; 21% in 1965; 2,000 ATMs in 1973, 60,000 in 1984
Electrical & Electronic Equip.	design & manufacture of all products	extensive
Electricity & Gas Utilities	extensive of analog & digital for energy mgmt, gas leak control, billing, meter reading	extensive
Hosiery	knitting, prpoduction processes	56% of machines driven by microprocessors by 1980, 36% by 1975; extensive use of microprocesses
Hydraulic cement	cement production, shipping	extensive in production, moderate in shipping apps.
Insurance	almost all functions, actuarial, billing, claims, underwriting, A/R rate & billing accounting, scheduling	extensive, all companies
Intercity Trucking		CPUs used by over 900 carriers, nearly all Class I carriers, growing in Class II companies moderate, more in newer facilities
Lumber & Wood	saw mill, plywood, millwork & cabinet operations (e.g., sawing.)	
Metalworking machinery	N/C, CAD/CAM	3% of all machine tools N/C driven; uses 30% of all machine tools in USA; CPUs moderately deployed
Motor Vehicles	CAD/CAM, manufacturing processes, robotics	in general use by all manufacturers; used 30% of all US robots

174

Industry	Applications	Usage
Petroleum Pipeline Transp.	highly automated processes for logistics, inventory	22% used CPUs in 1971
Petroleum Refining	monitoring & controlling refinery operations (analog too)	25% of all refineries by 1979 constituting 66% of industry crude capacity
Printing & publishing	composition & typesetting for newspapers, magazines, books; OCR & scanners	extensive, especially newspapers with 2,000 systems by 1979; limited OCR usage
Pulp, Paper, Paperboard	all production processes, materials handling, storage	extensive; 10% of all US process control equipment is in this industry; broadly diffused except for automated warehouse applications
Railroads	controlling car speeds, switching, traffic trend analysis, traffic control	extensive; 20% of all track CPU controlled; over 250 CPUs by 1974
Retail	store applications, POS, supermarket automation, EDI	extensive in large firms; 1 out of every 300 stores had CPU services in 1974, 1 out of 400 in 1968
Steel	production applications, also extensive analog computers used	extensive in hot strip rolling mills & blast furnaces; extensive use of 2nd generation CPUs
Telephone Communications	telephone switching, customer billing, line testing	extensive in all areas
Textiles	process control to operate machinery, computer-controlled production, materials handling	extensive in large plants
Tires & Inner Tubes	microprocessors in manufacturing, testing & inspection, CAD	extensive in manufacturing (10-20% of radial tire capacity); in 80% of all plants for testing & inspection; 75% of all design is done with CAD
Tranportation, Air	all aspects of design, manufacture, navigation & surveillance; automated airport terminal services	moderate to extensive; very limited airport services

Source: BLS studies.

175

Table 5.6
Reasons for Using Computers in Non-Manufacturing Industries, 1960–1980

Industry	Reasons
Banking	labor efficiency, new customer services, complexity of tasks
Electric & Gas Utilities	reduce labor requirements, improve service reliability
Insurance	paperwork productivity, vast data storage & retrieval operations
Petroleum Refining	lower operating costs, improve product quality, labor productivity
Petroleum Pipeline Transportation	efficiency & volume of operations (e.g., scheduling)
Printing & Publishing	applications, improved labor productivity
Railroads	reduce labor requirements, improve maintenance productivity, new services
Telephone Communications	increase service levels, labor & process productivity, reduce labor requirements

Source: BLS studies.

point-of-sale terminals for retail or ATMs in banking. But as Tables 5.6 and 5.7 suggest, just drawing on data gathered for the most extensive users of digital computers, other reasons were involved, which cut across all industries. The one nobody was willing to admit was the prestige of having a computer, probably because that was more of a consideration in the 1950s than in subsequent years. Furthermore, we have no data to suggest the extent of the consideration of prestige, but we can reasonably conclude that no company would spend millions of dollars on data processing just for reasons of prestige. Therefore, reasons cited in these tables are probably the primary ones for why computers were installed.

MICROCOMPUTERS, THE NEW DIGITAL COMPUTER, 1981–1995

While the digital computer is now 50 years old, we must acknowledge yet another anniversary: microcomputers, which have been around for twenty years! And yet they seem fresh, the new arrival in the information processing industry. To a large extent that sense of newness lies in the fact that for many people the PC was their introduction to computing. Even as I write these words, thousands of people each month acquire PCs for the first time, placing themselves (in

Table 5.7
Reasons for Using Computers in Manufacturing Industries, 1960–1980

Industry	Reasons
Electrical & Electronic Equipment	speed & capacity, employee productivity, control production processes
Motor Vehicles	reduce labor content, increase productivity, improve quality
Pulp, Paper, Paperboard	speed & capacity, employee productivity, control production processes
Steel	reduce labor costs, reduce raw material & energy costs, product quality
Tires & Inner Tubes	produict quality/complexity, labor productivity

Source: BLS studies.

effect) in the same circumstance of being on a technological frontier as did the programmers and the systems analysts who installed their first computers in the 1950s and early 1960s.

For purposes of this essay, let us separate home and school use from commercial uses of computers. Without delving into the rich history of PCs, suffice it to point out that while they were invented in the 1970s, and were first used by individuals enamored with this technology, they were not used widely in commercial settings until the early 1980s. Thus for our purposes the microcomputer, as the latest version of digital computers, became historically relevant in the 1980s. At the risk of being IBM-centric, they were not taken seriously by the business community in the United States until IBM entered the microcomputer market with the announcement of its first "Personal Computer" (an IBM-coined phrase) in August 1981. With that action, as commentators of the period noted, microcomputers were legitimated for commercial applications because of the "approval" of the leading hardware vendor.[55] In fact, microcomputers had already started to appear in commercial settings before IBM brought out the PC. IBM was simply responding to a new market for computing products and had to rush quickly to establish a marketing presence or lose the opportunity, much like it had to rush into the market for mainframes in the mid-1950s or forever be left behind.[56]

But first, a few facts document the arrival of the PC (I use the term PC to refer to all brands of microcomputers, not just IBM's). In 1981, 344,000 PCs were sold to businesses; the following year the number jumped to 926,000; in 1983 it exceeded 1.5 million. Growth in shipments continued to rise: nearly 2.4 million in 1984 and 3.3 million in 1985. Thus, within the first five years of significant adoption of these devices by businesses, nearly 7 million were in-

Table 5.8
Business Uses of PCs, 1980s

Accounting
Credit analysis
Database management
Financial analysis
Inventory control
Purchasing
Word processing
Other

stalled. Growth rates continued to rise each year through the next decade, bringing the population of these devices into the tens of millions! Today, we are also witnessing what may appear as the end of "dumb" desktop terminals (e.g., such as the IBM 3278 and 3279) which are being displaced by PCs.[57]

By the mid-1980s it was also becoming more obvious what size organizations were buying these machines: About a third of the firms with between 20 and 99 employees used these devices; nearly half in companies of between 100 and 500 employees; 72 percent of companies of between 500 and 1,000 employees, and 85 percent of companies that were larger.[58] The reason for pointing out these statistics is to demonstrate that the PC was penetrating all sizes of organizations. Second, the larger the institution, the more likely it was to have some PCs installed. In short, much like the experience with large digital mainframes of the 1950s, it was the large companies that first experimented with the new technology. It was many years before their acceptance was nearly total (invented in the mid-1970s, but not shipped in significant volumes until the early 1980s). In fact, the total number of units shipped in the United States to all industries (commercial and otherwise) were quite low in the early years: an estimated 20,000 in 1978 and 1979 each, 70,000 in 1980, bringing the total number of existing machines at the end of 1980 to 120,000, not a large number given the tens of millions that would exist a decade later.[59]

Table 5.8 displays the results of a survey done in 1985 answering the question: What were the business uses of PCs in 1983 and 1985, the years when companies finally concluded that this technology should be embraced and deployed rapidly? Coincidentally, the list of applications (with the exception of word processing) could have been produced for mainframe users of the late 1950s or early 1960s! The word processing exception can be accounted for by recognizing that typewriters could be displaced with typing software that was more flexible in function than a typewriter, an experience borne out by earlier word processing packages that had run on mainframes since universities like the Massachusetts Institute of Technology (MIT) developed online interactive systems in the 1950s.

While the application mix did not change fundamentally during the 1980s and early 1990s, the extent of adoption did. In a survey of IEEE *Spectrum* subscribers done in 1992, 91 percent of this technical community used PCs for scientific and engineering applications, graphics, and digital simulation. The most widely used tools were simple business software packages.[60] In another survey done that same year of 100 information systems managers from Fortune 1000 companies, investigators learned that 45 percent were shifting their users to PC-based environments. In a related study conducted by Internal Data Corporation (IDC) on a different IS management population, 45 percent said that in addition to PC-based platforms, they were going to continue concurrent use of digital mainframe environments.[61] The largest shift in functionality that occurred with PCs in the early 1990s was the networking of stand-alone systems into LANS and other networked configurations in all industries.[62]

Over the past three years yet another change occurred in the application of digital computing: mobility. All during the 1980s microcomputers remained essentially the same physical size, while their capacities and functions increased. But during the early 1990s, the physical size of these machines began to shrink in weight, from dozens of pounds to laptops of under 6 pounds, while functionality, capacity, and price performance continued to improve. The result was a shift to PCs that could be moved around with employees wherever they went— hence the notion of work mobility, which became so attractive by 1994–1995. Armed with telecommunications capability and large data storage, applications could now be performed outside the office. In addition to the traditional applications cited in Table 5.8, new ones could be performed. These included: access to mainframe data bases, product demonstrations (using graphics and video), order taking and transmission real-time in a customer's office, pen-based systems for data capture and transmittal (e.g., information on gas leaks in streets and writing speeding tickets), and faxing.[63]

The most visible of the early mobile workers to receive portable PCs were salesmen. There are more than 17 million of them in the United States. By 1991 this segment of workers, who traditionally had not used PCs in the 1980s, rapidly adopted them. As early as 1992 the reasons why became apparent: 255 sales people were surveyed in one instance, reporting that their use of PCs improved sales productivity by 25 percent, largely driven by the use of account handling and customer relations applications. Laptop usage climbed for this group from 36.2 percent in 1990 to over 50 percent in one year. This population, in 65 percent of the cases, accessed mainframe data bases on a routine basis using PCs.[64] Major sales organizations had equipped nearly 100 percent of their sales personnel with laptops by the end of 1994. For example, IBM's entire sales force worldwide used laptops. It had become standard operating procedure by the mid-1990s for sales forces selling industrial goods to use laptops regardless of what industry they worked in.[65] The same held true for most management consultants.

On this, the fiftieth anniversary of the arrival of digital computing, the technology continues to shrink with the arrival of "palm" computers which made their first appearance in 1992–1993 as digital calendars and for storing telephone lists. They rapidly expanded to provide additional applications such as E-mail, telephone communications, fax, and access to databases.[66] Even I/O had shrunk: portable HP printers the size of briefcases and similarly small tape and auxiliary hard drives for PCs.

CONCLUSION

What are the major lessons to be learned about digital computing in the commercial environment? What yet needs to be studied? For the historian digital computing is a wonderful example of a new and practical tool which rapidly made its way through the economy. At each new technological turn in the road, the technology was studied first before being adopted, and it always had to perform better and for less cost than its predecessor. But once deployed, users found new uses for digital computers not obvious at the time of acquisition. The adoption and use of digital computers followed very much the same pattern evident for other, non-computer technologies.[67] It also took about the same number of decades to permeate thoroughly the American economy as had other technologies such as radio, television, aircraft, and even electricity.[68]

Decisions to acquire various generations of technology essentially followed a similar pattern. First, information processing and technical management needed to learn about the new devices, whether in the 1950s with first-generation computing or in the 1970s with third-generation machines. Then, in the days of the PC, it was typically a technical constituency that initially looked at the new technology in much the same way, trying to understand its capabilities, comparing it against existing technologies, and then making acquisitions. In the case of PCs there was one difference to note: Most decisions to acquire made in the first decade of the device's existence were made by end users, not the data processing establishment, while the vast majority of mainframe decisions were made by the data processing organization.

In fact, a story yet to be documented by historians involves the political battles waged by data processing management in the 1980s to keep PCs out of corporate America because they posed a threat to the established data processing organizations and mainframe applications! By the late 1980s, data processing management had lost the battle, and was being ordered to network PCs, and to provide their insights on how to acquire, support, and apply this new variant of the digital computer.

Historians have yet to participate in the ongoing debate underway within the information processing community and among economists concerning the value of digital computing. Did commercial users of digital computers get their money's worth? It is a very important question that has yet to be answered. The issues are complicated, the analysis very technical and elaborate, and the debate one with a long history dating back to the days of the ENIAC.[69] Regardless of how the debate wanders in the years to come, the fact remains that by the start of the 1970s, it had become impossible for any commercial enterprise of over 50 employees to function competitively in the United States without using computers. They could not pay people, file tax information, bill customers, or manufacture products without these systems. And, as David F. Noble has so clearly demonstrated, certain lines of business could not even be entertained without the use of these machines (e.g., wing designs using CAD/CAM for U.S. military aircraft).[70] In short, the digital computer had become central to the functioning of American business.

But historians have other issues yet to face. We do not have a clear picture of how all these machines were used. Hopefully this chapter has demonstrated that looking at applications by industry suggests more than what machines were used for—rather, what they did to alter the complexity and course of events within industries. What we do know is that the commercial applications clustered around operational issues, which is why the studies should be industry specific. In addition, besides the issue of benefits derived, we know almost as little about the costs expended. These varied by industry and application, making the historical issues to be resolved complicated. Finally, there is the whole concern of how this technology was implemented and managed. We went from a data processing community of several thousand in the early 1950s[71] to one in the mid-1990s that boasted several million (a million alone just writing software products)—a large growth of many new professions derived directly from the existence of the digital computer.[72]

Turning an important thrust of this chapter's focus upside down—from looking at what made installation of commercial applications possible to what held them back—we could also ask: What prevented an even further dissimination of digital computing? All through the period from the early 1950s to the present, industry observers have commented on the lack of adequate numbers of programmers, computer literate end users, and so forth. Were skills a constraint or, as the technologists and economists argue, was progress impeded by the speed of introduction of new technical innovations? We simply do not have a good understanding of what might have been.[73] What we can be certain of, however, is that the constraints were not enough to keep the digital computer from becoming an icon for the late twentieth century or from clearly being the most important tool adopted by American industry in this century.

NOTES

1. On information processing industry structure and size, see James W. Cortada, ''An Introduction to the History of the Data Processing Industry,'' in his *Historical Dictionary of Data Processing* (Westport, Conn.: Greenwood Press, 1987): 1–44; on what is driving these expenditures see Norman Weizer et al., *The Arthur D. Little Forecast on Information Technology and Productivity: Making the Integrated Enterprise Work* (New York: John Wiley & Sons, 1991).

2. James W. Cortada, *TQM for Information Systems Management: Quality Practices for Continuous Improvement* (New York: McGraw-Hill, 1995): 1–18.

3. Tom Forester (ed.), *The Information Technology Revolution* (Cambridge, Mass: MIT Press, 1985) contains a collection of essays that also discuss who were the users of this technology.

4. Papers in the author's possession. Developed annually all through the 1960s–1980s, these were marketing estimates of market shares and opportunity.

5. For an introduction to this literature see Michael R. Williams, *A History of Computing Technology* (Englewood Cliffs, N.J.: Prentice-Hall, 1985) and Paul E. Ceruzzi, *Reckoners: The Prehistory of the Digital Computer, from Relays to the Stored Program Concept, 1935–1945* (Westport, Conn: Greenwood Press, 1983).

6. For example, James W. Cortada, *Before the Computer: IBM, NCR, Burroughs, and Remington Rand and the Industry They Created, 1865–1956* (Princeton, N.J.: Princeton University Press, 1993) and Martin Campbell-Kelly, *ICL: A Business and Technical History* (Oxford: Oxford University Press, 1989).

7. For the literature, see James W. Cortada, *A Bibliographic Guide to the History of Computing, Computers, and the Information Processing Industry* (Westport, Conn.: Greenwood Press, 1990): 396–491, and its sequel, *Second Bibliographic Guide to the History of Computing, Computers and the Information Processing Industry* (Westport, Conn.: Greenwood Press, 1996).

8. The models are Charles J. Bashe et al., *IBM's Early Computers* (Cambridge, Mass: MIT Press, 1986) and Emerson W. Pugh, Lyle R. Johnson, and John H. Palmer, *IBM's 360 and Early 370 Systems* (Cambridge, Mass: MIT Press, 1991).

9. James W. Cortada, *The Computer In the United States: From Laboratory to Market, 1930–1960*, (Armonk, N.Y., M. E. Sharpe, 1993): 107–124.

10. For example, see, "Answers by ENY; Electronic Numerical Integrator and Computer, ENIAC," *Newsweek* (February 18, 1946): 76; J. G. Brainerd and T. K. Sharpless, "The ENIAC," *Electrical Engineering* 67, no. 2 (February 1948): 163–172; and "Electronic Calculator: ENIAC," *Scientific American* 174 (June 1946): 248. For a full listing see Cortada, *A Bibliographic Guide*, 224–232.

11. William Aspray, "Introduction," in *Proceedings of A Symposium on Large-Scale Digital Calculating Machinery* (Cambridge, Mass.: MIT Press, 1985): ix–xxiii; Maurice Wilkes, *Memoirs of a Computer Pioneer* (Cambridge, Mass: MIT Press, 1985): 116–126, 160–183; a vast source is N. Metropolis, J. Howlett, and Gian-Carlo Rota (eds.), *A History of Computing in the Twentieth Century* (New York: Academic Press, 1980).

12. Cortada, *The Computer in The United States*, 102–107.

13. Ralph W. Fairbanks, "Electronics in the Modern Office," *HBR* 30, no. 5 (September–October 1952): 83–98 and John Diebold, "Automation: The New Technology," Ibid., 32, no. 6 (November–December 1963): 63–71. The *HBR* then published a variety of articles on the subject; for bibliography see Cortada, *The Computer in the United States*, 161, note 12.

14. Cortada, *The Computer in The United States*, 108.

15. Best summarized by Kenneth Flamm (actually an economist writing history), *Creating the Computer: Government, Industry, and High Technology* (Washington, D.C.: Brookings Institution, 1988).

16. General Electric, *The Next Step in Management: An Appraisal of Cybernetics* (General Electric, 1952, 1955): 91.

17. Ibid., p. 176.

18. Roddy F. Osborn, "GE and UNIVAC: Harnessing the High-Speed Computer," *Harvard Business Review*, 32, no. 4 (July-August 1954): 99–107; G. M. Sheean, "A Univac Progress Report," *Systems* 20 (March-April 1956): 334.

19. For an excellent introduction to the issues, see Robert J. Gordon, "The Postwar Evolution of Computer Prices," in Dale W. Jorgenson and Ralph Landau (eds.), *Technology and Capital Formation* (Cambridge, Mass.: MIT Press, 1989): 77–125.

20. One simple piece of supporting evidence is the large number of articles published on commercial applications in this period. For a sampling of this literature see Cortada, *A Bibliographic Guide*.

21. Cortada, *A Bibliographic Guide*, 403–419.

22. Joseph Pelej, "How Will Business Electronics Affect the Auditor's Work?" *Journal of Accountancy* 98 (July 1954): 36–44; Goodrich F. Cleaver, "Auditing and Electronic Data Processing," *Journal of Accountancy* 106 (November 1958): 48–54.

23. H. Thomas Johnson and Robert S. Kaplan, *Relevance Lost: The Rise and Fall of Management Accounting* (Boston: Harvard Business School Press, 1987): 1–3, 183–207.

24. For example, see Robert S. Alson et al., *Automation in Banking* (New Brunswick, N.J.: Rutgers University Press, 1963); Amy Weaver Fisher and James L. McKenney, "The Development of the ERMA Banking System: Lessons from History," *Annals of the History of Computing* 15, no. 1 (1993): 44–57.

25. "Automatic Banking," *Data Processing* no. 3 (July–December 1960): 156–169; Neal J. McDonald, "OnLine Savings & Loan System," *Datamation* 11, no. 10 (October 1965): 81–84; but see also Alson, *Automation in Banking*.

26. Robert V. Head, "Banking Automation: A Critical Appraisal," *Datamation* 11, no. 7 (July 1965): 24–28; American Bankers Association, *Automation and the Small Bank* (New York: American Bankers Association, 1964).

27. John J. Finelli, "Use of Electronics in the Insurance Business," in Adelbert G. Straub, Jr. (ed.), *Examination of Insurance Companies* (New York: New York State Insurance Department, 1954), especially volume 4, p. 649ff.; U.S. Bureau of Labor Statistics, *The Introduction of an Electronic Computer in a Large Insurance Company*, Report No. 2, *Studies of Automatic Technology* (Washington, D.C.: U.S. Government Printing Office, 1955); D. E. Slattery, "Optical Character Sensing for Life Insurance Premium Billing," in Charles H. Johnson (ed.), *Data Processing: 1960 Proceedings* (Mt. Prospect, Ill.: National Machine Accountants Association, 1960): 193–196; W. Everett, "The Effects of Electronics," *Best's Insurance News*, Life Edition (July 1962): 67–70; Life Office Management Association, "EDP in Life Insurance, Proceedings of Automation Forum," *Life Office Management Association* (New York: LOMA, 1962) and LOMA's report, *EDP Applications in Life Insurance Companies*, Report No. 10 (New York: LOMA, 1965).

28. *Reading Machines for Data Processing; Their Prospective Employment Effects*, Manpower Report No. 7, (Washington, D.C.: Office of Manpower, Automation and Training, U.S. Department of Labor, U.S. Government Printing Office, 1963); George E. Delehanty, "Office Automation and the Occupation Structure: A Case Study of Five Insurance Companies," *Industrial Management Review* 7, no. 2 (1966): 99–109.

29. The experiences of 159 case studies can be found in Lester Bittel et al., *Practical Automation: Methods for Increasing Plant Productivity* (New York: McGraw-Hill, 1957); George F. Hawley, *Automating the Manufacturing Process* (New York: Reinhold Publishing, 1959); David F. Noble, *Forces of Production: A Social History of Industrial Automation* (New York: Oxford University Press, 1984): 183, 329–332, 338, 350.

30. Louis E. Davis, "The Effects of Automation on Job Design," *Industrial Relations* 2, no. 1 (October 1962): 53–71; Malcolm L. Denise, "Automation and Employment: A Management Viewpoint," *The Annals of the American Academy of Political and Social Science* 340 (March 1962): 90–99.

31. For introductions to this study see Jerome A. Mark, "Measuring Productivity in Services Industries," in Bruce R. Guile and James Brian Quinn (eds.), *Technology in Services: Policies for Growth, Trade, and Employment* (Washington, D.C.: National Academy Press, 1988): 139–159; Bureau of Labor Statistics, *Technological Trends in Major American Industries*, Bulletin No. 1474 (Washington, D.C.: Government Printing Office, 1966): 1–13. For a listing of the large number of such studies see Bureau of Labor Statistics, *BLS Publications on Productivity and Technology*, Report No. 741 (Washington, D.C.: U.S. Government Printing Office, 1987, and subsequent editions).

32. See, for example, Albert W. Wilson, "New Computer Developments," *Pulp & Paper* (May 10, 1965): 33–34; Knut Angstrom, "Production Planning at Paper Mills," in A. B. Frielink (ed.), *Economics of Automatic Processing* (Amsterdam: North-Holland Publishing Co., 1965): 362–365.

33. See, for example, C. E. Bodington and T. E. Baker, "A History of Mathematical Programming in the Petroleum Industry," *Interfaces* 20, no. 4 (July-August 1990): 117–127; Dale O. Cooper and F. A. Romberg, "Advances in EDP in the Petroleum Industry: Part I: Mastering Change for Responsive Analysis Accounting," *Data Processing: Proceedings 1964* (New Orleans: Data Processing Management Association, 1964): 20–30; Thomas M. Stout, "Process Control: Past, Present, and Future," *The Annals of the American Academy of Political and Social Science* 340 (March 1962): 29–37; and for descriptions of 23 applications, see William E. Miller (ed.), *Digital Computer Applications to Process Control* (New York: Instrument Society of America, 1965); "Sixth Process Control Report," *Chemical Engineering* (June 7, 1965): 142–204.

34. See survey results, for example, in T. M. Whitin, "Report on an Inventory Management Survey," *Production and Inventory Management* 7, no. 1 (January 1966): 27–32.

35. National Industrial Conference Board, *Inventory Management in Industry*. Studies in Business Policy, No. 88 (New York: National Industrial Conference Board, 1958); J. F. Magee, *Production Planning and Inventory Control* (New York: McGraw-Hill, 1958); C. Holt et al., *Planning Production, Inventories, and Work Force* (Englewood Cliffs, N.J.: Prentice-Hall, 1960); R. G. Brown, *Smoothing, Forecasting and Prediction of Discrete Time Series* (Englewood Cliffs, N.J.: Prentice-Hall, 1963).

36. Howard E. Levine, "Computer Eases Service Firm's Growing Pains," *Rack Merchandising* (September 1965): 44, 46, 50; John S. Ewing and James Murphy, "Impact of Automation on United States Retail Food Distribution," *Journal of Retailing* (September 1965): 38–47.

37. Benham Eppes Morris wrote a thesis that circulated in the retail community in the United States during the mid-1950s, "Department Stores' Digital Information Processing by Digital Computer Techniques" (M.A. Thesis, MIT, 1952).

38. Cortada, *The Computer in the United States*, 102–124.

39. Dirk de Wit, *The Shaping of Automation: A Historical Analysis of the Interaction Between Technology and Organization, 1950–1985* (Rotterdam: Uitgeverij, 1994).

40. Flamm, *Creating the Computer*, 134–171.

41. Cortada, "An Introduction to the History of the Data Processing Industry," 9–22.

42. See the various essays in Metropolis, *A History of Computing in the Twentieth Century*, and Cortada, *The Computer in The United States*, 30–63.

43. Several dozen first-hand accounts have been published based on experiences in the United States. Four examples illustrate the issues involved: Harold F. Craig, *Administering Conversion to Electronic Accounting: A Case Study of a Large Office* (Boston: Division of Research, Harvard University, 1955); Dennis G. Price, "The Development of Computer Centralization," in A. B. Frielink (ed.), *Economics of Automatic Processing* (Amsterdam: North-Holland, 1965): 80–85; D. B. Baker, "Economic Considerations of Conversion," *Datamation* 12, no. 6 (June 1966): 30–48; and John E. Czerkies, "Conversion to a Third Generation System," in *Data Processing: Proceedings 1969* (Montreal: Data Processing Management Association, 1970): 227–236.

44. Franklin M. Fisher, James W. McKie, and Richard B. Mancke, *IBM and the U.S. Data Processing Industry: An Economic History* (New York: Praeger, 1983): 143–361.

45. R. L. Patrick, "Ten Years of Progress?" *Datamation* 13, no. 9 (September 1967): 22–23; Fisher, *IBM and the U.S. Data Processing Industry*, 117–118.

46. Tom Forester, *High-Tech Society: The Story of the Information Technology Revolution* (Cambridge, Mass: MIT Press, 1987): 148–151; Nancy Stern and Robert A. Stern, *Computers in Society* (Englewood Cliffs, N.J.: Prentice-Hall, 1983): 237–274; Lynn M. Salerno (ed.), *Catching Up With the Computer Revolution* (New York: John Wiley & Sons, 1983): 137–262.

47. Montgomery Phister, Jr., "Computer Industry," in Anthony Ralston and Edwin D. Reilly, Jr. (eds.), *Encyclopedia of Computer Science* (New York: Van Nostrand Reinhold, 1983): 339.

48. Cortada, "An Introduction to the History of the Data Processing Industry," 25.

49. Phister, "Computer Industry," 334.

50. Neil C. Churchill et al., *Computer-Based Information Systems for Management: A Survey* (New York: National Association of Accountants, 1968), serves as a quick introduction, but for a fuller accounting of the literature see Cortada, *A Bibliographic Guide*, 420–437, and a much expanded listing in the 1996 edition.

51. The literature is vast; to get a sense of what was going on see Robert V. Head, "Old Myths and New Realities in Business Applications," *Datamation* 13, no. 9 (September 1967): 26–28; Leonard Rico, *The Advance Against Paperwork: Computers, Systems, and Personnel* (Ann Arbor: Graduate School of Business Administration, University of Michigan, 1967); "The Office of the Future," *Dun's Review* (August 1979): 69–109; R. A. Hirschheim, *Office Automation: A Social and Organizational Perspective* (New York: John Wiley & Sons, 1985).

52. J. F. Rockart and D. W. DeLong, *Executive Support Systems: The Emergence of Top Management Computer Use* (Homewood, Ill.: Dow Jones-Irwin, 1988), is the best study on the subject.

53. The literature on this topic is substantial—several hundred titles per decade. Some of the more useful insights are provided by: Robert J. Rossheim, "The Next Plateau in File Organization," in *Data Processing: Proceedings 1965* (Philadelphia: Data Processing Management Association, 1965): 26–41; John W. Mauchly (co-developer of the ENIAC), "The Status of Computer Applications for Management," in *Data Processing: Proceedings 1965* (Dallas: Data Processing Management Association, 1966): 39–43; Russel L. Ackoff, "Management Misinformation Systems," *Management Science* 14, no. 4 (December 1967): B147–B156; D. B. Montgomery and G. L. Urban, *Management Science in Marketing* (Englewood Cliffs, N.J.: Prentice-Hall, 1969); Albert N. Schrieber

(ed.), *Corporate Simulation Models* (Seattle: Graduate School of Business Administration, University of Washington, 1970); Michael S. Morton, *Management Decision Systems: Computer Based Support for Decision Making* (Cambridge, Mass.: Harvard University, 1971); G. A. Gorry, "The Development of Managerial Models," *Sloan Management Review* 12, no. 2 (Winter 1971): 1–16; J. W. Traenkle et al., *The Use of Financial Models in Business* (New York: Financial Executives' Research Foundation, 1975); and P. G. W. Keen and M. S. Morton, *Decision Support Systems: An Organizational Perspective* (Reading, Mass.: Addison-Wesley, 1978).

54. For a sense of this important story see C. Robert McBrier, "A Concept for the Use of Electronics in Retailing," in *Data Processing: Proceedings 1963* (Detroit: Data Processing Management Association, 1963): 166–173; Donald H. Sanders, "Experiences of Small Retailers with Electronic Data Processing," *Journal of Retailing* 42, no. 1 (Spring 1966): 13–17, 61–62; Byron L. Carter, "Retail Systems," in *Data Processing: Proceedings 1967* (Boston: Data Processing Management Association, 1967): 335–339; William D. Power, "Retail Terminals—A POS Survey," *Datamation* 17 (July 1971): 22–31; Lawrence E. Hicks, *The Universal Product Code* (New York: American Management Association, 1975); National Retail Merchants Association, *Results of a Six-Month Test of the NRMA Ticketing Standard (OCR-A) in an Operating Department Store Environment* (New York: NRMA, 1977); Louis P. Bucklin, "Technological Change and Store Operations: The Supermarket Case," *Journal of Retailing* 56, no. 1 (Spring 1980): 3–15; Barry Bluestone et al., *The Retail Revolution* (Boston: Auburn House, 1981); and Brian L. Friedman, "Productivity Trends in Department Stores, 1967–86," *Monthly Labor Review* 111, no. 3 (March 1988): 17–21.

55. James Chposky and Ted Leonsis, *Blue Magic: The People, Power and Politics Behind the IBM Personal Computer* (New York: Facts on File Publications, 1988): 10–11; Regis McKenna, *Who's Afraid of Big Blue?* (Reading, Mass.: Addison Wesley, 1989): 32–33; Paul Carroll, *Big Blues: The Unmaking of IBM* (New York: Crown, 1993), passim.

56. Chposky and Leonsis, *Blue Magic*, 1–18.

57. Research done by Dunn & Bradstreet Corporation and appeared in *USA Today* (June 16, 1985): 5.

58. Ibid.

59. A. D. Little, Inc., published in Ulric Weil, *Information Systems in the 80's: Products, Markets, and Vendors,* (Englewood Cliffs, N.J.: Prentice-Hall, 1982): 214.

60. Gadi Kaplan, "Talking About Tools," *IEEE Spectrum* 29, no. 11 (November 1992): 32–33.

61. Monty Kersell, "Seperate Studies Mark Platform Shifts," *Info Canada* 17, no. 11 (November 1992): 24.

62. Robert Francis, "Downsizing: The Application Migration," *Datamation* 38, no. 23 (November 15, 1992): 36–48.

63. On February 11, 1994, the *Wall Street Journal* published 26 articles on the subject.

64. Thayer C. Taylor, "Computers," *Sales & Marketing Management* 114, no. 11 (September 1992): 110–112.

65. Sidney C. Lejfer, "Increasing Productivity by Using Sales Automation Software,"*Massachusetts CPA Review* 68, no. 1 (Winter 1994): 27–28.

66. See note 63.

67. George Basalla, *The Evolution of Technology* (Cambridge, Mass. Cambridge Uni-

versity Press, 1988): 207–218; Joel Mokyr, *The Lever of Riches: Technological Creativity and Economic Progress* (Oxford: Oxford University Press, 1990): 273–299.

68. Thomas P. Hughes, *American Genesis: A Century of Invention and Technological Enthusiasm, 1870–1970* (New York: Viking, 1989) is filled with examples.

69. The most detailed look at the issue has been made by Paul A. Strassman, *Information Payoff: The Transformation of Work in the Electronic Age* (New York: Free Press, 1985), and *The Business Value of Computers: An Executive's Guide* (New Canaan, Conn.: Information Economics Press, 1990).

70. David F. Noble, *Forces of Production: A Social History of Industrial Automation* (New York: Oxford University Press, 1984).

71. Montgomery Phister, Jr., *Data Processing Technology and Economics* (Santa Monica, Calif.: Santa Monica Publishing Company, 1976): 318–330.

72. Edward Yourdon, *Decline and Fall of the American Programmer* (Englewood Cliffs, N.J.: Yourdon Press, 1992): 25.

73. For this literature see Cortada, *A Bibliographic Guide*, chapters dealing with society and management of information processing.

III

The Management of Information Processing

Part III is devoted to issues concerning the management of computer-related assets. This section encompasses questions concerning the management of information processing departments, personnel matters, role in organizations, and other institutional relations. It is a subject area that has long drawn the attention of contemporary writers and observers of the information processing industry but which has been virtually untouched by historians. Yet the topic is so critical to any understanding of how best to deploy what has become a major asset in commercial enterprises today. The irony of the subject is that executives all through the period of the computer tried to pay attention to the experiences of their predecessors, looking for patterns of effective behavior, "rules of the road" with which to guide their exploitation of this technology.

We moved from the creation of large data centers in tabulating departments to support accounting functions reporting in to vice presidents of accounting, to large division-independent MIS organizations in the 1980s and 1990s. The topic of organization, while it has changed a great deal, is very important to historians because without organizational strategies for deploying technology, applications would not exist. Information processing organizations were those parts of companies and government agencies that wrote software, bought computers, dealt with vendors, and built and ran systems. It is this sector of the workforce that also employed millions of people in the second half of the twentieth century. Yet this vast subject has not been touched by historians. However, after understanding the value of applications, is the work of the historian so desperately needed both for the intellectual field of computer history and for the practical management of information processing.

To expand our understanding of the topic, Chapter 6 provides a brief overview of the issues we have to deal with. The material, while presented as if directed to an historian, is, in fact, drawn from the perspective of senior management because they are the people who have given the subject relevance by their concerns and through their investment of trillions of dollars on computing. The chapter will present an argument that there is much to be studied. It will also offer suggestions on where to start and how.

Chapter 7 presents the argument for why information is a corporate asset and how companies have looked at that issue. The chapter was originally written in the 1970s as defense of the notion of information as a corporate asset and was directed toward senior business management. Because it is couched in historical terms, the chapter could readily be expanded and updated to reflect a more historical view while preserving a "taste" of management issues at the height of the mainframe era.

Chapter 8 does what I proposed in Chapter 5. It is an initial effort to address issues associated with the history of the management of information processing, defining concerns and trends, and suggesting lines of future research. If we knew little about applications, we know less about the management of information processing. Thus this chapter is at best highly tentative, but, like Chapter 5, is based on contemporary material suggestive of what was happening.

The value of information drove the need for computing. Computing led to applications. Management of information processing made it possible to use computers in a manner acceptable to the managers of companies, universities, and government agencies. Thus, these chapters are linked by the reality of how things were done.

6

Issues to Be Studied in the History of Information Processing Management

The use of computers in the operation of American business required an army of specialists. These, in turn, called for a smaller army of managers and executives who ran information processing organizations. These departments and divisions likewise had to function within the broader context of the companies of which they were a part. Over time, information processing activities in one company had to link to those in other firms, requiring information management from supervisors to executives to embrace some common standards of performance, attitudes, and technical specifications and architectures across the breadth of American business. In short, without information processing organizations, companies would not have been able to use computers. In fact, one could go further and argue that computer technology would not have evolved to the point where individuals could have their own machines—the PC—because it was the symbiotic push/pull relationship of vendors and customers that caused computer technology to evolve over time in the ways it did.[1] Thus in order to understand fully how the computer came to be so important in the late twentieth century world, we need to complete the triangle of investigation, moving from just looking at the evolution of technology to examination of applications and, finally, to exploration of how this technology was run and managed organizationally.

It turns out that executives managing companies would agree with this assessment. When they wanted to exploit computers in any decade their tool was the information processing organization. They appointed managers for these departments, hired and fired employees in these same organizations, added and reduced budgets, and gave these I/T managers missions and instructions on what to do. In each decade, professors and consultants, like managers and executives, also turned to the organization and to the management of information processing as the way to understand what to do with computers. The technology was important and influenced what could be done; end users and applications were the basic business reasons for acquiring and using these machines and software, but it was the information processing organization that acquired, set up, delivered, and ran computer-based services. These generalizations apply as much to the 1950s as to the 1990s.

It is more than curious that if a cultural anthropologist or a sociologist were to study the characteristics and evolution of information processing organizations, they would probably observe three phenomenon. First, IS organizations change very slowly over time; their structure, job titles, and approaches to work evolved slower than the technology they used. Second, IS organizations developed their own values, culture, professional associations, social classes, criteria for success, and prejudices just as had other business people in their fields. Third, IS organizations took on a life of their own, constantly trying to expand and justify their value to the companies or government agencies of which they were a part.

If these three observations sound terribly similar to what one could observe in accounting, manufacturing, distribution, or marketing and sales, then we have begun to understand the significance of information processing organizations. They reflected as much the culture of the companies they served as they did particularistic attributes of their profession. In short, historians will come to find that IS departments were always an integral part of mainstream American business. If anything changed over time it was that they became even more important as they grew in size, as end user dependence on computing expanded, and because of the growth in percent of budgets allocated to them.

It was always accepted by many employees as given that data processing people were different, isolated from the mainstream of the corporation of which they were a part. In each decade you could find observations to that effect.[2] However, research done by business professors and historians, although limited, would suggest quite the contrary; namely, that these departments were as much a reflection of what the rest of the company or their industry was doing as any other profession/department.[3] The challenge for us, therefore, is to understand why this was the case. For management it suggests how best to deploy IS organizations in the future. It also is an example of imperfect understanding, because IS professionals accented differences between themselves and other parts of a company. Yet we know nobody operates in isolation. The impulse to create a professional identity was a strong one, but historians need to provide a balanced perspective.

ISSUES AT HAND

Chapter 4 makes a case for studying the history of how computers were used. Similar questions can be asked about how computer departments were staffed and run. We have the same questions concerning definitions, research methodologies, sources of information, and topic. Since historians have to deal with a topic covering over a half century, we should also want to know how the management of information processing changed over time. Did the technology cause changes, and, if so, how? At a very macro level there are several questions that must be answered:

- Who were these members of the computer world?
- What responsibilities were they given?
- What did they do, what role did they play?
- How were they organized and why?
- Where did they sit within the larger organization of their companies?
- Did the answers vary from one industry or period to another, and if so, how and why?

To a large extent what we are dealing with here is the sociology of technology and business management.

This is a profession that employed between 1.5 million and possibly 3 million people in the past half century (we do not know for sure the total). By any measure that is a very large number of people. They were in the majority better educated than many other professionals, generally had above average intelligence, and were spread across all industries in each decade, and around the world. Their influence was profound in most decades. Yet we know very little about the evolution of the various functions within information processing. How did the data processing manager evolve from a tabulator or systems supervisor of the 1930s and 1940s to the chief information officer of a large corporation in the 1990s? We need to understand the rise of the programmer, systems analyst, and machine room operator, to mention a few. What about the army of data entry clerks, tape librarians, Help Desk personnel, database managers, and so on? We know so much more about the evolution of military careers, biographies of key executives, and the professions of politics, science, government administration, farming, factory worker, teachers and professors, even librarians. We know very little about the IS professional. The issues associated with understanding the rise of the merchant, ranch and plantation foremen, law enforcement officials, Egyptian pharaohs, Roman armies, German professors, and nurses and doctors are the same for IS and for the same reasons.[4]

IS professionals and the organizations of which they were a part have become increasingly important in recent years because of the profound influence they exercise over the effectiveness of many companies. Soon after Louis V. Gerstner, Jr., became CEO of IBM in the early 1990s, he was disturbed to learn that almost 8 percent of the company's budget had been spent annually on internal use of information technology in the late 1980s-early 1990s. Nobody seemed surprised; after all, IBM makes computers. Whether it is 2 or 8 percent, either way it is a lot of money, people, and resources. CEOs want to use these resources as effectively and efficiently as possible. This constant was as true for senior managers at General Electric in the early 1950s when they pioneered use of commercial applications as it is for Gerstner running a $70 billion high-tech company in the 1990s.[5] A clear understanding of the mission and roles of information processing organizations represents an early basic step in appreciating how computers were deployed and how best they might be in the years to come.

Organizational considerations represent some of the most important focal points for executives. It is one of the few "buttons" they can push to make things happen. One could argue that it has been the favorite change and deployment tool of American executives in the twentieth century.[6] For that reason one would be more than justified in examining the structure of IS organizations. They are the channels for distributing responsibilities, budgets, and people. They are the tools used to define relationships among workers. Many of the guiding principles influencing IS structures were the same applied across other functions in American corporations. One influenced the other. How is not clear yet. What is certain, however, is that organizational evolutions in corporations can be likened to a biological metaphor: one part of the enterprise changes, leading to consequences in other departments and divisions, many unpredictable at the time they occurred. We are learning that the machine metaphor is not as useful as the biological in understanding organizational change, particularly as organizational change affected information processing.[7]

Any survey of the literature on IS organizations from the 1950s to the present suggests several dynamics at work which we do not fully understand. For one thing, centralized computing became the norm in the 1950s and 1960s because the technology was easiest to manage that way and most cost-effective. As computers became more distributed in the 1970s and 1980s, organizational changes occurred in response to this dynamic. For another, how IS organizations were structured also influenced the configuration of technology. Thus we find that vendors built equipment to satisfy the needs of large centralized IS organizations because these were their customers.[8] So we know that technology influences and was influenced by organizational dynamics.

The evolution of jobs within IS occurred for a variety of reasons, yet as the old saying goes, it seemed that the more things changed the more they stayed the same. Although we see that certain jobs (e.g., programmers) essentially retained the same responsibilities over many decades, the tools used by these professionals evolved radically over time. Many old-time programmers, however, might argue that nothing much had changed. What we have learned is that the kind of person who is successful in this profession is well defined and understood by sociologists of the job, but not within any historical context.[9] All through the 1950s and 1960s most commentators argued that there was a vast shortage of programmers. Technological innovations in hardware and software in the 1970s and 1980s, along with new techniques for designing and programming software, radically changed that situation by the end of the 1980s. It would be more than nice to understand better what happened. Are there lessons here for other labor-intensive technologies or jobs?

As will be demonstrated in the chapters that follow, the position of the information processing organization within enterprises is a fascinating story in itself. There is an obvious correlation between the increase in dependence on computing and the rise in stature of the information processing organization. We could see it simply by looking at who the data processing manager reported to over time, to the extent to which senior executives paid attention to information processing. That the dynamics of the information processing organization expanding in size, influence, and stature may represent the single most important new function created in American industry in this century. We do not have enough comparative studies of the role of the data processing organization to understand how this happened, let alone what it teaches us about the future.[10]

Finally—possibly ultimately—the central historical issue emerging from any consideration of management at large is the role of information. Computer people call it data, management wants information. A great story has yet to be told about the rise of machine-readable information (not to be confused with the history of computers). Thomas Watson, Sr., had the right idea in the late 1920s when he told his salesmen that only 5 percent of all accounting information was in punched cards. We need to take a similar view of all information in business in the late twentieth century, because if we just looked at sales of disk and tape drives, one would have to conclude that there was a vast migration of information to machine-readable form. To be sure other massive quantities of data were captured on paper, making this century clearly the most information-intensive of all. How people gathered, used, managed, and reacted to computer-based information is a subject that awaits what will probably have to be a small army of historians. As James Beniger and many others have suggested, the acquisition and effective management of data in ever-larger amounts made it possible for large corporations to exist successfully. The role of data, therefore, has to be studied in and of itself. How it moved into machine-readable form, was used, and its effects on human activity is a much larger story than the history of computer applications. One could easily see that a century from now that topic would be the central issue of interest to historians of twentieth century computing.

Thus, the history of how information was managed since the end of World War II is one of the most important themes in the history of modern business. Enough time has passed so that we can realize this. We needed time to elapse so that historians could come to understand the vastness of the topic. When we read in the newspapers that information doubles in a particular field every four years (e.g., in medicine) and that engineers are obsolete five years after they finish their college training, we can begin to appreciate the implications of the topic.

STRATEGIES FOR THE STUDY OF DATA PROCESSING MANAGEMENT

I would like to suggest that there is no single cookbook approach that can be taken. As suggested above, the topic is more than simply an examination of organization charts and job descriptions. There are various of topics that must be explored. As a first step, historians might begin by creating an inventory of subjects to study. Here is my initial list of suggestions:

- every basic job type in computing
- every basic job type in vendors of computers and software
- organizational structures within small and large IS shops
- role of IS organizations in corporations
- political dynamics of information processing
- role of machine-readable information in how management functioned in all departments
- role of machine-readable information in how nonmanagement functioned in all departments
- how dependence on machine-readable information increased and changed over time
- evolution of IS budgets
- cost justification process and politics concerning use of computers
- relations between IS organizations and end-user communities
- kinds of information captured in machine-readable form
- sociological and administrative effects of such data on people and organizations
- extent to which IS organizations helped, hurt, or had no impact on companies
- biographies of groups of workers
- biographies of individual IS managers, executives, technicians, and end users
- histories of individual data centers
- histories of how computer operations functioned
- history of programming
- history of systems design
- history of vendor/IS department relations
- role of industry associations on professionalization of IS jobs
- role of methodologies on IS personnel jobs and behavior
- how society came to value machine-readable information
- how society came to use such information
- consequences of machine-readable data on economic behavior
- generational differences between computer literate/illiterate employees

The list leads me to the conclusion that a variety of approaches will have to be taken. All the obvious strategies will be employed: biographies, case studies, sociological analysis, reviews of corporate archives, interviews, and so forth. It is also obvious that a broad range of historical methods will have to be applied, too: economic history, business history, intellectual history, history of technology and science, economic analysis of costs and benefits, history of accounting and budgets, psycho-history, and so forth. We will need to move from case studies to general accounts of what happened by industry and function and eventually move up to histories of how society used information as a whole.

If there is a line to pursue it might be the need for control of corporate operations. To be effective, executives and employees at large companies need information in order to deploy people and assets, to make decisions and pick markets, and to understand success, failures, problems, and opportunities. That set of issues sit at the nexus of capitalism and society's purposes, drawing the whole issue of information process to the center of economic and social activities in this century and beyond. Feedback and control, however, gives meaning to the history of computing, not the invention of machines. Therefore, questions can be asked and answered about how organizations deployed resources to ensure they had the kind of information needed to function. We can then judge the effectiveness and consequences of using computers to facilitate the gathering and use of information. The biological metaphor is clearly more appropriate than the more traditional machine motif. If there is anything we have learned about computing, particularly after the advent of online computing and PCs, it is that the use of data is an iterative process of understanding, exploitation, reaction, feedback, and renewed action. The machine model does not help us there; the biological makes perfect sense because that is the way our minds and nervous systems respond to information.

That point also draws our attention to another facet of the history of how information processing was managed. As we have learned more about the functioning of the human mind in the past generation, we have come to realize that no history of information processing organizations, people, or management processes is possible just relying on traditional historical tools. Our understanding of how the brain operates clearly must be factored into such studies. The role of societies and economies functioning interactively as if a much larger biological entity is no longer contested. A visual example illustrates the obvious. Next time you are flying at night and are approaching the runway at one or two thousand feet up, look out your window at the streets below and you will see vehicles rushing down roadways much like cells passing through the blood stream. Look at the houses and buildings and at the vast expanse lit up as if one complex entity, and it looks similar to an organism with muscles, bones, and organs. One does not have to have been the proud consumer of a bottle of wine onboard the airplane to see the analogy. We people are cells within a larger organism, all dependent on information not to crash our cars into each other, not to violate laws and rules, and to succeed in exploiting our individual advantages. The strategy of future historians will have to include interdisciplinary approaches if they are to understand fully what happened in information processing.

Because the value of information is so critical to the story, the role of computer-based information in organizations is a good point from which some historical studies can begin. Another is the sociological histories of IS departments within a company or industry. Periodization into eras does not appear at the moment to be as useful an approach as I suggested with the study of computer applications. This is because organizations and the roles of individuals did not change as quickly as did applications and technology. Some readers will differ with me because at the micro level of an individual department, change in management and operating styles of course did occur. One person came and went, organizations were bigger and smaller, and, of course, they were always busy acquiring new equipment. But what I just described occurred in the 1950s, 1960s, 1970s, 1980s, and 1990s, and often in much the same ways; or so the extant evidence suggests. A great deal of work needs to be done to defend or challenge this observation. How does the operation and changes that occurred in information processing compare to those in other functional areas of a corporation? These are good areas for initial investigation because they will provide both the building blocks for additional historically complex projects while adding to our store of knowledge useful to future managers.

CONCLUSION

Chapters 7 and 8 build one upon the other. The first suggests issues of concern in the area of how information was valued by corporations—basic to any understanding of how IS organizations functioned. The second deals with the more obvious bread-and-butter concerns of a conventional business historian. In both chapters I conclude that information processing is less a history of technology and more a study of business and social issues. If this book has a common theme, it is just that: The history of computing is not just about technology. Perched almost at the end of the twentieth century and, more importantly, with a half-century of experience with computers behind us, it is now very clear that the future of the history of computing is much larger and more important than earlier expectation, and terribly complex.

The body of readily available information to help the historian of the management of computing is vast and comes from many traditional disciplines. Business professors, consultants, sociologists, psychologist, medical doctors, and biologists, to mention a few, have conducted relevant research. Like the people they will study, however, historians have so much data to process and to make sense of. The ultimate challenge for them will be how to manage the large body of information that we have all come to rely on.

Further complicating the effort is the fact that even the nature of information is being redefined. The rise of chaos theory in physics is merely the start. Is

Ikujira Nonaka right in arguing that "an organization that creates information is nothing but an organization that allows a maximum of self-organizing order or information out of chaos?"[11] Or, was the creation of information processing management a practical search for what Matthew Fox has suggested we all want: wisdom? His notion is simple: "Wisdom is about living harmoniously in the universe, which is itself a place of order and justice that triumphs over chaos and employs chance for its ultimate purpose."[12]

NOTES

1. This is the heart of my argument in James W. Cortada, *The Computer in the United States: From Laboratory to Market, 1930–1960* (Armonk, N.Y.: M. E. Sharpe, 1993).

2. The source for such comments historically has been surveys of senior end-user executives, often by consultants and professors of business. A useful sense of the discontent that executives have felt with some IS organizations can be gleaned from industry surveys. For a listing of many of these, see James W. Cortada, *A Bibliographic Guide to the History of Computing, Computers, and the Information Processing Industry* (Westport, Conn.: Greenwood Press, 1990): 451–478, and the *Second Bibliographic Guide to the History of Computing, Computers, and the Information Processing Industry* (Westport, Conn.: Greenwood Press, 1996): 332–334.

3. Ibid.; but see also Harley Shaiken, *Work Transformed: Automation and Labor in the Computer Age* (Lexington, Mass.: Lexington Books, 1984); and Shoshana Zuboff, *In the Age of the Smart Machine: The Future of Work and Power* (New York: Basic Books, 1984).

4. We have no good models yet on how to do this in information processing. However, several examples exist from other professions. Drawing on business examples, see Alfred D. Chandler, Jr., *The Visible Hand: The Managerial Revolution in American Business* (Cambridge, Mass.: Harvard University Press, 1977); Daniel Nelson, *Managers and Workers: Origins of the New Factory System in the United States, 1880–1920* (Madison: University of Wisconsin Press, 1975); and Bernard Bailyn, *The New England Merchant in the Seventeenth Century* (Cambridge, Mass.: Harvard University Press, 1955); on the military see the excellent guide by John E. Jessup, Jr., and Robert W. Coakley, *A Guide to the Study and Use of Military History* (Washington, D.C.: U.S. Government Printing Office, 1979).

5. Paul A. Strassmann, *Information Payoff: The Transformation of Work in the Electronic Age* (New York: Free Press, 1985) and his *The Business Value of Computers: An Executive's Guide* (New Canaan, Conn.: The Information Economics Press, 1990).

6. The literature is vast and, as of the mid-1990s, change management appeared in all the key business surveys done in the United States to be the number one strategic issue on the minds of senior executives. The role of organizations is crucial to the issue. For a 1990s introduction to the topic, see Rosabeth Moss Kanter, Barry A. Stein, and Todd D. Jick, *The Challenge of Organizational Change: How Companies Experience It and Leaders Guide It* (New York: Free Press, 1992); for a more historical treatment, see Alfred D. Chandler, Jr., *Scale and Scope: The Dynamics of Industrial Capitalism* (Cambridge, Mass.: Harvard University Press, 1990).

7. For a fascinating demonstration of the biological metaphor for the office appliance

industry (precursor to the age of computers), see James R. Beniger, *The Control Revolution: Technological and Economic Origins of the Information Society* (Cambridge, Mass.: Harvard University Press, 1986).

8. Franklin M. Fisher, James W. McKie, and Richard B. Mancke, *IBM and the U.S. Data Processing Industry: An Economic History* (New York: Praeger, 1983) provides many instances; see also, Kenneth Flamm, *Creating the Computer: Government, Industry, and High Technology* (Washington, D.C.: Brookings Institution, 1988): 203–258. We still lack a comprehensive, up-to-date history of the industry; we only have pieces of the story.

9. There are many studies about the attributes of programmers. For example, see Philip Kraft, *Programmers and Managers: The Routinization of Computer Programming in the United States* (New York: Springer-Verlag, 1977) and Gerald Weinberg, *The Psychology of Computer Programming* (New York: Van Nostrand Reinhold, 1971).

10. One historian has looked at this issue by examining the experiences of several Dutch organizations over the course of several decades, offering us a possible model of how to go about such a study. See Dirk de Wit, *The Shaping of Automation: A Historical Analysis of the Interaction between Technology and Organization, 1950–1980* (Rotterdam: Hilversum Verloren, 1994).

11. Quoted in Margaret J. Wheatley, *Leadership and the New Science: Learning about Organization from an Orderly Universe* (San Francisco: Berrett-Koehler Publishers, 1994): 100.

12. His ideas are well explained in Matthew Fox, *Creation Spirituality* (San Francisco: Harper, 1991).

7

Information: The Corporate Asset

The case for treating machine-readable data as a corporate asset has long enjoyed a positive reception from American executives. It did not matter if one were looking at activities in the 1950s or at the "learning organizations" of the 1990s. The message was always the same: Know your markets, understand your customers and competition, and build up a bank of information that will make your operations more productive while providing customers with products they want to buy.[1] Conceptually, the notion of treating information as if it were like money, buildings, or inventory has never been problematic for executive management. Lower order issues were, however. For example, what should or should not be in a computer? How do you distribute information? What do you do with it? Can I get it cheaper? How do I deploy people and assets in charge of computers? How do I control the growth of costs for computing? How do employees learn and get information? One recent study, *The Information Mosaic*, focused on what people did use; its subtitle, *How Managers Get the Information They Really Need*, implied that maybe computers had given them data they did not want or use.[2] But nonetheless, there always existed a logic that reinforced the notion that information in a computer was of value, and worldwide, people invested over $4 trillion just in the hardware and software to house it.

This chapter was originally drafted at the start of the 1980s for executive management, and was part of a much larger discussion about the management of information processing, including IS organizations. While the text has been updated, the flavor of how management thought in the 1970s and 1980s is important to preserve because many in large organizations had gone through the mind-numbing experience in the 1960s of having expanded the use of computing by orders of magnitude and, then digesting the consequences of those actions as recently as the late 1970s. To a very large extent, computing at the start of the 1980s meant processing in large enterprises, such as at Fortune 1000 companies, major universities, hospitals, and government agencies. While many millions of dollars in minicomputers had been installed, most went into large enterprises, into engineering departments, or on shop floors, not into small employers. So the response to arguments for and against the value of computer-based information really concerned the larger enterprises of the industrialized world.

In the 1970s and 1980s few executives would ask why data processing needed to be justified. After a quarter century of spectacular growth as a productivity tool, for better or for worse, management had accepted the idea that information processing (in those days called simply DP) was an essential part of their lives. In fact, most would admit that information processing was well on its way to a dominant position in society. Chip technology had already come to control gas usage in our cars and the performance of microwave ovens; calculators had replaced most mental calculations. Some children were learning programming at school, and the home computer had become reality if, albeit, still a small reality.[3] However, what periodically needed to be redefined was how information processing in business and other organizations would continue to evolve so that the productive force that it represented could be harnessed most effectively for executive management. One of the greatest challenges facing executives was how to use computer technology, given the fact that its effect on their organizations would continue to grow regardless of any attempts to arrest it. Anything that is either useful or perceived to be effective was always employed, so the issue was to make the inevitable manageable and really productive.

These fundamental concerns had three facets in the 1970s and early 1980s.: The first was the concept of data processing—known then as management information systems (MIS) or, to be even more trendy, enterprise information systems (EIS)—as a corporate asset. Second, there were stages in the evolution of information processing within organizations that helped define the changing nature of DP applications.[4] Finally, there were growing numbers of observations on trends of dependency on DP which also contributed to our broader understanding of why information processing had become so useful, how one could determine its growth and applicability within an organization, and how outside pressures affected its use and management's reactions to it.[5]

INFORMATION AS AN ASSET

When information processing first emerged in business during the mid-1950s, the typical issue on the table was how such technology could be used to automate highly repetitive tasks and perform mathematical calculations quickly, usually for accounting departments. Similar questions continued to be asked during the 1960s, with an increasing number of answers emerging as the cost of computing dropped.[6] Computers penetrated manufacturing, sales, distribution, and many other areas by the early 1980s. The answers to these questions were phrased in terms of "applications" as they are today. The common tactic was to "apply" computers to accounting, then finance, inventory control, manufacturing work-in-process, and eventually the wide variety of uses we know today. But the issue of DP invariably focused on the use of computers to mechanize functions already existing in organizations, with minimal alterations to these processes. This perspective dominated thinking in the 1950s and 1960s. By the early 1970s, the variety of possible uses of computing caused vendors and industry pundits alike to speak of data processing creating new jobs, functions, and significant changes in the mission and structure of organizations.[7] By the end of that decade, this process logically had led to a new concept, that of information collected on all sorts of activities within an organization that could then be used to control and better manage a business.

By the early 1980s that thought was no longer a concept but a working definition of what data processing had to do for an organization. In short, it had become a strategic peg for executives to hang their DP hats on, a perspective from which to offer leadership to their companies. To put the concept in more formal terms, data processing had the mission of collecting and making available data from and to all parts of an organization so that management could have the information it needed to run and control the company. It had to support the tactical and strategic decision-making processes of all levels of management and do so in an efficient and cost-effective manner.[8]

A quick review of what MIS had come to mean by the start of the 1980s suggests the philosophical and, therefore, strategic base which governed many management decisions concerning data processing in many companies. The objective was to present management with meaningful and timely information to manage a business as effectively as possible. Anything beyond that appeared to detract from the productivity of DP. It was, for example, obviously both impractical and uneconomical to capture all forms of possible data floating around an organization and stuff them into a computer. Hence, the continued need for cost-justified selectivity in data and applications which remained a constant in the world of data processing. MIS implied giving management a tool—information as opposed to just raw data—with which to improve its decisions. Since decision making took place in essentially three forms—planning, execution, and control—it was critical that management ask for applications and information that improved the management and quality of these three elements. The hunt for the right data was not always clear and obvious, but gather data they did.[9]

By the early 1980s MIS had reached the point in its evolution where organizations could use data processing to help attain corporate objectives, help define tactics to implement these, and then monitor their execution. Most literature on data processing of the 1970s and early 1980s was concerned with monitoring the execution of tactical plans.[10] MIS contributed in theory, and sometimes in practice, to better decision making when it made available quality and selective information relevant to a specific decision. A more common example was the financial modeling approach that allowed a manager to define in detail multiple scenarios (rent, lease, purchase over any period of years).[11] Later, when PCs began to appear in businesses, one of the most popular of the early applications using spreadsheet packages like Visicalc.[12] So in point of fact, all through the 1960s and 1970s, and continuing into the 1980s, management most frequently believed that good information consisted of data when you needed it; that was accurate, relevant and, therefore believable; and that was concise in the form required.

ROLE OF DATA PROCESSING ORGANIZATIONS

Frequently, providing timely and relevant information involved pulling data together from independent applications that had evolved and grown over the years and doing so quickly. It might have meant allowing individuals in one division to have data from another, in making consolidations from many departments possible for a CEO. The clearest quick proof that this situation existed in an organization was by observing the number of terminals used by middle and upper management. The idea of a terminal on every desk was no longer a pipe dream by 1980 but a reality whose time was soon to come. An important survey done at the start of the decade cited many executives who had installed systems that allowed them access to various levels of information from a variety of departments and divisions.[13] This availability of information (as opposed to raw data) gave them the ability to understand their business to the degree of detail each wanted. They argued that this availability increased their ability to manage and control more effectively events within their companies. The editing and "sanitizing" that information traditionally went through for corporate political reasons as it rose slowly through many layers of an organization could then often be circumvented, giving the CEO new power through knowledge.[14] In hindsight we can also state, however, that most senior executives were very intimidated at the thought of sitting down at a terminal to extract data in the 1970s and early 1980s, a problem that it took the PC over a decade to overcome and even then, only partially.[15]

As the number of applications using computers grew in the 1960s and 1970s, it became increasingly obvious that the way companies ran had become highly dependent on computers. We did not need futurists such as Alvin Toffler and his book *Future Shock* to suggest what had already become so obvious: that our companies were becoming increasingly dependent on the information generated by computers just to function at operational levels and increasingly in areas of strategy formation and execution. An increasing number of decisions could not be made without facts that were stored in computers. The belief also gained wider currency in the 1960s and 1970s that decision making required more facts than in the past, in turn encouraging the gathering and manipulation of more data via computers.[16] Services increasingly could not be performed without dealing with terminals because the number of online applications was growing rapidly. Imagine trying to buy an airplane ticket in the 1970s or early 1980s without terminals. Management had also become dependent on elegant systems for making modular decisions that formed part of a much larger set of corporate strategies. Let there be no confusion about carts before horses: Our dependence on computers has not been a reliance on data processing but on the types of information generated by this technology. As the quantity and quality of this information grew during the 1970s, it became of major concern to management. Their reaction was to observe and control data processing more than ever before.[17]

No longer could computers be considered little black boxes in the basement or as tourist attractions behind vulnerable glass walls. DP managers began to be defrocked, their high priesthoods of mysterious technology stripped before a growing number of informed and concerned middle and upper managers intent on applying business controls. Evidence abounded on the conditions that forced an increasingly larger number of managers to pay attention to data processing. DP managers were no longer first- and second-line managers but rose to the ranks of executives, often as directors and vice presidents, and of MIS rather than of electronic data processing (EDP) or of DP.[18] In the United States alone, the share of total budgets spent on data processing around 1960 was hardly measurable; by the early 1980s, industries were reporting 0.8 to as high as 4 percent of budgets being invested in MIS.[19] Executive management's expectations in the early 1980s was that this percentage would grow all through the decade; in fact, it did.

Obviously, the concept of information as a corporate asset gained greater credence all through the 1960s and 1970s, particularly for senior executives. DP could put a company out of business or make it more profitable, more manageable, more competitive. Recognizing that information was a corporate resource was tantamount to having an intuitive grasp of the obvious. Too many millions of dollars had been invested in the development of applications across a wide spectrum of the business community, too many millions more paid out for hardware and people with job titles few understood, for any other conclusions to be reached. In slower-changing, more obtuse companies, reality may have struck home when DP disaster planners began justifying the expense to the organization in lost business and cash outlays if computers malfunctioned. By the early 1980s, the loss of a major data center could destroy a year's worth of business for a large corporation.[20] Our brave new world clearly called for new strategies if the 1980s were to be survived.

Various approaches were developed in response to the potential power of the computer. On the most conservative side, simple labor-saving automation projects were undertaken, usually involving clerical activities in which most corporate information that was in machine-readable form was of an accounting nature in both batch and online systems. At the other end of the spectrum there were professors, consultants, and a few organizations attempting to implement Total Systems (a term from the 1960s) in the belief that ultimately you could have computers do most of the work and make a vast array of decisions based on large numbers of data points. This extreme point of view was widely discussed in the 1960s as people imagined a situation in which computers could take econometric models, and respond with marketing and manufacturing actions.[21] Reality struck back and by the early 1970s people were settling for moving from one application to another, and by the end of the 1970s began lashing these systems together so that data could flow from one application to others by way of database management software tools.

But regardless of which camp management aligned with, executives with little or no knowledge of data processing could increasingly see as clearly as their more technically oriented peers that the lack of information could cripple their operations, drive the cost of business too high, and make competition tougher. That set of concerns led to one of the most pondered problems by executives at the end of the 1970s and start of the 1980s: how best to manage MIS. The most frequent response involved upgrading data processing managers from glorified computer baby-sitters and technical jockeys to business managers and integrating information from many sources into useful collections. Clusters of data (also called "databases"), when properly herded together, could be protected, used, changed, and cost-justified in a manner similar to other functions of a corporation. But two things had to happen to make this possible: first, management had to realize that their companies had large quantities of machine-readable data with which to run their businesses. Historians could calculate the quantity of data by simply cataloging the number of disk drives and feet of magnetic tape acquired in these years.[22] Second, manipulating data files such that online systems and multiple applications could be shared and coordinated required a whole new collection of software packages to manipulate information, called database managers.[23] These software tools began to appear in the 1960s and have continued to evolve and become more useful. These tools represent an unrecognized yet critical reason why so many applications became possible, particularly in the 1980s working on large mainframes.[24]

Those executives who wanted to exploit computer technology to the best of MIS's ability in the 1970s and 1980s first had to develop a workable perspective on data processing, and that invariably led to his or her acceptance of the notion that machine-readable information could be used to help run an organization effectively. Second, management time and effort had to be expended to manage this resource properly, just as for manufacturing, sales, finance, and other traditional sectors of a company. With information processing, therefore, any effort had to involve defining the nature and mission of MIS, continuously upgrade the quality of its leadership, and take advantage of new technologies (hardware and software) as they presented themselves. Their objective was to improve the quality of information, at some value that exceeded its costs. However, defining what was needed, what its value was, and its costs, proved very complicated in the 1970s and 1980s.

Historically, the industrialized world had seen both the cost and value of MIS increase. Cost had gone up because the use of data processing had increased faster than prices decreased with each new technological introduction, thus spurring continued use at a more rapid rate. Industry sales presented in Chapter 2 demonstrated growth rates of nearly 20 or more percent in the 1960s and 7 to 10 percent through most of the 1970s (except at the start of the decade during a U.S. recession), and double-digit growth in certain sectors of the information processing industry all through the 1980s.[25] Customers in the 1960s and 1970s generally saw value improve, although not always in such measurable forms as cost. Yet on the battlefields of a thousand applications, individually cost-justified over the years, the quantifiable and intangible benefits proved to be some of the most attractive investments that business could make in these years (1960s–1980s).

Just like a company, once it had money in its safe, needed an accountant and, finally, a chief financial officer, so, too, a similar phenomenon demonstrated the growing value of computer-based information. The requirements for MIS evolved to meet their growing significance. At first, management was usually satisfied to have data processing perform repetitive tasks previously done by armies of clerks. Accounting applications were the most widely employed.[26] Then came the requirement to analyze trends and patterns of behavior to improve functional productivity. The extension to manufacturing loading applications and floor systems to monitor production that told management what resources were available signaled a major thrust forward.[27] Then came decision-making demands—first in finance, with the introduction of models to cost out various scenarios, all the way to highly sophisticated ones on sales, expenses, budgets, industrial sectors, and even the national economy. Finally, by the early 1980s, many executives grasped the technological possibility of cost-justified integration of operational and control data with models, all packaged in relevant and timely reports which in turn could be presented to appropriate levels of management in some integrated fashion.[28] This approach was also accompanied by new applications that could actually perform operations, such as robots in manufacturing (see Table 7.1). The concept of MIS as a corporate asset had been brought to a new and significant level of responsibility and impact.

In summary, the increasing dependence of an organization on information processing, and the enormous explosion in cost-effectiveness of computers and related inventions that were easier to develop and that made decision making both at the tactical and strategic levels easier and even cost-justified, made it possible for management to accept the idea that information was something to be valued and used. Obviously, then, the question of how information can be managed better became one of the ''hot'' topics of the early 1980s, though it had become evident as early as the mid-1970s. Studies by such industry watchers of the period as James Martin, Charles P. Lecht, and John Diebold, and scholars looking at information handling in general (e.g., Fritz Machlup), began to confirm that companies were spending anywhere from 5 to 30 percent of their budgets just moving information around (e.g., phone calls, paper documents, and computer-based data), and increasing amounts through computers.[29] With

Table 7.1
Evolution of Applications, 1960s–1980s

1960s *Reports*	1970s *Applications*	1980s *Systems*
Accounting	Financial & Budgeting	Modeling
Bill of Materials	Manufacturing	Production
Order Entry	Customer Service	Office
Inventory Control	Distribution	Logistics
Standalone Reports	Integrated	Feeds Corporate
Batch	Query/On-line	Demand Query
		Models
No Data Integration	Database: Horizontal	Database: Vertical

that trend, the issue of managing the process no longer could be ignored. A new frontier in management had to be explored and conquered.

ROLE OF COMPUTER TECHNOLOGY IN THE MANAGEMENT OF DATA

Given the acceptance of information as a resource, the question frequently asked was: What were the emerging characteristics of a management information system that could serve as a resource for the company? For the period at the start of the 1980s, several observations were possible.

The most visible component of MIS was the computer. In the 1960s, an organization might have had one big computer; by the early 1980s they seemed to be all over the place—in offices, in data centers, buried in industrial equipment as microprocessors, in word processing devices, in hand calculators, and in novel, over-functioned clocks and Christmas presents. MIS was everywhere, no longer the private preserve of data processing departments. The cost of the hardware had dropped to the point where the average individual could now think of having a personal computer at home. The transaction $2 \times 2 = 4$, performed on a computer in 1950, would have cost about $1.50 (1950 purchasing power dollar). By the early 1980s, billions of similar transactions could be performed for a fraction of a penny and in a thousand times less of a second. Of course, people wanted to do many more such transactions which ensured that the overall budget for computers kept rising, escalating faster than the cost of a transaction kept falling. That is why many economic studies about the performance of computers in economic terms are superficial, even irrelevant, when looking at how companies deployed computers, whether in the 1960s, 1970s, 1980s, or 1990s.

A second characteristic of MIS was and continues to be programming, of applications or other software tools. Programs reside in computers that take in raw data and perform calculations we need for accounting, sales, manufacturing, finance, engineering, and so on, and have grown profoundly since 1960. Billions of dollars have been spent annually on this aspect of information processing. Any organization, as a horrible yet relevant rule of thumb, could assume that only one-third of its expenses on data processing had gone for hardware. This was as true in 1996 as in 1966. Clearly, the other two-thirds were spent on people to write and maintain software or on the purchase of programs from vendors. In other words, if a department had spent $4 million on a computer, it was probably running over $12 million in software and people expenses. Large mainframes of the late 1980s, valued at approximately $1-2 million each, sometimes had even more personnel and software baggage because of the accumulation of these over time, inflation in the cost of salaries, and the deflation in the price of hardware. Thus, software and people to work with it represented major expenses. Software increasingly became seen as investments of enormous value, returning benefits to corporations for many years, usually for far longer than the hardware in which it ran. Multimillion-dollar application packages might run for ten to fifteen years while mainframes were swapped out every three to five years in the 1970s and 1980s. Thus, software represented a major and valuable investment that continued to return benefits to the organization year after year.[30]

Along with applications software there emerged massive data file-handling programs. These took care of information rather than performing calculations on them. These packages eventually evolved into what, by the early 1980s, were called database managers. The concept was a simple one. You took groups of data, separated them from their programs, and protected and controlled who had access to them. Management provided the links so that programs could get to this information. Before databases one had information attached to programs. For example, a customer's address might have resided both in a mass mailing program and in an accounts receivable package. One had twice the cost of file maintenance and twice the opportunity to have the wrong address. By about 1980–1982, with one database a data center could have on copy of a customer's address, which either program could borrow for a calculation. The benefits of databases included less expense, greater accuracy, ease of use, and, most importantly accessibility for large models and inquiries such as I suggested above upper management wanted.[31] Experience with data processing that included databases resulted frequently in greater amounts of relevant information becoming available to larger user communities, more frequently and quickly, and at less expense. Commonly shared, databases had information that could be fed to a variety of users who might or might not have needed this information, depending on existing applications and knowing little or nothing about information processing. By the end of the 1980s, it was virtually impossible to find any major application that was written without some sort of database management approach to handling its information. In the 1990s, database management techniques were common in PCs where, for example, one could take data from a spreadsheet and bring it over to a word processing package, or drop it into a graphics presentation.

The explosion in the use of terminals, particularly in the 1970s, and of communications and data processing in the 1960s and 1970s and early 1980s in general was matched by the expansion of database managers. With the increasing number of users able to get to data and even to write programs, the role of MIS management changed. During the 1950s and most of the 1960s, DP departments did the majority of programming for commercial applications and captured all the data required for these, getting the information into computers. By the early 1980s, MIS, along with many end users of computer applications, wrote programs and maintained data files. During the era of the microcomputer, that was always the case. Databases remained the preserve of MIS in the 1980s, and for good reason. A strong characteristic of a database was its centrality, which implies central control, and what better technical reserve of experience and capability was there in most organizations than within the MIS department? This approach continued to prove effective and essential to the integrity and accuracy of information in the 1970s and through most of the 1980s, not to be undone until distributed local area networks (LANs) and software to disperse files in a shared manner came along as an effective alternative (although not a replacement) in the 1990s. In the 1970s and 1980s, DP organizations consequently spent more time protecting and managing a company's data than convincing users of the value of doing new things with computers.

By the mid-1970s, MIS had become responsible for all information in computers, just as finance had been for decades for money. By the end of the 1980s, MIS had governance and policy responsibility for computer-based information regardless in which computer they resided, even microcomputers which placed the DP professionals in the position of feeling responsible for how PCs were used. The logic was simple enough: Only if MIS used their professional capabilities could one be assured that the benefits of a database could be repeated: reduced redundancy of data, increased reliability of software, increased control through one organizational point of access, availability to a larger community of users on upper management's say-so, and reduction in the high cost of maintaining and repairing old programs. This approach also made it possible for MIS to organize information in groups for multi-functional purposes rather than leaving it in the more traditional per-application organization.[32] By structuring the organization of data, executives had the capability to move information horizontally and vertically across the enterprise to various users and applications (as suggested by Table 7.2).

From the point of view of strategy and policy, a manager could consider establishing data management as a formal, well-defined function and initiative. The advice of the period was, if hardware and programs were going to be dispersed through an organization, why not try to manage the inevitable when it first became an issue? In reality, most MIS directors of the 1970s and early 1980s did not believe information processing would become so dispersed to call

Table 7.2
Typical Organization of Data

Characteristics	Organizational	Control	Strategic
Highly	Accounting	Budgeting	Models
Structured	Order Entry	Sales Forecasting	Business
			Direction
Partially	Plant	Production Planning	Acquisitions
Organized	Scheduling		
Ad Hoc	Costing	Sales	Research

for that approach. The dissemination of microcomputers at a speed far exceeding the deployment of any previous information technology cured that myopia by the late 1980s. In fact, haphazard growth often occurred as end users bought minis and micros out of impatience with the slowness that MIS demonstrated in providing new applications or access to data. The result of end-user initiatives was later great expense when end users wanted compatibility with and connectivity to other machines, when senior executives saw data flying around unprotected and redundant, and after expenses rose for machines that were being used in a limited fashion for spreadsheets and some word processing. Reality in data management never matched the advice given at the time.[33]

A third characteristic of MIS by the early 1980s concerned its distribution throughout an organization. With hardware increasingly appearing all over a company, bought by end users and no longer just by the MIS organization, computing was taking place in a wide variety and number of offices and departments, not just in the data center or in engineering laboratories. Clearly, from the mid-1970s forward, not only was there movement of information inside an organization, rather than simply within a data processing department, but management expected such movement to accelerate. In hindsight, that is exactly what happened all through the 1980s and early 1990s. The installation of telecommunication networks in the 1970s and 1980s (e.g., cables, telephone lines, and satellites) allowed tens of thousands of terminals in the United States, and additional thousands in Europe, to talk with banks of centralized or dispersed computers, thereby moving increasingly massive quantities of information up and down organizations.[34] Over the years a variety of communications software evolved to meet the logical challenge of moving data safely, quickly, and cost-effectively through a building, across a town, or around the world.

The other technical facet of MIS that made it possible for machine-readable data to become a corporate asset was the system control program (SCP). All computers and information processing hardware have, in effect, a software traffic policeman called an SCP to coordinate the flow of information and application software in and out of computers, through dependent peripheral equipment and components, and throughout communications networks. SCPs were developed by computer manufacturers, as were most telecommunications and database management software, with some notable exceptions.[35] SCPs were provided by machine developers for mainframes in the 1960s to the present, just as SCPs were by providers of minis (1960s to the present) and PC vendors of the 1970s–1990s. DP staffs in large information processing organizations spent as much time in the care and feeding of such software as they did in either maintaining existing stockpiles of application programs or writing new ones in the 1960s and 1970s, and to a declining extent all through the 1980s and into the 1990s. That was a critical fact in the 1970s and 1980s, for example, when an MIS manager complained that despite large staffs and tons of equipment, his or her department did not have the staff to write some new application. In providing support and guidance to such a data processing manager it became imperative to stress the need to adopt methods and policies that drove down the amount of time and resources expended in maintaining existing programs. Experts in the field of computing produced a library of advice on these issues from the late 1950s to the present.[36] Beginning in the mid-1970s, the need for software tools to assist in the work effort resulted in the creation of new programs and managerial procedures in data processing that drove down maintenance activities. In the 1970s, the average data processing organization spent about 70 percent of its manpower in running or maintaining existing programs (SCPs and applications). By the mid-1980s some data centers had pushed that percentage down to as low as 45 percent, so progress was possible. However, even in the mid-1990s, software maintenance activities were routinely closer to what had existed in the 1970s.

GROWTH IN INFORMATION PROCESSING

In summary, the concept of information as a corporate asset evolved in response to increased dependence on information processing, its attractive cost performance in the 1960s and 1970s, its contribution to human and organizational productivity (in all decades), and its general ability to meet the requirements of most forms of jobs and decisions (1970s to the present). By the early to mid-1980s, MIS was being used to plan strategic and tactical moves, execute them, and monitor and control events along the way. General management increasingly tried to manage MIS and to define its mission with the same discipline imposed on sales, manufacturing, distribution, accounting, and finance.

Expectations among information industry watchers in the 1970s and 1980s, which they were relaying to executive end users, were that all enterprises and government agencies would acquire more computers and have more data in machine-readable form, treating these trends as an almost inevitable process. The conventional wisdom was that migration would be through stages in the development of operational applications for the lower levels of an organization followed by evolution into data management systems that deliver strategic planning tools to middle and upper management.[37] In hindsight several things happened. First, the trend occurred, more computers and data files were acquired. Second, as had happened in the 1960s, lower level operational applications continued to be installed all through the 1970s and 1980s. Third, decision-making applications also appeared but their golden age came not with the arrival of databases but with the personal computer. By the end of the 1980s, the PC had frequently become the technical platform of choice for "what if" analysis for much small and mundane decision making using spreadsheet software.[38]

Fourth, databases became popular and effective, applied slowly in the 1970s and then, by the end of the 1980s, routinely applied to all major applications. They constituted the tool that made it possible to lash major applications together—for example, information on customers, billing, phone center applications, executive financial reporting, product design, work in process inventory, production schedules, manufacturing status, and finished inventory applications. Historians will probably conclude in the future that database software had a profound influence on the use of computers right on the eve of the arrival of the PC.

The reference to the almost inevitable growth of information processing frequently stuck in the throats of executives as an uncontrollable phenomenon. No executive likes not having options. But what occurred in the 1970s and 1980s frequently were several changes to business which did indeed make it almost inevitable that much information would have to be managed through use of computers. In certain industries, work simply could only be done using computers for technical or legal reasons—airplane wing design or guiding rockets to the moon, for example. In others, it was the price of admission to a marketplace demanding such services—automated teller machines in banking, computer-based reservations in various travel industries, for example. In others, by the end of the 1980s, new practices existed—inventory forecasting and control shared among suppliers and manufacturers in the automotive industry, or electronic interchange between large retail store systems and their suppliers, for example. The personal computer also represented a unique challenge for executives; nobody could stop for long its acquisition. End users usually had enough budgetary authority to make individual decisions to acquire PCs, and so these machines began to seep into organizations. In other cases, information processing departments facilitated the process by negotiating large purchase agreements with Apple, IBM, and others. In most companies and government agencies no formal attempt was made even to inventory how many there were until the late 1980s. Then people were horrified to find out that, in some companies, the amount of horsepower in PCs came close to what the IS director had in his or her glass house! In short, in some companies while the IS manager was buying a $1 million computer from his IBM sales representative, users were spending nearly the same amount in a variety of microcomputers from a half-dozen vendors. Senior executives began to recognize the pattern in growth of computing by the late 1970s, and remained watchful, concerned, or upset all through the 1980s.

To a certain extent the problem they faced was that money was spent on machine-readable data without the kinds of formal justification exercises that had characterized the early acquisitions of computers. To control the spiraling growth in data processing expenditures, they frequently imposed chargeout systems, beginning in the 1970s.[39] Essentially the way this worked was that a data center would charge end users a monthly fee for using the data center's computers, adding new applications and files, and for sharing the overhead of the entire facility. Such a strategy worked in some cases to constrain expenses but, while the hard data are not in, it appeared in aggregate to do little because the sales of disk drives, computers, and terminals kept growing all through the 1970s, and in the 1980s end users also invested in personal computers along with continued investments in mainframe applications.

Most MIS directors in large companies surveyed in the early 1980s indicated that if they continued with their current cost-justified (or at least authorized) plans and with no new pressures or technologies appearing on the horizon, they would have to increase their computing power by a minimum factor of four in the 1980s. The pent-up demand for applications therefore constituted about a 400 percent increase in computing over the vast quantities of installed applications of the early 1980s. Uninstalled backlogs of applications at the time often exceeded either the value of already installed systems, or, more frequently measured by the time it would take to write and install them, three or more years.

The major computer and software vendors understood the value of computer-based information to their customers. They had forecasts counting new housing starts and factory chimneys and worrying about GNP and other variables to predict the amount of computing that would be needed or could be sold. Historically, forecasters grossly *underestimated* the amount of computing power customers acquired. Yet despite that maladjustment in forecasting, they frequently predicted growths of ten times existing power in the late 1970s-early 1980s. Thus from a number of perspectives, computing power was predicted to grow all during the 1970s and 1980s in response to a continued and massive move of data into machine-readable form.[40] In the decade prior to widespread use of personal computers, such massive growth in computing power proved essential to drive large database systems as well as the complex applications that were being developed to move operational applications into more integrated, vertically mobile data files that were strategic planning and control tools. Thus, information processing continued to evolve, as always, yet by the early 1980s as a communications vehicle for the transmittal of information across a variety of departments and offices of an organization. That same process of communications continued right through the period of the personal computer. By the mid-1990s the language of this process included such vocabulary as "groupware," and LANs, all new words to describe a historic process underway for over a generation.

Figure 7.1
Information Migration from Paper to Computer

Type of Data	Operation	Management Control	Planning
Source	Internal	◄───────►	External
Scope	Narrow/Specific	◄───────►	Broad/Varied
Organization	Historic/Present	◄───────►	Future
Time Frame	Immediate	◄───────►	Aged
Needed Precision	Extensive	◄───────►	Minor
Frequency of Use	Very	◄───────►	Occasional

CONCLUSION

By the early 1980s, online, terminal-activated systems with massive databases were becoming increasingly familiar. They served interests in business less expensively and more effectively than some documents, newspapers, television, or the telephone. One by-product already in evidence was the integration of multiple types of computers and programs throughout the organization. A second advantageous evolution already evident was the distribution of databases across a variety of systems, thereby making it possible for departments and divisions to stockpile their own mountains of (hopefully) meaningful machine-readable information.

While this is not the place to discuss in detail the nature of the kind of data considered a corporate asset, it might be useful to realize that the large mainframe applications of the 1960s–1980s frequently did lead to a mosaic of machine-readable information. Figure 7.1 suggests a model historians might consider using when they finally map out the huge migration of information from paper to computer. They will also have to document the enormous expense of these files because they are the reason why companies continuously spent anywhere from 0.8 to over 7 percent of their total operating budgets on computing since the early 1960s. It is also why information processing was a trillion dollar industry in the late 1990s.

NOTES

1. For a broad listing of the literature covering the 1950s–1990s, see James W. Cortada, *Second Bibliographic Guide to the History of Computing, Computers, and the Information Processing Industry* (Westport, Conn.: Greenwood Press, 1996): 298–302, 374.

2. Sharon M. McKinnon and William J. Bruns, Jr., *The Information Mosaic: How Managers Get the Information They Really Need* (Boston: Harvard Business School Press, 1992).

3. The literature is vast; however, as examples, see Irene Tavis (ed.), *The Computer*

Impact (Englewood Cliffs, N.J.: Prentice-Hall, 1970); Charles R. Walker (ed.), *Technology, Industry, and Man: The Age of Acceleration* (New York: McGraw-Hill, 1968); Gunter Friedrichs and Adam Schaff, *Microelectronics and Society for Better or for Worse: A Report to the Club of Rome* (Oxford: Pergamon Press, 1982); Tom Forester (ed.), *The Microelectronics Revolution: The Complete Guide to the New Technology and Its Impact on Society* (Oxford: Basil Blackwell, 1980); and Donald P. Lauda and Robert D. Ryan (ed.), *Advancing Technology: Its Impact on Society* (Dubuque, Iowa: Wm. C. Brown Company, 1971).

4. See the widely read article on stages of information processing by Richard L. Nolan, "Managing the Crisis in Data Processing," *Harvard Business Review* (March–April, 1979): 115–126; also see the useful arguments of G. Anthony Gorry and Michael S. Scott Morton, "A Framework for Management Information Systems," *Sloan Management Review* (Fall 1971): 21–36.

5. An example that straddled the 1970s and 1980s of this kind of assessments is by Myles E. Walsh, *Understanding Computers: What Managers and Users Need to Know* (New York: John Wiley & Sons, 1981).

6. F. R. Crawford, *Introduction to Data Processing* (Englewood Cliffs, N.J.: Prentice-Hall, 1968): 3–14; Roger Nett and Stanley A. Hetzler, *An Introduction to Electronic Data Processing* (New York: Free Press, 1959): 138–178; John Dearden, *Computers in Business Management* (Homewood, Ill.: Dow Jones-Irwin, 1966): 113–182; Donald H. Sanders, *Computers in Business: An Introduction* (New York: McGraw-Hill, 1968): 1–12, 239–278; and for a series of articles published in the 1970s and early 1980s, see Lynn M. Salerno (ed.), *Catching Up with the Computer Revolution* (New York: John Wiley & Sons, 1983).

7. See, for example, T. A. Dolotta et al., *Data Processing in 1980–1985: A Study of Potential Limitations to Progress* (New York: John Wiley & Sons, 1976); Cortada, *Second Bibliographic Guide*, 254–275.

8. Brandt Allen, "An Unmanaged Computer System Can Stop You Dead," *Harvard Business Review* (November-December 1982): 76–87; James W. Cortada, *Strategic Data Processing: Considerations for Management* (New York: Prentice-Hall, 1984): 12–19, 53–84.

9. Cortada, *Second Bibliographic Guide*, 340–348, 374.

10. James Martin, *Design and Strategy for Distributed Data Processing* (Englewood Cliffs, N.J.: Prentice-Hall, 1981); C. Warren Axlerod, *Computer Productivity: A Planning Guide for Cost-Effective Management* (New York: John Wiley & Sons, 1982); James I. Cash, Jr., F. Warren McFarlan, and James L. McKenney, *Corporate Information Systems Management: The Issues Facing Senior Executives* (Homewood, Ill.: Dow Jones-Irwin, 1983).

11. James W. Cortada, *A Bibliographic Guide to the History of Computer Applications, 1950–1990* (Westport, Conn.: Greenwood Press, 1996): 170.

12. J. E. Goodman and J. Bolovdy, "25 Top Personal Finance Programs," *Money* 13 (November 1984): 130–132ff.

13. John F. Rockart and Michael E. Treacy, "The CEO Goes On-line," *Harvard Business Review* (January–February 1982): 82–88.

14. Ibid.; however, see also for an earlier time, J. Kanter, *Management-Oriented Management Information Systems* (Englewood Cliffs, N.J.: Prentice-Hall, 1972).

15. The effects of computing on individuals has recently become a growth area in the research on computer applications. For two useful studies, see Shoshana Zuboff, *In the*

Age of the Smart Machine: The Future of Work and Power (New York: Basic Books, 1984); Thomas K. Landauer, *The Trouble with Computers: Usefulness, Usability, and Productivity* (Cambridge, Mass.: MIT Press, 1995).

16. Harley Shaiken, *Work Transformed: Automation and Labor in the Computer Age* (Lexington, Mass.: Lexington Books, 1984) suggests the increasing role of computers in business life and culminates with conventional wisdom including extensive use of data. See also a textbook, Gregory M. Bounds, Gregory H. Dobbins, and Oscar S. Fowler, *Management: A Total Quality Perspective* (Cincinnati, Ohio: South-Western College Publishing, 1995).

17. Allen, ''An Unmanaged Computer System Can Stop You Dead,'' 76–87. A very early discussion of computer-based productivity issues can be found in William J. Abernathy, *The Productivity Dilemma* (Baltimore: Johns Hopkins University Press, 1978); but see also Joel E. Ross, *Productivity, People and Profits* (Reston, Va.: Reston, 1981).

18. Ibid.

19. Richard L. Nolan, *Management Accounting and Control of Data Processing* (New York: National Association of Accountants, June 1977); David P. Norton and Kenneth G. Rau, *A Guide to EDP Performance Management* (Wellesley, Mass.: Q.E.D. Information Sciences, 1978); and James W. Cortada, *EDP Costs and Charges* (Englewood Cliffs, N.J.: Prentice-Hall, 1980).

20. James W. Cortada, *Managing DP Hardware: Capacity Planning, Cost Justification, Availability, and Energy Management* (Englewood Cliffs, N.J.: Prentice-Hall, 1983): 323–367. This volume presents the only discussion of the issue published up through the early 1980s.

21. Cortada, *A Bibliographic Guide to the History of Computer Applications*, 27–40, 57, 68.

22. There are a number of guides to volumes of devices sold. The most complete is by Montgomery Phister, Jr., *Data Processing Technology and Economics* (Santa Monica, Calif.: Santa Monica Publishing Co., 1974, 1975, 1976, 1979).

23. J. P. Fry and E. H. Sibley, ''Evolution of Data-Base Management Systems,'' *Computing Surveys* 8, no. 1 (March 1976): 7–42; W. C. McGee, ''Data Base Technology,'' *IBM Journal of Research and Development* 25, no. 5 (September 1981): 505–519; and M. Lynne Neufeld and Martha Cornog, ''Database History: From Dinosaurs to Compact Discs,'' *Journal of the American Society for Information Science* 37, no. 4 (1986): 183–190.

24. For an historical perspective on the evolution of software see Edward Yourdon, *Classics of Software Engineering* (New York: Yourdon, Press, 1979) and his sequel, *Papers of the Revolution* (New York: Yourdon Press, 1982). Yourdon is a prolific commentator on programming methodologies.

25. Two classic studies are William F. Sharpe, *The Economics of Computers* (New York: Columbia University Press, 1969) and Gerald W. Brock, *The U.S. Computer Industry: A Study of Market Power* (Cambridge, Mass.: Ballinger Publishing Co., 1975). Less known but very useful is Charles P. Lecht, *The Waves of Change: A Techno-Economic Analysis of the Data Processing Industry* (New York: Advanced Computer Techniques Corp., 1977); Computerworld, *The Age of MIS* (Farmingham, Mass.: IDG Communications, 1987); and Egil Juliussen et al., *Computer Industry Almanac* (Dallas: Computer Industry Almanac, 1987).

26. For a sampling of this class of applications, see David H. Li, *Accounting, Com-*

puters, Management Information Systems (New York: McGraw-Hill, 1968); and his *Accounting and the Computer* (New York: American Institute of Certified Public Accountants, 1966).

27. For a sampling of this class of applications, see Donald W. Brewer, *The Impact of the Electronic Computer Upon the Production Control Function* (Rock Island, Ill.: U.S. Management Engineering Training Agency, 1968); and John N. Taussig, *EDP Applications for the Manufacturing Function* (New York: American Management Association, 1966).

28. The literature is massive; see Cortada, *A Bibliographic Guide.*

29. James Martin, *Telematic Society: A Challenge for Tomorrow* (Englewood Cliffs, N.J.: Prentice-Hall, 1978); Lecht, *The Waves of Change*; John Diebold's classic, *Automation: The Advent of the Automatic Factory* (New York: D. Van Nostrand, 1952); and the first of many studies by Fritz Machlup, *The Production and Distribution of Knowledge in the United States* (Princeton, N.J.: Princeton University Press, 1962), with other related studies published into the 1980s.

30. For an introduction to the topic—one whose economics have hardly been studied by historians—see Stephen E. Siwek and Harold W. Furchtgott-Roth, *International Trade in Computer Software* (Westport, Conn.: Quorum Books, 1993); a partial exception is a study by economists looking at the historical record, Franklin M. Fisher, James W. McKie, and Richard B. Mancke, *IBM and the U.S. Data Processing Industry: An Economic History* (New York: Praeger, 1983): passim. I have listed additional citations in the *Bibliographic Guide to the History of Computing, Computers, and the Information Processing Industry* (Westport, Conn.: Greenwood Press, 1990): 396–491, and in *Second Bibliographic Guide*, 276–279.

31. McGee, "Data Base Technology," 505–519.

32. One of the most prolific commentators on the subject was James Martin who, between the 1960s and the 1990s, published more than 80 books. Any one of his publications from the 1980s and 1990s lists his many books, almost all published by Prentice-Hall.

33. See, for example, Thomas H. Davenport, Michael Hammer, and Tauno J. Metsisto, "How Executives Can Shape Their Company's Information System," *Harvard Business Review* (March–April 1989): 130–134; Harlan Cleveland, *The Knowledge Executive: Leadership in an Information Society* (New York: Truman Talley Books/E. P. Dutton, 1985); E. W. Martin, "Critical Success Factors of Chief MIS/DP Executives," *MIS Quarterly* 6, no. 2 (June 1982): 1–9 and the sequel, "Critical Success Factors of Chief MIS/DP Executives—An Addendum," *MIS Quarterly* 6, no. 4 (December 1982): 79–81; and R. L. Nolan, "The Plight of the EDP Manager," *Harvard Business Review* 51 (May 1973): 143–152.

34. See Chapter 4 on applications.

35. N. Weizer, "A History of Operating Systems," *Datamation* 27, no. 1 (January 1981): 119–126.

36. For an exposure to the growing list of citations on this topic, see Cortada, *Second Bibliographic Guide*, 285–377.

37. The entire body of publications by James Martin, for example, was typical of the period. For additional bibliography, see Cortada, *Second Bibliographic Guide*, 261, 279, 358.

38. See my comments in Chapters 1 and 2 for bibliography.

39. Dan Bernard et al., *Charging for Computer Services. Principles and Guidelines* (New York: PBI Books, 1971); N. Statland et al., "Guidelines for Cost Accounting Practices for Data Processing," *Data Base* 8, no. 3 (Winter 1977), supplement.

40. Dolotta, *Data Processing in 1980–1985*, passim.

8

Evolution of Information Processing Management, 1945–1995

The management of the trillions of dollars of investments made by organizations in information processing over the past half-century have barely been studied by historians. As with the topic of computer applications, those who have studied I/T have been either business professors or consultants. Historians have yet to come up to the plate.[1] The topic is important for the reasons suggested in Chapter 7. What historians will want to do is link the experience of managing information technology to the mainstream of management practices of the second half of the twentieth century, because information systems management increasingly became part of the mainstream of corporate America, bringing their organizations into the heart of many enterprises.

Since this chapter is an introduction to the history of the topic, it is at best a sampling of the issues that require detailed examination. For our purposes, however, three sets of issues are examined:

- evolution of information processing organizations and where they fit into corporate enterprises
- rise of the key professions within the information processing community
- key issues associated with the management of information processing.

Many other topics could be examined. These include end-user relations with information processing, effects of computers on various communities of workers, and the role of I/T management practices on how organizations function. Those will have to wait as we deal with more basic bread-and-butter issues.

The bulk of my comments below focus on large North American companies for two reasons. First, for the majority of the period in question they were the largest and most important users of computers. In fact, from the 1950s to the mid-1980s, they dominated the acquisition and use of such technology. Only with the arrival of less expensive mid-sized general processors in the late 1960s and early 1970s and PCs in large quantities in the early 1980s did it become possible for increasingly smaller firms to use computers. Second, for the larger enterprises we have the greatest amount of documentation.

DATA PROCESSING ORGANIZATIONS BEFORE THE COMPUTER

Computers were first adopted by organizations that had extensive experience with information handling technologies, such as IBM tabulators and accounting equipment from Burroughs and NCR.[2] Primarily from World War I forward, these large enterprises developed a wide variety of business practices designed to exploit effectively these kinds of technology, with the result that by the time the computer arrived, there already were organizations in place that did data processing. They had different names—such as the punch card department, IBM department, and so on—but they did essentially the same things: gathered data, put it into machine-readable form, and produced reports. These were the same functions performed with computers. As in the early days of computers, these departments were typically housed in two organizations: in engineering/manufacturing divisions and in accounting/finance departments. Either way, they performed data processing (DP) services for many branches of a company. Thus, when the computer came along, the new processing machines were invariably put into these departments.

The decision to do that was driven as much by the nature of the technology itself as by who knew what to do with it. Early computer systems used many input and output devices familiar to the data processing community of the precomputer era. The most obvious example was the use of punch cards as input to tabulators and later to computers. "Computer reports" had also been produced during the pre-computer era. So the initial thinking was that computers could continue to do much of the earlier work faster with some familiar technological features. The second reason concerned who knew about data input and output. While much has been written about how a new generation of engineers came into existence who knew about computers,[3] the fact remains that when computers were used initially in commercial operations, these people and their machines came under the control of long-established data centers. The majority of these "shops" were also part of the accounting and financial organizations because these were the departments that typically had relied the most on the use of computing equipment in order to do their work prior to the arrival of the computer. They were also the departments that exploited computers the most in the first two decades of their availability. As suggested in Chapter 5 on applications, accounting and financial (and related applications, e.g., inventory control and purchasing) uses made it usually most practical to assign management of the computer into these parts of the organization.

Lest there be confusion, trends in organization over time should be understood. First, small accounting equipment turned up in an enterprise wherever there was simple mathematics going on. Thus cash registers were in stores, adding machines in most departments. These types of machines hardly influenced the organization of a company or department. And, of course, accountants were extensive users of this technology. Second, the larger and more complex calculating equipment became, the more such technology influenced organizational structures because management always wanted to leverage the technology for efficiency.

Just after the end of World War I, one study of business organizations noted that statistical and accounting work tended to be centralized. It cited the experiences of the National Cloak and Suit Company, Postal Life Insurance Company, United States Rubber Company, Curtis Publishing, Equitable Life Insurance Company, Funk and Wagnalls, and others.[4] In the mid-1930s, organization charts for accounting departments demonstrated that tabulating functions were part of the organization.[5] During the early decades of the twentieth century there also emerged the function of the "system man" who, in effect, did the same kind of work "systems analysts" did in the age of the computer. In 1936 one author described what the "system man" did:

In the design of accounting systems, the system man has a choice of a great many different kinds, styles, and applications of forms, filing devices, binders, and machines for carrying out the clerical work and physical operation of the various accounting and statistical procedures. To make a successful selection, he must know what equipment and devices are available for particular tasks and at what cost they can be employed. The selection of accounting method and the selection of accounting equipment are complementary tasks.[6]

The message remained essentially the same for the next several decades. One of the most highly respected commentators on accounting in the 1940s, Leon E. Vannais, also linked his profession and machines together. He saw the accountant as the leader in determining how best to use punch card technology: "In considering punched-card procedures the problem of 'what to punch' in cards is in many ways the same problem which confronts accountants when they must decide 'what to record'."[7] In 1961, a leading expert on computing, James D. Gallagher, was advising his readers that:

The ultimate goal of an effective management information system is to keep all levels of management completely informed on all developments in the business which affect them. To do this, the data-processing personnel and those entering information into the system should know exactly what data to collect and which to tabulate, and management on its part has the obligation to be able to write down its actual requirements for internal information.[8]

These pre-computer organizations had machine operators (such as keypunch operators) who "fed" data into the devices, maintenance personnel, file clerks, systems analysts, and application specialists (e.g., cost accountants). They were, in short, integral parts of the accounting, finance, or shop floor departments who they served. As will be demonstrated below, these functions came over intact into the era of the computer.

EVOLUTION OF THE DATA PROCESSING ORGANIZATION

When historians think about the evolution of an organization they have to conceive their notions in terms of the role and significance of a particular function since, in most enterprises, form did follow function. In the case of information processing, data processing professionals started low in the organization and rose in importance over the long period from the 1940s to the 1990s. How they were managed by senior executives evolved as well, as these leaders started from knowing nothing about computers to reaching a point where they saw information processing as a strategically important part of the business but often not managed to their satisfaction. Information processing grew to such a level of importance in a short period of time that general management never quite knew how best to deploy it. They were always catching up with the technology's changes.

Looking at roles and organizational structures provides yet another window into the life of business structures. A substantial amount of anecdotal evidence suggests what happened. Two models for the early positioning of information processing organizations seemed to co-exist. The first was driven by the economies of scale and function of computers and the second by where data processing began the computer era.

Computers were first installed in commercial settings in the early to mid-1950s. By about 1957 it had become evident to many companies that the huge cost of acquiring and caring of computers called for centralized operations. The issue of centralization versus decentralization of computing remained an active topic from the beginning and continues to this day. It is normally driven by a discussion of the economics of having large computers versus distributed computers performing the work required by end users. Politics and turf battles also complicated the discussion. But the heart of the debate always centered on the economics of computing. One observer of the industry in the 1950s noted that his contemporaries were learning that "centralization of data processing and the methods and procedures function is often necessary so as to obtain the most economical use of automatic data-processing equipment."[9] He also noted, however, that the economies of scale forcing centralization did create political and managerial problems if the culture of the company was that of a decentralized firm.[10] Limited evidence suggests, however, that if the culture of a company was decentralized, then the requirements of data processing changed and sometimes conformed to the firm's needs. Nonetheless, that kind of response did create communications problems that limited the quality of some computer applications.[11] A group of professors at the Harvard Business School in the 1980s with many years of experience watching this industry concluded that in the 1950s the economies of scale had favored glass house consolidations and that until those economies of scale changed in favor of decentralized computing, organizational proclivities did not.[12]

The second organizational trend concerned residence within the accounting function. Typically, initial interest in computers led senior management to commission a study of the possible advantages and uses of computers. Such studies were normally undertaken by the accounting or finance function of the company, often with direct support from engineering functions. The rationale was that the technical horsepower in computing already resided in accounting.[13] That circumstance, therefore, made it almost inevitable that the financial community would end up with responsibility for using computers once the studies indicated the advantages of such devices. One data processing manager of the 1950s commented in 1960:

In the past, the responsibility for data processing quite often has been assigned to the function or department which first uses the equipment involved, or which uses data-processing the most.

Traditionally, the responsibility for data processing has been assigned to financial departments. The reasons stated for this are that financial departments have generally been held responsible for the development of business systems. In addition, financial departments are charged with the basic responsibility for the maintenance and protection of company assets, the establishment of inventory policies, and other general responsibilities which affect all phases of the business. Most companies, from a corporate viewpoint, have found that the potential of the data-processing program can be best exploited where the financial department is held responsible for the development of an integrated systems program because of the over-all interests of the financial department in all phases of the business.[14]

Paul A. Strassmann, who eventually became the senior information processing executive at Xerox in the 1970s, made the same observation about the early years. Names changed from machine accounting to data processing to management information systems (MIS), but more frequently than not, during the years from the 1950s to the 1980s, information processing and finance were closely linked.[15]

What did these early organizations have to do? From about 1950 to 1960 one could generalize that data processing worked with computers for the first time, and thus lacked any deep understanding of this new technology. Management in these companies and government agencies had to (1) select, acquire, and maintain such technology, and (2) design, code, and operate applications that increased company efficiencies. During the 1950s and 1960s, the role of data processing was defined in an evolutionary way. Automating systems and procedures emerged as the key functions. Using computers confused the process.

One business professor in the 1960s, looking back on the early years, observed that "top management has failed to develop policies to guide systems activities or to become actively involved with them. Middle managers trained in systems, initially permitted to implement computer technology pretty much as they wished, are coming under closer line management control."[16]

But, as computers became increasingly important to the operations of the enterprise, the role of data processing management (and consequently of their organizations) changed. DP managers rose in stature. In a survey done in the mid-1960s of 288 firms, researchers turned over the fact that 117 DP managers were now second-line managers, and another 110 third-line managers. Five had become senior executives, while 49 were still fourth-level management.[17] So the rise in stature of the data processing community was well underway. We care about the issue because position was an indicator of value, of importance within any organization. Another student of the period confirmed the rise of the stature of data processing managers driven by five factors:

1. institutional traditions, accomplishments, and age of systems group already in place prior to the introduction of computers

2. number and degree of sophistication of new computer-based applications

3. time lapsed since the first computer was introduced into the organization

4. personal status and abilities of the data processing manager who owned the "systems group"

5. importance of data processing to senior management.[18]

All through the 1960s and 1970s, the elevation of the data processing manager continued to the point when, in the late 1970s, such managers frequently had become senior vice presidents of major corporations, a position many continued to attain in the 1990s.[19]

The reason for evolution of information technology in an organization, as reflected in the reporting position of the DP manager, related to the scope of responsibilities. During the decade of the 1960s, these managers were responsible for the wide proliferation of computers mentioned in almost every chapter of this book. They continued to be responsible for the selection, installation, and maintenance of this technology. They designed massive systems, hired over a million workers, and controlled billions of dollars of budgets. During the 1970s, they became managers of MIS—information—not simply baby-sitters of hardware and data entry clerks. They began to control vast quantities of a corporation's data and implemented systems that began to differentiate the competitive capabilities of their companies. All through the 1970s and 1980s, computing became distributed, first through minicomputers and later personal computers, stretching the influence of MIS across broader sectors of a company.[20]

By the early 1990s some one-third of all capital expenditures in the United States were being made by this group of managers.[21] That amount accounted only for the capital part of the budget, typically about one-third of what these techno-management teams spent. All through the 1960s and 1970s a big portion of a data processing expense budget went for the preparation of data, such as keypunching and checkers. As late as 1980, data processing managers were still committing between 20 and 40 percent of their resources (primarily people) to activities preceding actual processing of data by computers. After the 1970s, many costs for data entry shifted to end users, including some programming after the arrival of the personal computer. These shifts in expenses are one reason why economists and business managers in the 1990s have had so much difficulty understanding what information systems (IS) managers are spending for computers.[22]

These IS organizations became report factories, producing paychecks, accounting and inventory reports, production schedules, and shipping manifests, all within a tightly scheduled calendar in the 1950s through the 1970s. As the 1980s progressed, much of the reporting could be drawn down at will from computer systems by end users. But in the earlier decades it was the mysterious black hole of data processing that produced these materials. As such, information processing organizations tended to operate in some isolation from the rest of the corporation. This disconnect from the culture of the rest of the enterprise has yet to be studied by historians. Yet it is an important feature of information processing. Two observers of the period described it this way:

Fit into the tight schedule of this centralized computer shop was the periodic production of a stack of management reports on their highly recognizable, light green and white striped paper. Sometimes weighing many pounds, but very often providing little useful information, these reports were rolled out on a daily, weekly, or monthly schedule.[23]

They also reminded us that end users frequently could not get to the data they wanted in this kind of batch environment, let alone even physically enter the data center. But that began to change with the installation of terminals and online systems. By the mid-1980s nearly 20 percent of all information workers had access to information via terminals.[24] A decade later almost all who needed access had it.

Despite the enormous investments made in computers, relations between data processing organizations and the rest of the company were anything but smooth. In each decade contemporary commentators reported problems. A sampling of remarks suggests some of the problems. From the 1950s:

The punch card or computer installation normally is in the controller's department, which is not absolutely a necessity, and sometimes hinders management's operation.

True, the controller has more requirements by law for tax reports, interstate commerce reports, etc., etc., than do other departments of the organization, but the other departments of the organization are the revenue producing departments which need data and up-to-the-minute facts to make the decisions to make a profit.

When the punch card or computer installation is within the controller's shop, the reports that management asks for are sometimes rejected because there is not enough time, it costs too much, or they just don't want to do it. This, to me, is not serving the company's best interests to do a job regardless of who is in charge.[25]

From the 1960s, the highly respected Richard Nolan remembered that senior management made data processing managers scapegoats for problems, in part out of confusion about what the data processing manager's role should be.[26] In the 1970s he reflected a widely held opinion about management's relations with information processing:

The EDP manager is being poorly managed in the organization. Senior management is ill-informed on the processes and risks of using new computer technology. Consequently, the EDP manager may be held accountable for effects beyond his control.[27]

The counter argument, as expressed by Paul Strassmann, holds that data processing managers had a poor track record for accounting for their contributions. Even John Diebold, long a proponent of the benefits of computers, criticized the financial community that ran computers, arguing that they did not have the breadth of understanding or authority to support the entire enterprise, with the result that "their departmental position arouses the antipathy of their peers." Further, "they lack the entrepreneur's view of the enterprise as a whole."[28] Other functions in a company had simply done a better job in justifying the value of their contributions. In a survey of twenty data processing managers, Nolan discovered that seven had been fired within the past year, eleven changed firms within the previous three years, and only two had been in their jobs for five or more years. In four firings "the impetus for firing originated with a senior management ill-equipped to deal with a set of problems that involved the EDP department which had suddenly become very visible."[29] All during the period 1950–1995, MIS managers' jobs had become more complicated. They managed low-skill data entry clerks all the way up to highly skilled technical personnel. Their budgets ranged from 0.5 percent of a corporation's total operating budget to over 5 percent. During the 1950s and 1960s the key skill required of them was knowledge of computing, afterwards increasingly general business management since most basic accounting applications had been computerized. Now the requirement was to link applications across departments to use computing as a competitive weapon (1990s).

Information processing managers seemed under constant siege in the 1970s and 1980s. International Data Corporation (IDC), a highly respected research arm in the information processing industry, reported in 1983 that end users were now buying hardware on their own, outside the control of information processing organizations. In 1982, for example, 85 percent of all personal computers were acquired directly by end users.[30] Purchases of personal computers grew tenfold before the end of the decade, many bought without any influence from the information processing department. By the early 1990s, MIS directors had nearly a decade of experience and frustration defending their "value add."[31]

The number of documented case studies of data processing management operations is extensive and need not detain us here. However, in many of these instances, the authors were data processing managers. They have frequently written incisively about their roles, making this kind of material of enormous value to future business historians.[32] These studies include organization charts, mission statements, and comments about daily activities. They are clear statements to the effect that computer technology was not a techno-centric topic but increasingly a collection of important business-centric issues. Even end users commented on data processing management organizations. For instance, Terrance Hanold, president of the Pillsbury Company in the late 1960s and early 1970s, represented a new breed of commentators on computers—executive end users—who took a personal and necessary interest in computing. In an address to financial managers he argued that "business information, then, requires the systematic collection of data and its systematic processing according to a series of intellectually valid methods."[33] Hanold said that in this company, "the General Manager must assume responsibility for the definition of the information and processing requirements of his operation."[34] In other words, information processing had become too critical to leave to an accounting department to handle; computers were too vital to the organization. In a survey of where IS sat in the organization in 1974, 10 percent reported directly to the president, 2 percent to the CEO's office; another 7 percent were attached directly to executive vice presidents; and 14 percent still were under the direct supervision of controllers.[35]

DATA PROCESSING PERSONNEL

The first step in the process of studying the history of data processing personnel is to understand what functions they performed. These were varied, providing employment for many. One of the initial observations we can make is that computing-related professions grew rapidly, and during the late 1960s and most of the 1970s, the inability of the American economy to provide additional workers may have constrained an even more rapid expansion in the use of computers, despite annual growths in the adoption of computers that normally were in double-digit ranges of 10 to 28 percent.

The data processing manager was in charge of all computing operations. Over the decades this position evolved. In the beginning these managers came out of an accounting or tabulating machine heritage and ran small departments, frequently of fewer than 100 employees. All during the 1950s, 1960s, and early 1970s, the one major change was growth in the size of departments in large American and Western European corporations. By the end of the 1970s it was not unusual to see MIS directors—now executives—running multiple departments, including a variety of administrative functions. In the 1980s they began to acquire responsibility for all information technology (e.g., telephone systems). By the end of the decade some were called Chief Information Officers or, more simply, CIOs.

By the middle of the 1960s there were some 30,000 supervisors, managers, and executives in information processing in the United States; one estimate from the period put the shortfall of managers at 10,000.[36] In the years 1959–1963, when so many second-generation computers were installed, one could see the same thing happening to data processing managers as had occurred in other functional areas: As spans of control grew (as measured by the number of people in the department and the size of the budget controlled by DP) so, too, did salaries. In this four-year period salaries for data processing management rose on average by 20 percent, the same rate as for senior technical staff. The number of machines installed did not dramatically influence the rise in salaries. Thus we could conclude that the management of people was the greater economic value to a business.[37]

Systems analysts designed software applications and grew out of the pre-computer-era job of the ''methods department'' that essentially did the same kind of work using tabulators, for example. The role emerged at the dawn of computing and has remained essentially the same to the present. In 1966 there were an estimated 60,000 of these workers in the United States and an additional 35,000 were needed.[38] One could see, therefore, given the fact that companies could not exploit computers without an adequate supply of these kinds of people, how important they were. They were the keyhole through which organizations had to squeeze through to get any practical value out of computers. One student of the profession in the mid-1960s, Leonard Rico, described their role this way: The ''system analyst is the chief specialist responsible for implementing computerization in a firm.'' He found that they did four things: determined the feasibility of a company using a computer, managed the conversion to its use, tested new applications before they went ''live,'' and maintained both applications and systems.[39]

They became a large workforce—in 1971 some 150,000. Ninety percent were men and, increasingly over time, had college or advanced degrees in computer-related topics. In the 1950s and 1960s most were high school and college graduates. The latter typically had technical degrees. Beginning in the 1960s and continuing to the present, as programs in computer science became available in colleges and universities, training in this subject increasingly became the norm.[40] Another study suggested that in 1970 there were 171,000 systems analysts employed in the United States and that by 1980 the number had grown to 283,000, up over 60 percent.[41] By the mid-1980s, this population had climbed to over 400,000. Paul Strassmann calculated that there were 479,000 in 1988.[42]

Perhaps no occupation is more visible in the information processing world than that of the programmer. No population grew so fast and became so visible as this one. Programmers have essentially played the same role for five decades. They took the work of the analysts and wrote software programs to instruct computers what to do. There were several hundred at the start of the 1950s and several thousand programmers in the early 1950s. One estimate holds that in 1960 there were 120,000, with an unfilled demand for an additional 50,000.[43] Another study noted that in 1970 there were 163,000 and in 1980 more than 317,000, up over 94 percent![44] All through the half-century the vast majority were men; we have a statistic for 1971 of 79 percent male.[45] That circumstance began to change at the end of the 1980s, but programming remains, as of this writing (1996), a male-dominated profession. That population continued to grow in the early 1980s at the same rate as systems analysts. All during the second half of the twentieth century programmers made up between 25 and 35 percent of the total data processing population. All during the same period, data processing managers bewailed the shortage of programmers. One commentator in the 1960s argued (with some hyperbole) that the problem cut across all professions in computing:

We can all agree that the need for machine operators, computer programmers, and systems personnel is acute and becoming worse. I know companies that will hire, on the spot, anyone that has seen a computer or who has an uncle that has taught him the word 'modular' or 'binary.'[46]

No population of information processing workers created more controversy. For one thing, many were migrants, moving from one job to another with little loyalty to the companies they worked for in an era when job hopping generated higher salaries. This phenomenon is one that will have to be studied by historians because job movement disrupted programming and software maintenance operations. Until the arrival of both the personal computer and many new software tools in the late 1980s, programmers were in chronic short supply. While they remained so during the late 1980s and into the 1990s, technology began to ease the pressure. In the 1980s and 1990s Third World programmers, as in India, began entering the profession, drawing off some work that otherwise would have been done by American programmers.[47]

For another, programmers were frequently accused of writing software that was not end-user friendly, that appealed only to their technical proclivities. This charge has been leveled against them for decades. Even Jay Forrester, builder of the Whirlwind computer in the early 1950s, was harsh on programmers in the 1960s:

My experience is that one gets totally different computer programs and operating systems, depending on whether the design is from the viewpoint of a programming group which is also setting system specifications or whether the programmers are responsive to system specifications from managers who put people and customers first and expect the machines to serve rather than dominate.[48]

The complaints are still around in the 1990s.[49] Yet salaries have continued to reflect the demand for more programmers, regardless of criticisms. For example, in 1959 a lead programmer made about $118 per week; by the end of 1974, that had grown to $246, about double.[50]

Next in the pecking order of a data center world are computer operators. These are the people who actually run the machines, load tapes onto tape drives, push buttons at computer consoles, load paper into printers, schedule programs to run on computers, and plan and install new or additional hardware. Like the other occupations, their functions have remained essentially the same, despite the fact that beginning in the late 1970s they also ran Help Desks which assisted end users with their computer-related problems, often because of the increased use of terminals. These people often had run tabulating equipment prior to the 1950s and simply migrated over to computers.[51] Estimates of numbers of these workers are hard to come by for the early years because of the large variety of functions and job titles involved. However, estimates of how many there were in about 1970–1971 range from 165,000 to over 200,000, with their number doubling by the start of the 1980s.[52] We know very little about this group. A few articles have appeared over the years about the culture of data centers, often characterizing this as a world isolated from the mainstream of the company.[53] Within this group were tape librarians and clerks all the way up to supervisors of computer operations, often third- or fourth-level management. By the start of the 1970s, systems analysts responsible for maintaining operating systems and other sub-systems (e.g., such as databases with the head technicians called database managers) came under computer operations.

The last major group to look at are the data entry clerks. All during the 1950s through the 1970s they were typically called keypunch operators, later data entry clerks. They performed the task of collecting data and then typing it into machines that punched cards, and loaded data into disk drives, diskettes, and other machine-readable forms. In the pecking order of a data processing center, they were at the bottom. They cost the least, although there were many of them, and they required the least amount of technical knowledge. The main skill they needed was typing ability. In the early 1950s, many had been keypunching data onto cards to feed tabulators. After the arrival of the computer they continued to do exactly the same job on the same data entry equipment. That did not begin to change until the 1960s when other forms of data entry equipment began to appear; but they all had the familiar typewriter keyboard or adding machine pad. Not until the wide adoption of personal computers, with their attendant requirement for understanding how to use data capture software, did the profession begin to acquire a more technical edge.

In the early 1950s there were tens of thousand of keypunch operators working in the United States. Theirs was a labor-intensive job and many were required. One survey suggested that in 1971 there were 440,000 out of one million data processing employees.[54] Another study based on U.S. Bureau of the Census data had a similar number—396,056—for 1970 and 394,815 in 1980—essentially flat.[55] The reason why this population leveled off in the 1970s is because much data entry was shifted to end users employing terminals and thus was not counted in the statistics. Another reason lay in the wide adoption of key-to-disk data entry equipment beginning in the second half of the 1970s which increased the productivity of a typical data entry clerk by about 40 percent. In short, the amount of data needed to "feed" a computer had not gone down; it simply came from a different mix of sources.

What is most interesting about this community of workers is their makeup. All through the half-century under study, the majority of them were women, just like clerks and secretaries in other functions across corporate America. One study, based on data for 1971, reported that 99 percent were women.[56] Turnover was high, pay was low. In this respect, these workers were much like their clerical colleagues in other departments. Thus we see across all the professions in computing that the more technical or higher ranked a position became, the more likely it was to be occupied by a man.

For all these populations, recruiting and training early became a major focus area since the requirement for qualified personnel always seemed to lag behind availability. Leonard Rico described the consequence:

With electronic data processing, the availability of skills of often determines the rate at which the new technology may be exploited. Computerized firms have more and tougher staffing problems as the human factor of production rather than technology has been recognized as a major bottleneck retarding progress.[57]

In the 1950s and 1960s most recruitment occurred from within organizations installing computers, later from a national labor pool. College education by the 1960s had become a prerequisite for most candidates as well. These professionals represented 4 to 5 percent of all office workers in some industries, like insurance. Testing for aptitude grew in importance in the 1960s and, by the 1970s, graduates with computer science degrees became more widely available.[58]

As the data on application adoptions suggested in Chapter 5, one would expect to see where data processing people were employed correlated to application usage. In fact, the extant evidence suggests this is the case. At the height of the mainframe era—circa mid-1980s—the total population of computer professionals reached an estimated 1.15 million, with a bullish expectation of a greater than 50 percent growth coming by 1995. Of this 1.15 million, some 217,000 worked for manufacturing and service organizations (e.g., IBM, Automatic Data Processing [ADP]), the rest for corporate users of computers. The U.S. government was the single largest employer of computer professionals (about 6.5 percent), of which half worked for the military. Service industries employed about 27 percent of the total, manufacturing 20 percent, finance, insurance, and real estate another 14.8 percent, and the distribution and retail trades 13.3 percent. All other employers by industry were single digits (e.g., state and local government, transportation, utilities, education, health, and mining).[59] The lesson from these data is clear: Here we have additional evidence of the extent of adoption of computers across the breadth of the American economy within one generation of the introduction of this new technology.

Focusing on this community of workers—and deliberately leaving out any discussion about people who built, sold, and maintained this technology—we can make several other observations. In the beginning, use of computers was seen as a way of increasing a company's overall productivity and, in fact, automation of work in the 1950s and 1960s simply encouraged further use of computers. In turn that led to additional hires of information processing professionals. In this sense, what happened with computing was no different from what had become evident elsewhere in the economy. For example, the introduction of more advanced earth-moving equipment made it possible to build more and grander highways in the United States. More reliable and less expensive telephone service led to more phone calls. The availability of more sophisticated banking services and technologies encouraged greater use of check-writing services and credit card transactions.[60] The broad range of many technology-driven activities generally contributed to an increase in the number of professional and clerical workforces in the years 1955–1974. Thus one could conclude that computers did not cause jobs to go away; in fact, the opposite occurred. In the ten years between 1974 and 1984, outlays for information technology grew at an annual rate of 15 percent, roughly two-thirds of which went for people. After 1984, expenditures slowed, closer to 6 percent per year.[61] Data for the late 1980s and early 1990s suggest that regardless of any concerns regarding increases (or lack of), investments in computing, and associated peripherals, personnel continued unabated.[62]

What remains confusing is the role of the personal computer on personnel in the information processing professions. We know, for example, that in the beginning DP managers fought the introduction of PCs as a threat to their empires and ability to support information processing. We also know that they had resisted migration to end-user systems relying on terminals for similar reasons: control and data integrity. But by the early 1990s, the number of PCs installed in American industry that now had to be connected together to share information had created new issues. Do you put support for end-users at the end of a telephone at a Help Desk or do you deliver support physically around the corporation? Both strategies have been employed, resulting in new job classifications that exist alongside the more traditional ones described above. We know almost nothing about these new jobs. The issue of who controls computing is as intense a debate today as it was a half-century ago. The contemporary literature comments extensively on the problem.[63]

Of greater interest to historians will be the linking of management's tasks to those of the corporation as a whole. How people were deployed in the final analysis will probably draw the greater interest because it is the interaction at the nexus of end-user information needs and data processing professionals. We do not yet have good models by which to measure the evolution of information processing management. Richard Nolan's four stages of information processing has been widely adopted by executive management across American industry as a way of looking at the role of information technology.[64] To a large extent the central issue has been the management of the diffusion of technology. While space does not permit a detailed diffusion of the four stages, briefly stated they are:

- technology identification and investment
- technological learning and adoption
- rationalization/management control
- maturity/widespread technology transfer

In Stage 1 management worries about such issues as who should be responsible for the care and feeding of the computer. In Stage 2 the issue shifts more to how best to manage computer people. In Stage 3 one asks, ''How do you make sure that the organization can 'afford' the computer?'' In Stage 4 you become more interested in maximizing exploitation of the technology.[65] While the model was developed in the age of the centralized computer centers, these issues remained the same in the 1990s, a period characterized by the extensive use of personal computers and network-centric applications. We need to take these kinds of business models and apply them to the historical assessment of information processing management. Nowhere does this seem so obvious than in the study of how data processing personnel worked.

MANAGEMENT ISSUES

Many of these issues have been suggested or discussed above. However, others will require fuller treatment by historians because they link to broader business organizational concerns.

Budget issues are closely linked to perceptions of productivity and cost justification—a subject worthy of its own book, while many have already been published on the productivity issue.[66] In the information processing world, a measure of the extent of computing is typically what percent of a company's budget is spent by the IS department. This number varies from one industry to another. For example, manufacturing companies historically have spent between 0.8 and 2 percent on information processing departments, while banks have usually hovered between 2 and 5 percent. The extant evidence today suggests that after the early 1960s—the years before ones of major expansion in computing—the percents remained relatively stable. First, we will want to validate that hypothesis in the years to come, and second understand why. Distribution of budget is an important part of the answer. We know that about a third of all expenses went for hardware and software, the other two-thirds for people, facilities, and services. There are many hidden costs that never make it into the information processing department's budget that, if understood, may radically change our views about productivity and the benefits of computing. Disturbing anecdotal evidence suggests the need for this kind of analysis. For example, Donald I. Lowry, a manager at Procter and Gamble in the mid-1960s, argued that staffs were the lion's share of his expense and that for every dollar of hardware and related equipment costs, he or someone else in the firm had to spend another $1.50 investing in human skills required to produce an adequate return.[67] To what extent were there hidden costs for information processing in other corporations?

Official IS budgets represent a complex topic, too. A study conducted by the American Federation of Information Processing Societies (AFIPS) suggested that slightly over 2 percent of the U.S. gross national product (GNP) was being spent on computing in 1971. Payroll amounted to $8.3 billion, overhead about $5 billion, and goods and services another $10.3 billion.[68] The hardware/software side of the budget churned and changed greatly as older technologies were replaced, often with more (rather than less) hardware and software. The cost of computing dropped about 25 percent each year from the 1950s through the 1970s per unit of processing power. This was by far in excess of any other major technology or industry. Another study put the decline at 19 percent between 1954 and 1984. Yet at the same time the cost of software absorbed a greater share of expenditures. It began as a minor cost; some vendors like IBM even gave it away in exchange for customers acquiring hardware. By 1973 software was absorbing 5 percent of systems costs; By 1978, 80 percent of systems cost was absorbed by software. Two years later it exceeded 90 percent. Part of the reason for software going up in cost, to quote William J. Baumol and his colleagues who have studied the economics of computing, is that software development was a "handicraft activity and is, so far, a stagnant service."[69] Since software was labor-intensive, one could easily see how personnel costs rose faster than any other component of the IS budget, often by over 2.5 percent compounded from the 1950s to the present. Citing data from the Diebold Group from 1988, Baumol's team suggested that in large data center operations between 1971 and 1981, on average the share of computer operations budgets devoted to hardware fell from 35 percent in 1971 to 27 percent in 1981; that the share of computer operations people (such as keypunch operators) fell from 29 percent in 1971 to 18 percent in 1981. The proportion of the budget spent by these organizations on systems development people remained the same, however: 25 percent in 1971 and 24 percent in 1981.[70]

Even the software portion was constantly changing. People wrote most of their applications in the early years, but as time went on they acquired commercially available software packages. By the 1980s this strategy was being applied extensively. In 1983, 25 percent of all major applications in the United States came from purchased software, in 1988, 44 percent.[71] Why? Packages were faster to install. In the late 1980s it normally took between 3 and 5 years to write major applications, but businesses were operating in much faster cycles and thus needed software to match the speed of change occurring in other parts of the company. Hardware, software, and personnel budgetary dynamics leads us to one conclusion: that budgeting in information processing is a complicated topic that will require careful and extensive study.

Richard Nolan looked at budget patterns for his four stages to define the budgetary patterns of growth from 1959 to 1972 in several companies. He discovered that in Stage 1 annual increases after first installation of computers were slow but consistent; in Stage 2 there was a tremendous increase in expenditures (often 50 percent or more per year); in Stage 3 there were decreasing annual increases or decreases from previous years; and in Stage 4 firms showed slow, even no growth. Nolan argues that these kinds of data suggest how senior management was managing information processing, demonstrating close alignment in planning, organizing, and controlling. In the 1970s Nolan attempted to establish a normative theory of data processing management—a goal not yet really achieved even in the mid-1990s by anybody—but what he suggested is worth pursuing. He believed that IS budgets could serve as ''a surrogate for the collective effect of multiple situational variables, such as industry, dollar sales, products, business strategy, management, and technology.''[72] His stages were very realistic, along with his descriptions of what was going on in each: Stage 1 is *initiation* when the first computer is installed; Stage 2 *contagion*, ''intense system development,'' which accounts for the rapid rise in expenditures and move from capital (e.g., hardware and data centers) to operating budget (e.g., people); Stage 3 is *control*, when expenditures are reined in; and Stage 4 is *integration*, when the focus is on ''user/service orientation,'' in other words on results.[73]

Other experts on budgets view this topic as the preferred way to understand better the role and contribution of information processing. For example, Paul Strassmann, a highly respected critic of computing's productivity, also likes to chase budgets because ''In the absence of reliable productivity measures, industrial-age executives became convinced that the preferred way to control computers was through project authorization procedures which reduced the risks of computerization to a minimum.''[74] Of course, he also saw problems with linking budgets and projects too closely: ''Investment-oriented executives failed to recognize that computerization is an incremental, continuous and evolutionary organizational learning process that requires better controls over operating results for the entire business.''[75] Yet their desire to control new investments led them to establish ''the information system as a discrete and separate function, instead of integrating it into every manager's job.''[76] If we needed another reason to take seriously information processing budgets, Strassmann's comments—Strassmann has been an IS executive for decades—is evidence enough.

Even closer to the central arguments about the costs and benefits of information processing is the debate over cost justification. The subject is also linked to the discussion about productivity of computers, a topic I have alluded to throughout this book. The topic of justification is also another way of identifying why people wanted to use computers and other technologies, what their expectations were of technology, and the consequences of their use. In short, the topic is massive, complicated, and may, in the final analysis, be the way that will be favored by students of business operations for understanding the role and impact of computers on commercial operations.

What was management thinking of during the early stages of computer implementation? In Chapter 5 we briefly discussed this topic, but a little closer look demonstrates the linkage of budgeting and application considerations. My own research suggests that there is a typology of cost justification; however, further investigation will be required in order to flush out the model. Briefly put, systems were justified for purposes of efficiency, effectiveness, and innovation, typically when looking at applications in all periods. The evidence for computers being installed to save cash is weak, hence, I believe, why economists and others have had a field day with the productivity issue. Efficiency—savings in operating expenses—was ostensibly the most widely used criterion in the 1950s and 1960s, although few firms ever quantified after the fact that they saved money.

A second source of justification was corporate image, that of a technical, state-of-the-art, "modern" enterprise installing trendy technology. A. R. Zipf, executive vice president at the Bank of America in the 1960s, and in the 1950s the vice president responsible for introducing computers to this company, was very harsh about what happened in 1955:

This was the year that computer hysteria swept the business world. Banking was no exception. Businesses large and small, all over the United States, joined in a stampede to reap the benefits of the new computer technology. All were enchanted with pastel cabinets, spinning tapes, and flashing lights. All too often, computer systems were installed without even rudimentary thought about their cost, their efficiency, and most important, their applicability to the job that needed to be done.[77]

Admittedly beyond prestige there was the innocence of the new technology. John Diebold, a leading proponent of the value of automation in this period, complained about people not understanding how to exploit the technology. In fact, he warned that computers would profoundly change things in a controversial and well-read book called *Automation*, published in 1952.[78]

Innovation—otherwise frequently referred to as using computers for competitive advantage—emerged in three forms. The first involved the replacement of older technology with newer, such as punch card tabulators with computers and, later, newer computers for older ones. The second form was the extension of technology forward to do new tasks not done before, such as new decision-support applications in the 1960s and 1970s. The third concerned changes in how processes in organizations worked. At about the time I was thinking in these terms (mid-1980s), Peter G. Sassone at Georgia Institute of Technology was developing a similar typology based on a much broader research initiative.[79]

What appears to have emerged over the past half-century, however, is growing evidence that justification for technology was closely linked to personnel matters. Central to the work done by David F. Noble on computers and automation, for example, is the idea that management wanted to reduce the amount of labor and labor content in production in order to maintain control over the business out of their irritation with all the strikes of the 1930s and 1940s. Thus they went after automation as a strategy for fixing labor problems, not just to reduce costs. Noble argued that separation of work tasks lowered the amount of skill required to do many jobs. Making machines more intelligent also reduced the amount of knowledge and the number of workers required to do many jobs. He concluded that "the trend toward job degradation and automation accelerated in the two decades following World War II."[80] He further argued:

The impulse to automate was encouraged by a time-honored manufacturing philosophy that favors machinery over people, by the competitive drive to keep up with technical advances, by the subsidized effort to meet military performance specifications, by the technical enthusiasms of automation promoters and practitioners, and by the continuing struggle of management to gain greater control over production, weaken the power of unions, and otherwise adjust a recalcitrant work force to the realities of lower pay, tighter discipline, and frequently layoffs.[81]

His argument is intriguing and since it was well presented, will require additional attention and validation.

The more traditional interpretation is that management was simply applying technology to improve people productivity because that is what good managers do. Yet costs for one type of worker (e.g., factory and clerical) were often offset by an enormous increase in expensive data processing professionals. Strassmann argues that if the strategy was to reduce labor content to improve productivity, management failed. He contends that "they failed in dealing with the rising costs of professional staffs which were excluded from productivity calculations because their output was intangible."[82] He concludes that by 1975 overall costs of people were higher, that the computer did not help the cause of reduced labor cost.

So who is right? I would contend that Noble and Strassmann have to be taken seriously, but more like Monday-morning quarterbacks reflecting on the game already played. If one looks at the case studies written at the time decisions were made, the intent of management appeared to resemble more closely three objectives: a sincere desire to lower personnel expenses, the need to do things that could not be accomplished without this technology, and admittedly, a certain amount of vanity in applying the latest technology. This interpretation appears to allow us to reconcile what the documentation of the period presents with the findings of economists concerned about productivity issues, and others like Noble and Strassmann who find other motives at work.

The hunt for intent thus must take into account contemporary comments. For example, read what one business professor doing research on computing usage in the mid-1950s wrote:

Usually a company's decision to acquire automatic equipment was based on estimates of the cost and savings associated with the performance of the equipment on a specific application. The selection of the application to be studied was based on several considerations: the prospect of substantial dollar savings, the usefulness for 'large volume' applications and application using fairly standard procedures, and planned limitation of automatic processing to those applications which would not affect customer relations in the event of equipment breakdown.[83]

That statement could have been written in any year, even in 1996. Five years after this statement was penned, another author wrote that the primary reason for computing projects was "to control paperwork and clerical costs." He noted that "the substantial increase in clerical workforce and in the number and sheer volume of working documents and reports required to keep an enterprise functioning today is assuming serious proportions."[84]

In 1988 another observer commented that "the technology has been used primarily to meet the mushrooming demands of handling information. Businesses now are faced with the task of controlling 400 billion documents, a number that is expected to increase at the rate of 72 billion per year."[85] Rico in 1967 argued the same point: "Mechanization is encouraged by the rapid growth in both the number of white collar workers and in overhead costs."[86] The number of citations and quotes that could be offered of a similar vein would easily fill up many more pages, but the point has been made. While other reasons also existed, this prevalence of cost displacement has been advanced by too many people to be ignored.

Associated with the whole question of justification is the issue of who was doing the justification. Scholars know too little about this topic. We know, for instance, that in each decade most of the justification studies were either done by data processing professionals or at least involved them in the process. But who really made the decisions? Diebold surveyed 2,500 executives in 140 American and foreign companies to get at the answer in the late 1960s and discovered that "technicians, not members of management, are setting goals for computers. This is one of the prime reasons why companies often fail to realize the true potential from their data-processing investment."[87] If this can be validated, does this explain, as Diebold would suggest, why end users more often than not were disgruntled with what they got from their information processing colleagues? One student of computing wrote at the start of the 1960s that "management is frequently forced to hunt through a haystack of irrelevant information in its reports in order to find for itself the needle of pertinent fact."[88] We just quoted Strassmann on complaints circa 1980s. In the 1970s Nolan expressed similar concerns with how justification was taking place.[89] Thomas J. Watson, Jr., chief executive office at IBM through the early decades of the computer, recalled that management in general rushed forward to the computer with almost abandon: "By the mid-'50s, 'computer' was becoming a magic word as popular as vitamins. The executives rightly believed that the companies of the future were going to be computer run." "It became the conventional wisdom that management ran a bigger risk by waiting to computerize than by taking the plunge."[90] Strassmann commented on the 1970s and 1980s in a similar way: "I find that not much has changed over the last two decades in how proposals are approved."[91]

CONCLUSION

We could deal with many other topics associated with the management of computing, such as centralized versus decentralized computing, the politics of glass house management, and the changing nature of relations with end users (particularly complicated by technology in the form of terminals and then PCs). There are questions about project management techniques, later the role of quality management practices, and in the 1990s the strategic "fit" of information technology into flattened companies with partnerships and alliances outside the traditional corporate boundaries. Those will all have to await their own historians.

However, I would like to conclude by suggesting that the kinds of issues discussed in this chapter have less to do with computers and more are characterized as business issues of the type one would find in other parts of corporations. What gives the subject relevance is the fact that all departments of corporations became increasingly dependent on computers in order to do their work. Shoshana Zuboff may have inadvertently documented the significance of my statement when she pointed out that in 1980 over 10 million American workers used terminals and that this number was approaching 25 million by 1990. She also acknowledged that her numbers were conservative since another study in the late 1980s suggested that the number would approach 50 million.[92] They were all wrong; the number in the mid-1990s was closer to 70 million. But it does not matter whose numbers you use, they all are very large and lead us to the same conclusion: that computers touched the lives of more workers than executives or business historians have previously realized. Since the mechanism for delivery of computing services was, almost from the beginning, a data processing department, the role of that organization is a subject of profound importance to any understanding of how a technology like the computer was diffused so rapidly into the American economy.

Because the use of computers proved so extensive, many of the managerial habits of the information processing community were adopted outside the IS organization if for no other reason than to deal with the computer experts. Project management techniques have long been a subject of great interest to information processing managers because these methodologies were necessary in order to write complicated applications and implement large and expensive systems. Many of their practices have been adopted by other groups, such as by engineers and manufacturing personnel. The evidence for such adoptions appeared almost from the beginning. By the early 1990s, one could also observe large numbers of words from the computing community now in the mainstream of American speech.[93] Many of the tools of quality management and process re-engineering of the 1980s and 1990s also came out of the information processing community.[94] What we do not understand yet is the process by which these concepts were diffused thanks to the influence of information processing professionals. But the point is, many of their habits and attitudes have influenced how companies do their work. That alone should cause all of us to understand better the process at work.

Finally, the number of people who have worked in information processing makes the topic important. I have liberally used the number one million workers employed in the computing profession; I believe the number too conservative. Then there are the vendors of such equipment—always a number in the hundreds of thousands. IBM alone had 404,000 employees in 1987 and, if you add those who had already worked at the company or had retired over the years, the number is closer to a half million. And that was only one company! Then add in the number of PC users, employees who use terminals and other computer devices, and now we are dealing with the majority of the working adult population of the industrialized world by the early 1990s. Then there are the children in school who, beginning in the late 1970s, began to be exposed to computers. Add in college and university students, the majority of whom today interact with computers, and with over a third owning such devices, and the evidence mounts that the business of computing is more than just interesting or important, it is a ubiquitous facet of our lives.

NOTES

1. One notable exception, and a model to emulate, is Dirk de Wit, who looked at the role of information processing in several Dutch organizations, covering several decades, in *The Shaping of Automation: A Historical Analysis of the Interaction between Technology* and *Organization, 1950–1985* (Rotterdam: Hilversum, 1994).

2. James W. Cortada, *Before the Computer: IBM, NCR, Burroughs, and Remington Rand and the Industry They Created, 1865–1956* (Princeton, N.J.: Princeton University Press, 1993): 128–136, 266–268, passim.

3. See, for example, Herman Lukoff, *From Dits to Bits: A Personal History of the Electronic Computer* (Portland: Robotics Press, 1979); Herman H. Goldstine, *The Computer from Pascal to von Neumann* (Princeton, N.J.: Princeton University Press, 1972); and David E. Lundstrom, *A Few Good Men from Univac* (Cambridge, Mass.: MIT Press, 1987).

4. *Office Management* (New York: Alexander Hamilton Institute, 1919): 257

5. See, for example, the widely read text of the period by J. Brooks Heckert, *Accounting Systems Design and Installation* (New York: Ronald Press, 1936): 476–477.

6. Ibid., 478.

7. Leon E. Vannais, "The Accountant's Responsibility in Planning Successful Punched-Card Installations," *Journal of Accountancy* 88, no. 5 (November 1949): 402.

8. James D. Gallagher, *Management Information Systems and the Computer* (New York: American Management Association, 1961): 17.

9. Peter R. Laubach, *Company Investigations of Automatic Data Processing* (Boston: Division of Research, Harvard Business School, 1957): 220.

10. Ibid., 220–221.

11. James D. Gallagher, "Organization of the Data-Processing Function," in Donald G. Malcolm et al. (eds.), *Symposium on Management Information and Control Systems* (New York: John Wiley & Sons, 1960): 120–134.

12. James I. Cash, Jr., et al., *Corporate Information Systems Management* (Homewood, Ill.: Dow Jones-Irwin, 1988): 106.

13. Laubach, *Company Investigations of Automatic Data Processing*, 154. This commentator noted that "most of the project personnel had accounting backgrounds," Ibid., 156. See also, James W. Cortada, *The Computer in the United States: From Laboratory to Market, 1930 to 1960* (Armonk, N.Y.: M. E. Shape, 1993): 112–116.

14. Gallagher, "Organization of the Data-Processing Function," 120–134. Gallagher was the data processing manager in the 1950s for Lockheed Aircraft Corporation, an important early user of computers.

15. Paul A. Strassmann, *The Business Value of Computers* (New Canaan, Conn.: The Information Economics Press, 1990): 31–32.

16. Leonard Rico, *The Advance Against Paperwork: Computers, Systems, and Personnel* (Ann Arbor: University of Michigan, 1967): 305.

17. M. Valliant Higginson, "Managing with E.D.P.: A Look at the State of the Art," *American Management Association Research Study 71* (New York: American Management Association, 1965): 35.

18. Rico, *The Advance Against Paperwork*, 111–112.

19. Richard L. Nolan, "Managing the Computer Resource: A Stage Hypothesis," in his *Managing the Data Resource Function* (St. Paul: West Publishers, 1974): 59–60.

20. James R. Johnson, "The Changing DP Organization," *Datamation* (January 1975): 81.

21. Strassmann, *The Business Value of Computers*, 25.

22. Ibid., 18–19, 20–24.

23. John F. Rockert and Christine V. Bullen (eds.), *The Rise of Managerial Computing* (Homewood, Ill: Dow Jones-Irwin, 1986): vii–viii.

24. Ibid., viii.

25. R. C. Head, "Systems and Development for E.D.P.," in Charles H. Johnson (ed.), *Data Processing: 1960 Proceedings* (Mt. Prospect, Ill.: National Machine Accountants Association, 1960): 168.

26. Richard L. Nolan, "Plight of the EDP Manager," in his *Managing the Data Resource Function* (St. Paul: West Publishing, 1974): 109–126.

27. Ibid., 107.

28. John Diebold, *Business Decisions and Technological Change* (New York: Praeger, 1970): 93.

29. Ibid., 109.

30. "Computer Shock Hits the Office," *Business Week,* August 8, 1983.

31. Strassmann, *The Business Value of Computers*, passim; see also, James W. Cortada, *TQM for Information Systems Management* (New York: McGraw-Hill, 1995): 92–114, 137–144.

32. For an extensive listing of this literature, see James W. Cortada, *Second Bibliographic Guide to the History of Computing, Computers, and Information Processing* (Westport, Conn.: Greenwood Press, 1996): 285–377. For a couple of early, useful ex-

amples see Robert H. Gregory, "Sylvania's Data Processing Center: Data Processing—Its Role in Administration," in Donald G. Malcolm et al. (eds.), *Symposium on Management Information and Control Systems* (New York: John Wiley & Sons, 1960): 157–168; D. Viesi, "Progress in Automation with Banco di Roma," A. B. Frielink (ed.), *Economics of Automatic Data Processing* (Amsterdam: North-Holland Publishing Co., 1965): 358–361: and from the Manager of Data Processing and Systems at Procter and Gamble, C. A. Swanson, "A Decade of EDP Management: From Concepts to Results," *Data Processing Proceedings 1965* (Dallas: DPMA, 1966): 498–515.

33. Terrance Hanold, "An Executive View of MIS," *Datamation* 18, no. 11 (November 1972): 66.

34. Ibid., 69.

35. Robert J. Greene, "The DP Manager's Status," *Datamation* 20, no. 6 (June 1974): 66–67.

36. Dick H. Brandon, "Jobs and Careers in Data Processing," *Computers and Automation* (September 1966): 25.

37. Charles W. Gilbert, "Salary Trends in Data Processing," *Data Processing: Proceedings 1963* (Detroit: DPMA, 1963): 10.

38. Brandon, "Jobs and Careers in Data Processing," 25.

39. Rico, *The Advance Against Paperwork*, 129–130.

40. Bruce Gilchrist and Richard E. Weber, *The State of the Computer Industry in the United States: Data for 1971 and Projections for 1976* (Montvale, N.J.: AFIPS, 1973): 28, 30.

41. Leslie Albin and Kathleen M. Gagne (eds.), *Information Processing in the United States: A Quantitative Summary* (Reston, Va.: AFIPS, 1985): 32.

42. Strassmann, *The Business Value of Computers*, 296, 315.

43. Brandon, "Jobs and Careers in Data Processing," 25. Experts do not agree on the numbers and thus more historical research will have to be done. For example, another authority placed the programmer population in 1955 at 10,000 and in 1960 at 60,000; M. S. Mahoney, "History of Computing in the History of Technology," *Annals of the History of Computing* 10, no. 2 (1988): 120.

44. Albin and Gagne, *Information Processing in the United States*, 32.

45. Gilchrist and Weber, *The State of the Computer Industry in the United States*, 30.

46. Rico, *The Advance Against Paperwork*, 233.

47. Edward Yourdon, *Decline and Fall of the American Programmer* (Englewood Cliffs, N.J.: Yourdon Press/Prentice-Hall, 1992): 279–312.

48. Quoted in George E. Delehanty, "Computers and the Organization Structure in Life Insurance Firms: The External and Internal Economic Impact," in Charles A. Meyers (ed.), *The Impact of Computers on Management* (Cambridge, Mass.: MIT Press, 1967): 100.

49. For example, see Yourdon, *Decline and Fall of the American Programmer*.

50. Montgomery Phister, Jr., *Data Processing Technology and Economics* (Santa Monica, Calif.: Santa Monica Publishing Company, 1976): 329.

51. Rico, *The Advance Against Paperwork*, 234; U.S. Bureau of Labor Statistics *Bulletin Number 1276* (Washington, D.C.: U.S. Department of Labor, May 1960): 3.

52. Gilchrist and Weber, *The State of the Computer Industry in the United States*, 28; Albin and Gagne, *Information Processing in the United States*, 32; and Phister, *Technology and Economics*, 321–324.

53. See, for instance, Philip H. Dorn, "EDP Professionals—The Blurred Image," *Datamation* 17, no. 1 (January 1, 1971): 22–24; and Louis B. Marienthal, "The Internal Isolation of the DP Department," Ibid., 25–28.

54. Gilchrist and Weber, *The State of the Computer Industry in the United States*, 28.

55. Albin and Gagne, *Information Processing in the United States*, 32.

56. Gilchrist and Weber, *The State of the Computer Industry in the United States*, 30.

57. Rico, *The Advance Against Paperwork*, 233.

58. Ibid., 239–246; Richard W. Riche and William E. Alli, "Office Automation in the Federal Government," *Monthly Labor Review* 83, no. 9 (September 1960): 937.

59. Ablin and Gagne, *Information Processing in the United States*, 5.

60. Phister, *Technology and Economics*, 57.

61. Strassmann, *The Business Value of Computers*, 56 and drawn from "Has High-Tech America Passed Its High-Water Mark?" *Business Week* (February 5, 1990): 18.

62. Thomas K. Landauer, *The Trouble with Computers* (Cambridge, Mass: MIT Press, 1995): 13–46.

63. Cortada, *Second Bibliographic Guide*, 305–332.

64. Cyrus F. Gibson and Richard L. Nolan, "Managing the Four Stages of EDP Growth," *Harvard Business Review* (January–February 1974) was reprinted in Lynn M. Sallano (ed.), *Catching Up with the Computer Revolution* (New York.: John Wiley & Sons, 1983): 25–43.

65. Cyrus F. Gibson and Richard L. Nolan, "Behavioral and Organizational Issues in the Stages of Managing the Computer Resource," in Richard L. Nolan, *Managing the Data Resource Function*, 63–86.

66. Cortada, *Second Bibliographic Guide*, 298–302.

67. Hershner Cross et al., *Computers and Management* (Boston: Ha vard University Graduate School of Business Administration, 1967): 34–35.

68. Gilchrist and Weber, *The State of the Computer Industry in the United States*, 24.

69. William J. Baumol et al., *Productivity and American Leadership* (Cambridge, Mass.: MIT Press, 1989): 136–137; statistics are from the same source, 135.

70. Ibid., 142.

71. C. Hartog and R. Klepper, "Business Squeeze Pushes Software Sales Up 184%," *Computerworld* (August 22, 1988): 55.

72. Richard L. Nolan, "Managing the Computer Resource: A Stage Hypothesis," in his *Managing the Data Resource Function*, 47–61. Quote is from p. 52.

73. Ibid., 52–53.

74. Strassmann, *The Business Value of Computers*, 79.

75. Ibid., 79.

76. Ibid., 80.

77. Quoted in Cross, *Computers and Management*, 54.

78. John Diebold, *Automation: The Advent of the Automatic Factory* (New York: D. Van Nostrand, 1952): 32.

79. See his paper "Cost Benefit Analysis for Office Information Systems," College of Management, Georgia Institute of Technology, May 1984.

80. David F. Noble, *Forces of Production: A Social History of Industrial Automation* (New York: Oxford University Press, 1986): 39.

81. Ibid., 41.

82. Strassmann, *The Business Value of Computers*, 77.

83. Peter B. Laubach, *Company Investigations of Automatic Data Processing* (Boston: Harvard Business School Division of Research, 1957): ii.

84. James D. Gallagher, *Management Information Systems and the Computer* (New York: American Management Association, 1961): 43–44.

85. Shoshana Zuboff, *In the Age of the Smart Machine* (New York: Basic Books, 1988): 417.

86. Rico, *The Advance Against Paperwork*, 18.

87. Diebold, *Business Decisions and Technological Change*, 55; for the case study he wrote, 55–57.

88. Quoted in Gallagher, *Management Information Systems and the Computer*, 59.

89. K. Eric Knutsen and Richard L. Nolan, "On Cost/Benefit of Computer-Based Systems," in Nolan, *Managing the Data Resource Function*, 281–282, passim.

90. Thomas J. Watson, Jr. and Peter Petre, *Father, Son & Co: My Life at IBM and Beyond* (New York: Bantam Books, 1990): 241.

91. Strassmann, *The Business Value of Computers*, 32.

92. Zuboff, *In the Age of the Smart Machine*, 416.

93. Use of computing language in mainstream conversation has hardly been studied, although we are beginning to see publications appear on the language of computing. See, for example, John A. Berry, *Technobabble* (Cambridge, Mass.: MIT Press, 1991), which is outstanding; but also see Eric Raymond's absolutely entertaining and well-informed collection of materials, *The New Hacker's Dictionary* (Cambridge, Mass.: MIT Press, 1991). Almost from the beginning, dictionaries have been published. One of the best is *Dictionary of Computing* (Oxford: Oxford University Press, 1983). For an early listing of dictionaries of computer language, see Cortada, A *Bibliographic Guide*: 17–20.

94. For examples, see Raymond L. Manganelli and Mark M. Klein, *The Reengineering Handbook: A Step-by-Step Guide to Business Transformation* (New York: AMACOM, 1994); and James W. Cortada and John Woods, *McGraw-Hill Encyclopedia of Quality Terms and Concepts* (New York: McGraw-Hill, 1995).

Bibliographic Essay

Debate on issues inevitably winds up in written form. The discussion about how a topic, such as computers or the general history of technology and business, is largely framed within articles and books gives us a picture of how issues have changed over time. To a large extent this book has been a bibliographic essay on how to look at the history of computing not solely as a topic in the history of technology, but as a major part of the experience of modern business. To demonstrate that point of view, much of the literature on the topic has been recruited in defense of the task. That is why each chapter has been heavily laced with notes and why, as part of this effort, I have published two book-length bibliographies at the same time.

The purpose of this bibliographic essay is to suggest publications that can quickly get you to discussions of major themes. For more detailed material, consult the previous chapters and their notes. Also, the most important studies on modern computing and business history are very well documented with bibliographies—a hallmark of modern historiographical research from both Europe and North America!

With businesses growing in size, beginning in the nineteenth century and continuing unabated to the present, the requirement for complex organizational structures, widespread distribution of information, and application of productivity-generating technologies all came together very quickly starting in the mid-1800s. Our attention was drawn to the issues resulting in the rise of a managerial class—for many the first modern information workers—by Professor Alfred D. Chandler, Jr., in his award-winning *The Visible Hand: The Managerial Revolution in American Business* (Cambridge, Mass.: Harvard University Press, 1977). It was clearly the most important history of American business published to that time. He continued to explore the role of large corporations in a sequel, *Scale and Scope: The Dynamics of Industrial Capitalism* (Cambridge, Mass.: Harvard University Press, 1990). In this second volume, the author clearly demonstrated the level of global commitment that large corporations made in technology, organization, people, distribution, manufacturing, and communications in order to succeed in their lines of work. The role of information and communications in business was further defined in two important studies that followed in his tracks. The first, by James R. Beniger, an expert on communications, entitled *The Control Revolution: Technological and Economic Origins of the Information Society* (Cambridge, Mass.: Harvard University Press, 1986), argued effectively that as organizations expanded in size and complexity, their need for control over operations grew, leading to the development of a wide variety of mechanical aids to communication almost simultaneously with the growth of these institutions. He included many devices from typewriters and adding machines to telephones, television, and computers. Then JoAnne Yates, writing a history of case studies of how communications occurred in American corporations, gave us specific examples of how both paper-based and technology-based communications apparatus played crucial roles in the daily lives of business people. In her book, *Control through Communication: The Rise of System in American Management* (Baltimore: The Johns Hopkins University Press, 1989), she took us through the development and use of 3 × 5 cards and spiral notebooks, for example, to systems views of how data flowed through corporations.

What is important to recognize is this group of books clearly demonstrated that information technology played an early and important role in businesses, from the 1860s to the arrival of the computer. I took a look at the same demand for information handling by examining the information processing industry as it existed before computers were used. In *Before the Computer: IBM, NCR, Burroughs, and Remington Rand and the Industry They Created, 1865–1956* (Princeton, N.J.: Princeton University Press, 1993), I attempted to demonstrate that businesses relied extensively on a vast array of information technologies prior to the arrival of the computer, and second that the information processing vendors of the period—the same looked at by Chandler, Beniger, and Yates—were driven by major issues of concern to their customers.

Then we get to the period of the computer. The literature is vast—as suggested in this book—but the issue turns on the business applications of computers. Three books, out of hundreds, conveniently illustrate the business issues from the perspective of business managers. The first, *Catching Up with the Computer Revolution* (New York: John Wiley & Sons, 1983), edited by Lynn M. Salerno, is a reprint of many important articles on computing published in the *Harvard Business Review* during the 1970s and 1980s. It is an excellent window into the issues confronting management during the 1960s, 1970s, and 1980s. The struggle over what kind of technology to buy and use is endless. A book written to help business managers figure out what to acquire and how technology is evolving suggests the kinds of issues raised since the 1950s, even though this volume concerns the 1990s: Norman Weizer et al., *The Arthur D. Little Forecast on Information Technology & Productivity: Making the Integrated Enterprise Work* (New York: John Wiley & Sons, 1991). Since we are all interested in what is next in computing, an important peak at the future, rooted carefully in practices of the 1980s and 1990s, can be found in Nicholas Negroponte's, *Being Digital* (New York: Alfred A. Knopf, 1995). The author, a professor of Media Technology at MIT, in addition to discussing the future of computing, shares many stories about modern computing and, most important, argues the case for the centrality of digital information in our futures. Interestingly, the author's comments are not terribly different from what others were arguing would be the case as early as the 1950s.

Placing computing into the broader context of contemporary society is a task already started by historians, economists, and technologies. Tom Forester, who has published extensively on computing, wrote a useful introduction to the role of computers in modern society in *High-Tech Society* (Cambridge, Mass.: MIT Press, 1987). The part played by

American government agencies in bringing the computer into wide use was studied by Kenneth Flamm while he was at the Brookings Institution: *Targeting the Computer: Government Support and International Competition* (Washington, D.C.: The Brookings Institution, 1987) and *Creating the Computer: Government, Industry, and High Technology* (Washington, D.C.: The Brookings Institution, 1988). For a pioneering study on how organizations responded to the computer, see a Dutch study, based on European cases, by Dirk de Wit, *The Shaping of Automation: A Historical Analysis of the Interaction between Technology and Organization, 1950–1985* (Roterdam: Hilversum Verloren, 1994). For a similar one done with American cases, see James L. McKenney, Duncan C. Copeland, and Richard O. Mason, *Waves of Change: Business Evolution through Information Technology* (Boston: Harvard Business School Press, 1995).

The role of the computer in business is also the story of how vendors interacted with customers to develop, market, and support the use of computing. Since that aspect of the story is not well understood—hence a major reason for the book you are reading—the historical literature is slim. I began to address the issues associated with the development of computers in a business context in my *The Computer in the United States: From Laboratory to Market, 1930 to 1960* (Armonk, N.Y.: M. E. Sharpe, 1993). For a window into European affairs, an excellent survey is by Martin Campbell-Kelly, *ICL: A Business and Technical History* (Oxford: Clarendon Press, Oxford University Press, 1989), which covers activities from the 1880s through the 1980s. Since it is impossible to discuss business and computing without looking at IBM, see the most current history of the firm by a retired IBM executive and a highly admired historian of its technology, Emerson W. Pugh, *Building IBM: Shaping an Industry and Its Technology* (Cambridge, Mass: MIT Press, 1995).

The economics of computing has left a long trail of articles and books, much of it redundant in their refrains from one decade to another. However, four books clearly introduce the historical issues. The first profoundly important publication came from Fritz Machlup, *The Production and Distribution of Knowledge in the United States* (Princeton, N.J.: Princeton University Press, 1962), in which we have one of the earliest studies of the idea that information was a business activity of major significance. One can trace the subsequent three-decade debate about "knowledge workers" to his work. One of the most thorough early studies on the economics of computing and consequences for business was written by William F. Sharpe, another economist, in *The Economics of Computers* (New York: Columbia University Press, 1969). This study is an excellent introduction to the complex economic arguments about the dynamics of declining costs of computing transactions and their effects on acquisition of such equipment. The next important study, written by an IS executive, Paul A. Strassmann, called the *Information Payoff: The Transformation of Work in the Electronic Age* (New York: Free Press, 1985), discusses when computing will deliver tangible benefits. Instead of looking to technological innovations, he argued that organizations needed to change workflows, structures, and roles, representing an important turn in the road toward looking at computing as a major business issue. The fourth book to look at was written by Thomas K. Landauer, *The Trouble with Computers: Usefulness, Usability, and Productivity* (Cambridge, Mass.: MIT Press, 1995). While the author's intent was to argue that people would use computers more if they were easier to work with, in the process he provides an excellent summary of the various arguments for and against computing, and the economic implications for businesses.

And for those who are interested in histories of computers? A number of books are readily available. For a history of many computing devices, see the very readable book by Michael R. Williams, a leading authority on the history of computers, *A History of Computing Technology* (Englewood Cliffs, N.J.: Prentice-Hall, 1985). For a well-done account of the computer industry and society's response to the technology written by a journalist, see Katharine Davis Fishman, *The Computer Establishment* (New York: Harper & Row, 1981). A beautifully written account that places extensive emphasis on the era of the microcomputer is by Stan Augarten, *Bit by Bit: An Illustrated History of Computers* (New York: Ticknor and Fields, 1984). Finally, for a wide-ranging history of devices, their use, and covering such other items as television, radio, movies, telephones and computers, see a gem-of-a-book by Steven Lubar, a curator at the Smithsonian Institution, *Infoculture: The Smithsonian Book of Information Age Inventions* (Boston: Houghton Mifflin, 1993).

There is a vast body of business literature on computer industry activities, some of which are very well done and important. There has been a continuous stream of memoirs and books by industry giants. Three important ones are worth looking at by those interested in the history of computers as a business topic. The head of IBM from the mid-1950s to the early 1970s—during the period when IBM moved into the computer business—wrote an outstanding business memoir: Thomas J. Watson, Jr., and Peter Petre, *Father, Son & Co.: My Life at IBM and Beyond* (New York: Bantam, 1990). One of the co-founders of Hewlett-Packard, David Packard, wrote a magnificent memoir covering the period from the 1930s to the 1990s, *The HP Way: How Bill Hewlett and I Built Our Company* (New York: Harper Business, 1995). No discussion of the microcomputer era would be complete without some comment about or by Bill Gates. He, too, has written a book describing his vision of the future of computing, *The Road Ahead* (New York: Viking, 1995). While many books have been published on the industry's activities of the past two decades, most are inward focused, looking at industry-related events in almost total isolation of broader business and societal considerations. Two recent additions to the literature are an exception. Charles H. Ferguson and Charles R. Morris wrote a fascinating book on the industry of the 1980s and 1990s, *Computer Wars: How the West Can Win in a Post-IBM World* (New York: Times Books, 1993). A thoughtful book on the management practices of Microsoft, and which are applicable to the management of many companies, is the theme of *Microsoft Secrets: How the World's Most Powerful Software Company Creates Technology, Shapes Markets, and Manages People* (New York: Free Press, 1995).

To understand the interrelationship of technology and business practices begins to get at the heart of the issue of what technology is and how it functions—a field that has been getting increased attention over the past two decades from historians, economists, business professors and consultants, and corporations at large. The topic is made more complicated by the fact that technology evolved from craft-based to science-based very quickly, within one century. The challenge ahead for experts on technology is to synthesize what we already know about the topic. George Basalla, professor of the history of technology at the University of Delaware, has written a wonderful history of how technology evolves, *The Evolution of Technology* (Cambridge: Cambridge University Press, 1988). Two other studies on the history of technology demonstrate the effects of technology on human events. First, Joel Mokyr, an economic historian, shows the effects of technology on the wealth of nations, *The Lever of Riches* (Oxford: Oxford University Press, 1990). An American historian, Daniel R. Headrick, has demonstrated how the British Empire was able to expand using technology, for example the steamboat, giving us additional lessons on the role of technology as a whole: *The Tools of Empire: Technology and European Imperialism in the Nineteenth Century* (Oxford: Oxford University Press, 1981). When to move from one technology to another is always a thorny problem for businesses, particularly those whose products are high-tech. Pioneering work on the role of change and innovation, today always with a high technology content, is examined by Richard N. Foster, a leading change consultant, *Innovation: The Attacker's Advantage* (New York: Simon and Schuster, 1986). For a wide-ranging collection of essays by different authors on the evolution of technology, see George Bugliarello and Dean B. Doner (eds.), *The History and Philosophy of Technology* (Urbana: University of Illinois Press, 1979). For examples of how science-based technology affects corporations, see David A. Hounshell and John Kenly Smith, Jr., *Science and Corporate Strategy* (Cambridge: Cambridge University Press, 1988), which discusses research and development at DuPont from 1902 to 1980; for a collection of case studies of many technologies discussing discovery, innovation, and risk of change, see Newton Copp and Andrew Zanella, *Discovery, Innovation, and Risk: Case Studies in Science and Technology* (Cambridge, Mass.: MIT Press, 1993); and on commercially popular computers, Charles J. Bashe et al, *IBM'S Early Computers* (Cambridge, Mass.: MIT Press, 1986) and the sequel by Emerson W. Pugh, Lyle R., Johnson, and John H. Palmer, *IBM's 360 and Early 370 Systems* (Cambridge, Mass.: MIT Press, 1991).

Since information processing technology is only one set of tools and innovations influencing how businesses operate in a society, there are broader issues to deal with. Change and its effects are looked at by a group of writers in Wiebe E. Bijker and John Law (eds.), *Shaping Technology/Building Society: Studies in Sociotechnical Change* (Cambridge, Mass.: MIT Press, 1992); for a similar discussion in historical context, see Wiebe E. Bijker, Thomas P. Hughes, and Trevor Pinch (eds.), *The Social Construction of Technological Systems* (Cambridge, Mass.: MIT Press, 1987); and for a collection of papers dealing with the issue of how society does and should exploit technology as public policy, see Lewis M. Branscomb (ed.), *Empowering Technology: Implementing a U.S. Strategy* (Cambridge, Mass.: MIT Press, 1993). This last book is chuck full of comments on and analyses of information technology.

Computers are not the only information technologies humankind has used. Other technologies have been studied very well, from the pencil to the book. Understanding how these collateral technologies evolved tells us a great deal about the role of information processing in commerce and as a business topic. Pencils, telegraphs, and books were not invented in isolation; they were products sold and used, with profound economic and social consequences. There is a fascinating, indeed outstanding, study of the humble little pencil written by an engineer worth reading for many reasons, including entertainment: Henry Petroski, *The Pencil: A History of Design and Circumstance* (New York: Alfred A. Knopf, 1992). One of the most stimulating books to appear in recent years on books, writing, and other forms of data capture is by a French historian, Henri-Jean Martin, long a student of the history of the book, *The History and Power of Writing*, English translation, by Lydia G. Cochrane (Chicago: University of Chicago Press, 1994). These are the most interesting recent books. However, there is a constant flood of new publications appearing about television, telegraph, telecommunications, typewriters, adding machines and calculators, pens, paper, books, and other information-handling media. The literature is so vast that it would require another book just to describe it.

So how do you keep up with new material which we know will continue appearing? First, a useful source on computer history is the *IEEE Annals of the History of Com-*

puting, which contains articles and book reviews, published quarterly. Second, there are several book publishers which have carved out the entire subject of technology as a special area of emphasis: Cambridge University Press and MIT Press are the two obvious, but almost every publisher today feels compelled to publish on the topic. Greenwood Press, long recognized as a leading supplier of reference works, has published nearly a dozen publications on the history of information processing. *Harvard Business Review* and *Sloan Management Review* publish a great deal on the role of information technology. Online bibliographies are a useful source and now the Internet is becoming so as well. Every major technology center, including the Charles Babbage Institute, has a "page on the web." Relying on an older "technology platform," called paper, I have published several bibliographies on the computer, drawing on all disciplines for content. They are organized by topic, are annotated, and are fully indexed. They are: *A Bibliographic Guide to the History of Computing, Computers, and the Information Processing Industry* (Westport, Conn.: Greenwood Press, 1990), its sequel, *Second Bibliographic Guide to the History of Computing, Computers, and the Information Processing Industry* (Westport, Conn.: Greenwood Press, 1996), and *A Bibliographic Guide to the History of Computer Applications, 1950–1990* (Westport, Conn.: Greenwood Press, 1996).

In the 1990s researchers working on the history of technology are in general moving closer to discussions about economics, society, and business than before. At the same time, business school professors, economists, business consultants, managers, and executives profoundly influenced by the increasing influence of technology are also moving closer to the study of the history of technology. In short, the whole theme of computers or, put more broadly, technology, has been studied from the perspective of many different intellectual disciplines and now these separate views are beginning to merge, providing historians and business leaders with a better understanding of the subject. One can expect that the discussion will continue to expand, providing more literature to put within our frame of reference.

Index

ABC, 92

Accounting: early applications, 163; home for many DP departments, 225; used equipment, 223

Accounting machines, early history of, 16–17

Acton, Lord, quoted, 2

Adding machines, made like typewriters, 115

Adoption of computers, by businesses, 160

Advertisements, for information processing products, 122

Aiken, Howard H., 118

ALGOL, 63

Amdahl Corporation, role of (1970s), 79

American Federation of Information Processing Societies (AFIPS), 53; on preserving materials, 26; study on I/T expenditures (1970s), 236

American Telephone and Telegraph Corporation (AT&T), 66, 92; antitrust problems of, 78, 103; archives of, 30; cross-licensed transistors, 115; model study of, 30; R&D at (1920s–1930s), 108–109; size (1960s), 70; supports history, 104

Ameritech, 92

Ampex, 72

Annals of the History of Computing: described, 4; published memoirs, 23

Antitrust division: pattern of behavior, 103; suits in information processing industry, 77–78

APL, 26, 63

Apple Computer, 81, 86, 90, 213; access for journalists at, 104

Applications: chronology of, 25; earliest uses (1945–1952), 161–162; effect on product demand, 120; history of, 139–157; how justified in 1980s, 88; in 1950s, 68; initial commercial uses (1952–1965), 162–167; need to study (1800s–early 1900s), 14–25; phases in history of, 146–151; role of databases in, 213; status of its history, 26; strategy for study of, 151–154; trends in use, 202–203; wide adoption by corporations (1965–1981), 167–170

Archives: European holdings, 17–19; limited for post-1960, 23; problem of, 27–31

Artificial intelligence, status of its history, 26

About the Author

JAMES W. CORTADA is a member of the IBM Consulting Group and the author of over a dozen books on the history and management of information. His most recent books include *Before the Computer* (1993); *The Computer in the United States* (1993); *TQM for Information Systems Management* (1995); *Second Bibliographic Guide to the History of Computing, Computers, and the Information Processing Industry* (Greenwood, 1996); and *A Bibliographic Guide to the History of Computer Applications, 1950–1990* (Greenwood, 1996). Dr. Cortada also serves on the editorial boards of several journals, including the *IEEE Annals of the History of Computing*.

ISBN 0-313-29950-1

EAN

9 780313 299506

HARDCOVER BAR CODE